Post True Stories of Daring and Adventure

Post True Stories of

Daring
and
Adventure

SELECTED BY THE EDITORS OF
THE SATURDAY EVENING POST

CURTIS BOOKS, A DIVISION OF
THE CURTIS PUBLISHING COMPANY

THE WORLD PUBLISHING COMPANY
CLEVELAND AND NEW YORK

Published by The World Publishing Company
2231 West 110th Street, Cleveland, Ohio 44102

Published simultaneously in Canada by
Nelson, Foster & Scott Ltd.

Library of Congress Catalog Card Number: 67–25794

ACKNOWLEDGMENTS

"The Unknown War." Reprinted by permission of The Macmil-
lan Company from *The Sledge Patrol* by David Howarth. Copy-
right © 1957 by David Howarth.

"One Man Against the Sea." Permission to reprint granted by
Paul R. Reynolds, Inc., 599 Fifth Avenue, New York, New
York 10017.

"We Rowed Across the North Atlantic," by Captain John Ridgway, with James Atwater. Reprinted by permission of Orbit
Press Features, London.

Contents

Foreword

What is it that drives a man to attempt to conquer the Atlantic in a small boat or to set out across the Pacific alone on a raft? What compels men to climb impossible mountains, to soar toward the stratosphere in a free balloon, to squeeze through tiny spaces deep in the earth? The cynic says they do it for money, and surely in an age when heroism is commercially successful this can be a motive. But if so, how do you explain John Ridgway and Chay Blyth, who decided to row nearly 3,000 miles in a 16-foot boat with no guarantee that they would live, let alone make any money out of it? Amateur psychiatrists will find some deeper motive—a need to prove masculinity, perhaps; they will see symbolism in the high mountain or the damp isolation of the cave.

The men themselves usually cannot say why they take these risks. When asked why he wanted to climb Everest, George Leigh Mallory offered the now-classic "Because it is there," and beleaguered adventurers have been quoting him ever since. But is that a reason, or is it simply an attempt to express the inexpressible?

Perhaps there is no simple explanation. Perhaps one must feel viscerally that it is worthwhile to be the first man on top of Everest, to have driven faster or soared higher or dived deeper than any other human being. There is a feeling that comes over a man who has conquered a mountain or broken a record, a marvelous sense of accomplishment, even of exhilaration, that they say is like no emotion they have known before. Perhaps the driving force is a search for this feeling.

It may be, as some have said, that it is no more complicated than a desire for fame and the acclaim that comes with it. Fame may be transitory, and it may bring more trouble than glory (think of Charles Lindbergh) ; it may even seem an ignoble motive. But for some it must be there.

Most men, of course, would never risk their lives for fame, or glory, or even money. Some of these men, if they suddenly found themselves alone on the ocean, or abandoned in a wilderness, would soon give up and die. Others, though, would fight to stay alive until they lost consciousness. Men have performed great feats of strength and endurance when their cause looked hopeless and death seemed inevitable, and those who survived have looked back and wondered how they were able to do it.

If it were possible to say just why a man will risk his life to reach some undefined and seemingly worthless goal, or why he will keep going when there seems no hope of victory or even survival, we might be able to say more about the nature of man himself. All we know is that we have always striven to explore the unknown, to go where no man has gone before, to do what no one has ever done. And this mysterious compulsion has taken us to every corner of the earth, it has taught us to fly, to explore the depths of the ocean, to leave the earth itself and dream of standing on the planets.

Most of us, of course, do nothing more adventurous than driving a freeway, or climbing a ladder to remove a second-floor storm window, and must enjoy our dangers vicariously. Fortunately, most men who dare great deeds come back with the strong desire to tell others what they have done, and over the years the editors of *The Saturday Evening Post* have been proud to publish many of these stories. This book, we think, contains our best. Even though the men all have different explanations for their actions, and some have no explanations at all, their accounts may offer yet another clue in man's attempt to understand his own nature.

—THE EDITORS

We Rowed Across the North Atlantic

BY CAPTAIN JOHN RIDGWAY
WITH JAMES ATWATER

At 5:30 P.M. on June 4, 1966, two men rowed a heavily laden dory through the inlet at Orleans on Cape Cod and headed out to sea. The men were Captain John Ridgway and Sergeant Chay Blyth, two British paratroopers, and their goal was to row home to England, a 3,000-mile trip across the North Atlantic, one of the most treacherous bodies of waters in the world.

What was more, Ridgway and Blyth were actually entering a race. Their opponents were two other British oarsmen, David Johnstone and John Hoare, who had started out two weeks earlier from Virginia Beach, Va. Each team wanted to become the first to row the Atlantic since 1896. This is the story of how Ridgway and Blyth succeeded.

Their opponents were not so fortunate. On October 15, a Canadian warship found their small boat bobbing, empty, on the open sea. The last entry in its log was dated September 3— the very day that Ridgway and Blyth landed triumphantly on the Irish coast. The capricious sea had allowed one team its victory—and taken its toll of the other.

I REMEMBER that the weather was fair and the waves were calm when we began the long row home. The few small boats that escorted us out of Orleans gradually began to turn back, one by one. I noted in my log that "we passed four rather mystified

1

fishing boats" and then, rather suddenly, Sergeant Chay Blyth and I were alone.

The full implications of our plans—that we were actually going to try to row the Atlantic—didn't dawn on me that first day, nor did we think much about the grandeur or the power of the sea. Our initial reaction as we set out was simply one of relief that we were getting on with the job after all the hectic weeks of preparation. We were afraid that we might already be far behind Johnstone and Hoare. Although they had begun in Virginia Beach, some 500 miles to the south of us, they were much nearer the Gulf Stream, the great current of water that sweeps up the coast of the United States and then curves east toward Europe.

I suppose there is nothing more pointless than to try to row across the Atlantic. With its sharp bow and flaring sides, our dory, the *English Rose III,* rode the waves like a chip, which meant that we were constantly in motion, even on a gentle sea. I was sick four times that first day out. Our systems had to learn to adjust to the ceaseless movement—up and down, up and down, up and down—as we climbed the side of a wave that loomed above us like a hill and then slid swiftly down the other side.

In a storm, *Rosie* was swept along like a surfboard. The most vivid memory I have of the North Atlantic is the force of a wave driven by a storm, and the sound, the ferocious, intimidating sound of it. At the beach, a wave breaks on the shore and then disappears. On the open sea, the wave breaks with a roar, the water tumbles down into the trough, and then the wave picks itself up again and comes on silently. You can hear it coming at you through the night from very far off—a crash and then silence, a crash and silence. It sounds like a very fast train, not a train going nonstop but one that pauses and then continues and pauses again. Then you hear the wave crash nearby, and you know that the next time it is going to hit you.

Occasionally the waves would actually break right over *Rosie,* filling her like a bathtub with a half foot or more of cold, salt water. But more often *Rosie* would somehow manage to get up on top of the breaking wave, and then there would be a tremendous rush of white all around you. The dory would be flung forward, and all you could do was to hold on for your life, literally.

But even when the sea was absolutely calm, life in our dory was wretched. *Rosie* was only 20 feet long to begin with, and watertight compartments at each end reduced our living space to an area of about 10 feet by 5 feet. We found on our first night that this open cockpit was so cluttered with lashed-down gear that there was no place to stretch out. Our sleeping that night, and every other night, was done in a bent position with our knees drawn up and the backs of our necks resting on some equipment, usually one of the spare oars, so that we often woke up with headaches.

We had to learn to sleep, row, eat, to exist in wet clothes. We were constantly being soaked through by rain and waves. A canopy rigged upon a metal framework covered about half of the cockpit, but it gave us only minimal protection. We precariously cooked our meals of dehydrated British Army rations on a small camping stove fired by compressed gas.

So when you think of the conditions of the trip, rowing the Atlantic does seem pointless—pointless in a commercial sense, that is, and today only commerce seems to matter. But the trip did make sense to me aesthetically. I'm an experience seeker. I'd guess that's all I am—a physical experience seeker.

I really was born out of my time. There's no vacancy in this modern age for anyone like me at all. I'm very much a dreamer. What one has to be today is a technocrat, which is completely divorced from my kind of life. I grew up imagining myself climbing Everest or sledding to the South Pole or canoeing down the Amazon. But most of these things had been done when I became a man. There were very few things left to do that didn't require the enormous expense of mounting an entire expedition. That's why I jumped at the idea of rowing the Atlantic when I heard that Johnstone was planning to do it. It was exactly right. I could afford it—it only cost me about $1,500 altogether—and it was a proper test for Chay and myself.

Each of us loves to be faced by a physical challenge, to get to the point where we're so fatigued that we're sort of lifted out of ourselves and can observe our reactions from a distance, as it were. I get a great sense of elation from being absolutely shattered by exhaustion—and then to be able to keep on going, to know that I'll go on endlessly. Chay gets the same feeling. He says that it's a form of masochism, really, and I suppose he's right. Perhaps we are social misfits. The exhaustion and the knowledge that I can go on gives me a kind of pleasure that I've never experienced in anything else in my life. It can make me almost cry with emotion.

I developed this obsession to keep on going when I was still in school and discovered that I would never be really very good at sports. I don't have a good body—my arms aren't very strong, I'm long in the wrong places, and I have sort of funny feet. When I was nine years old, a shoe clerk took one look at my feet and told my mother they should be reversed—the right one really belonged on the left leg, and vice versa. And I never had what I almost worshiped in an athlete—the graceful movement of it. I got on the first teams in Rugby and cricket only by constant training, training, training.

I was captain of boxing at Sandhurst, the Royal Military academy, but only through persistence. I was a great loser; I've got some terrific trophies for losing. In one tournament someone broke my nose with his head. I won that fight and the next, and in the final I fought a pretty good bloke. My nose was in a hell of a state by then. I could hear the bones grate when I was hit.

The referee stopped the fight in the last round with one minute to go. It was the only time I was ever stopped and I had a kind of nervous breakdown, I'm ashamed to say, right there in the ring, which from a British point of view is disgraceful. Tears streaming down my face, and so on. They took me to the dressing room, and I just cried and cried. I couldn't believe that I had been stopped.

When I joined the paratroopers, I became very interested in tuning the body. I did long marches in the mountains with a 50-pound pack on my back, and it was like having a big engine inside you that would take a long time to warm up, and then you'd feel that you could go on endlessly.

I was always looking for ways to test myself, to see what I could stand up to. In 1960, Colin Thompson, a fellow officer in the paratroops, and I entered the 125-mile nonstop canoe race down the Thames. We did it in about 26 hours and finished 15th out of 110.

Later I started a 70-mile nonstop canoe race for the parachute brigade. We did it in the winter in the dark. I canoed with Blyth, a Scot who had been in my platoon as a private when I was a 2nd lieutenant. I had rather got used to the idea of not winning by that time, but Blyth wanted to win. We turned over in the dark in a whirlpool and very nearly drowned. It was a half hour before we got out. Despite the loss of time, Blyth still was determined to win. We finished in utter exhaustion, but we came in first.

When I heard in 1965 that Dave Johnstone was planning to row across the Atlantic, I volunteered to go along with him. There were other volunteers, and Johnstone and I never did get together. Then, early last spring, I read that he was planning to make the trip with John Hoare. I became determined to beat them.

Although I wanted Blyth to go with me, I didn't feel that I could ask him because he was married. But he came up to me one day and said, "I hear you're looking for someone to row across the Atlantic. I'm your man."

And I said, "All right, it's settled." Just as quickly as that. We didn't even have to shake hands on it.

Chay not only had never been on the sea, he didn't know how to row. I had never done any really serious ocean rowing. But this lack of experience worried neither of us. We believed that rowing skill would be incidental. Much more vital, we were certain, would be the determination to survive. We knew we could survive. We don't quit. We always finish. That's what our life is all about.

The Army agreed to give us leave without pay for the trip, but no one would sponsor us. No newspaper would pay our expenses in advance, because no one was prepared to under-write two suicides. We got together $600 to buy a plywood dory, which, I understand, was quite different from the design that Johnstone used. His boat, which was especially built for the crossing, was 15½ feet long, nearly five feet shorter than our dory, and seemed to squat in the water instead of riding on top of it. The boat had a closed cabin, while we, of course, had just a canopy.

We decided to leave from Cape Cod simply because that was the spot Johnstone had picked originally. When he switched to Virginia Beach at the last minute, apparently because it was closer to the Gulf Stream, we couldn't follow him there because we didn't have any more money.

I had read, of course, about the marvelous fishermen on Cape Cod who had used dories years ago, and I practically prayed that some of these people would still be alive. And some of them were, men in their 70's and 80's who still had the great, thick-skinned hands of a dory fisherman.

They came forward eagerly to help. Alton Kenney, who is 70 himself, took us in at his boatyard in Chatham, just down from Orleans. "I wasn't born in a dory," he said, "but damned close to it." And then there were men like Allie Hunter, who was 82 and had been a fisherman most of his life, and Joe Stapleton and Bill Stephens, both around 70, and both men who had rowed dories on the Grand Banks years ago. These were good men. I think the only good people in this world are the people who have known suffering, and these dorymen know what suffering is all about, my Christ they do. Some of them had been out in their dories in the dead of winter when a blizzard had hit. The storms separated them from their mother ships, and they were completely on their own, with no supplies, for the three or four days until they could reach land. These men knew the stagger-ing ability of the dory to put up with heavy seas. One man I remember said that he had been in three 70-mile-an-hour hurri-canes in a dory, and if any boat could do it a dory could.

These old Cape Codders, and some younger men too, would sit by the hour around that stove, that marvelous old stove, talking about our trip, and they'd say, "We know you guys are sincere, and we're going to do what we can, as fast as we can, to give you a fightin' chance."

And that's what they did. My God, they did. Several of them took us out on Pleasant Bay to give us rowing lessons. We had the idea that you had to lean far forward and then really pull and lean far backward. But Joe Stapleton and the other men said that if you're going to row for a long, long distance, the idea is to concentrate on just keeping the boat moving. Just sit up straight—and row with short strokes. If you pulled too hard, they told us, you'd raise blisters in a mile or two.

They built up the freeboard by about 14 inches to give the cockpit more protection against the waves. They put in thick pieces of oak to reinforce the hull, and it was really powerfully put in. There was a great deal of comfort in seeing this solid oak go into *Rosie*.

I had arrived with a strip of wood that I had been told should be added as a sort of keel to help the boat track in a straight line. They all got together, sitting around that stove, and talked it over and then they said, "You don't want a keel—we've come out against that." They said a keel would hold the dory too stiff on the wave, that the force would turn us over. The beauty of a dory was that it could slide down the sea, they explained, just slip sideways off the thing, and a keel would prevent that.

What we wanted, they said, was a rudder, and then there was a tremendous argument about the shape of it. You know, this was life and death to both parties. We also had brought over oars specially made by the leading British manufacturer. They were beautiful things with stainless-steel fittings, and they had pins that would hold them fast to the side of the boat. The Cape Codders really got excited when they saw those. If you use those, they said, you're going to die. It will be suicide. They said you couldn't have an oar that would not jump out, because you'll be hit by a sea sooner or later that will either break the oar, or break the side of the boat, or break you.

Then there was a great debate over whether we should use open oarlocks or old-fashioned thole pins, which are really just two wooden pins stuck in the gunwales to hold the oar. Some of the older men, and the younger men too, argued that oarlocks were too modern and newfangled. They said the whole world will think there are fools on Cape Cod—we can't possibly let you go with oarlocks. But the other side won the argument, and we ended up using open oarlocks. We discarded our British oars altogether. Instead we used the American kind made of solid ash. We carried some spare sets lashed to the inside of the cockpit.

To keep us attached to the boat, the Cape Codders worked out a system of harnesses hitched to 20-foot safety lines that were long enough so that we would not be caught under the dory if it turned over. We carried a compass mounted before the rower nearest the bow. We had four radios. The first was a "coffee-grinder" set that you had to crank when you wanted to send a message. We never used it, nor did we talk to anyone by radio during the entire trip. We carried a transistor receiver to pick up the exact time, which we needed to navigate accurately. And we carried two small radios that we never expected to use—search-and-rescue equipment that sent out a signal when you pulled the handle. The last thing we wanted to do was to ask someone to come save our miserable skins and risk being drowned.

We had foul-weather clothes that eventually became so worn that we had to hold them together by tape. To keep out the cold, we took along some heavy warm-up suits that runners use. We also carried plastic-coated blankets; as time went on, they became riddled with holes.

To start out, we took some fresh fruit, vegetables and eggs. When they were gone, we began to eat the dehydrated Army rations, which were stored in a number of plastic boxes and lashed to the insides of our cockpit. We carried a gallon of water a day per man for 60 days, or about half a ton of water, which turned out to be far too much. We found that we sometimes were using only a few pints a day per man. To lighten the boat, we eventually poured a lot of our water into the sea.

One of the last things given to us by the Cape Codders was a brass plaque screwed into the wall of a watertight compartment at one end of the boat. It said, OH GOD, THY SEA IS SO GREAT, AND MY BOAT IS SO SMALL. Somehow I found the words comforting.

I've always had tremendous respect for water. It's the enormous power of it, not only of the sea, but of an ordinary stretch of river. I live up on the northern coast of Scotland, and even on a calm day it's deeply impressing to see the Atlantic hitting the rocks, to see the way the water drops back from the cliffs and then sucks up again, the enormous, unharnessed power of it.

I find water deeply moving. I don't know just why this is— perhaps just because I'm English. I don't think I'm afraid of water, but anyone who feels this way about something has to go out and challenge it.

Before we left, the Cape Codders didn't give us any tips on how to survive on the water. I think we impressed them with the basic fact that we were mentally prepared to survive. We didn't make any pretense of being boat handlers, or anything like that. And the men who really knew weren't worried about the rowing. The rowing was nothing, really.

And so on Saturday, June 4th, the Cape Codders shook our hands and escorted us onto the fringe of the North Atlantic and left us on our own. We weren't afraid; we were just glad to be getting on with it.

On the second day it began to blow, and by the third day we learned what an Atlantic gale is like. We put out our sea anchor and holed up under our canvas. Twice in the night Chay called out in his sleep for us to hold on. That night, for the first time, we heard the great storm waves coming at us, the thunderous crash somewhere in the darkness, and then the ominous silence as it re-formed to come on again.

The dory began riding broadside to the seas, and I thought, "This *cannot* be!" I was very worried that we'd be swamped. But she slid down the sides of the waves, just the way the Cape Codders had said she would if we left the keel off.

The sea was flecked with white caps when we awoke the next morning. We soon discovered that the storm had torn away our sea anchor, one of the three we carried. Suddenly we were very keen indeed to attach to the boat the two St. Christopher medals that the Cape Codders had given us. There was an unseemly scramble to find a screw for one of the medals; in fact, we moved just about all of our gear to find it.

That first storm pushed us north a good ways—how far I wasn't quite certain because my sextant began giving me some startling readings. At one point I calculated we were in the middle of Vermont. It wasn't until later that I discovered that the storm had knocked a screw out of line.

Early on we talked mainly about getting to the Gulf Stream. We had a bottle of wine we were going to drink when we got there, and we worked out marvelous fantasies about the way the stream would look—a kind of river of blue water in the gray ocean, with Coca-Cola machines on it and tables under palm trees and girls sunbathing. We were going to get into the stream, drink our wine, and then be carried to England as though we were on a conveyor belt.

But we obviously were making little progress in those first few days, and we became very dejected. On June 9th, I figured we were only about 100 miles off the coast of Maine, if that, and we both became worried about being carried ashore, perhaps being swept into the Bay of Fundy by those fearful tides. And then the embarrassment of it. The people coming down to us and saying, "Well, you tried and you failed."

We Rowed Across the North Atlantic / 9

The sun was hot, very hot, on June 9th, and we were quite discouraged. I think it was one of the lowest points of the trip. We said to hell with it, we'll take a sleep and then we'll have a go. And so we took a nap for an hour. When we set off again there was an immediate improvement. We saw a seaplane, and some fishing boats in the distance and schools of porpoises, and I said, "Ah, the Gulf Stream."

But it wasn't. And then, after a while, we heard on our transistor radio that Hurricane Alma was due to hit us some-time during the next few hours. Chay said we should immedi-ately go over our gear and lash everything down, and I said, "Let's take some photographs."

Chay sat there in bewilderment. "Take some photographs!" he said. "Take some photographs!"

But that's what I did. I knew it would take only a few minutes to get as ready for Alma as we could ever get, and that there was really nothing to be done. I'm not a nerveless person—I'm very conscious of fear. I'm frightened of parachuting; I don't like doing it at all. But when I'm faced with really acute danger, I'm able to stop worrying and to relax and rather enjoy it. I know that I've done all I can do to help myself, and the situation is out of my hands.

That night, with Alma due sometime before morning, we tied everything down. We put out our second sea anchor, slipped into our safety belts and went to sleep. There was nothing much else that we could do.

Alma woke us up the next morning with a huge wave that half filled the boat. Luckily, Alma was dying when she got to us, and it wasn't as bad or as dramatic as we thought it might be. *Rosie* took the seas beautifully, and we soared up the sides of waves that were 20 or 30 feet high and slid down the other side. The sea was one long roller coaster. We still weren't talking to *Rosie* at this point, urging her to take an unusually big wave that we could see making for us. I think we three were all still separate; two separate men, and each of us separate from the boat. Later we would all seem to blend into one, one entity against the sea, but that would not be for some time.

Each of us was recording his private feelings in separate logs that neither of us showed the other until the trip was done. We wanted to feel free to say exactly what we felt as we went along. "The waves were big—about 30 feet," Chay wrote of Alma. "I got a little apprehensive about them. I think it will take a lot to turn the boat over. When it does happen, it will cause some problems. I think we might lose more kit than we imagine.

"I pray quite a lot now. All that is in mind is to finish and get on land again. Having never been to sea before, it is all rather fearful.

"It was a cold, cramped night. We broke into our main rations, had fudge and curry. Cheered us up no end. A hot meal makes a fantastic difference."

Curry turned out to be the staff of life for us. From that point on, we tried to have hot curry every day, plus a hot breakfast and a third hot meal, if we could. The hot food became essential to us. We soon found that sugar is great for giving you a little bit of energy, but for the power you need you really have to have meat.

On June 15th, the day after Alma left, we met the *Winchester*, a trawler out of Boston, and received some absolutely shattering news. After 12 days we were only 180 miles east of Boston. In fact, we had come only about 120 miles from Cape Cod. It was either on this day, or soon after, that I made the calculation that at that rate we wouldn't reach England until March.

This was the point that Chay really got hold of the situation. I think his fear of an embarrassment was probably even stronger than mine, and mine was pretty strong. We really came to grips with the thing, really screwed ourselves down. We developed this mania to keep on rowing, and we rowed as hard during the next few days as we ever did on the trip.

Up until that point, we both had been sleeping at night. Now we began taking turns rowing all night long—two hours of rowing, and then two hours of sleep, and so on. We had such a mania to keep rowing that we tried not to lose a stroke. When we changed over, one man would be poised to take one oar and then the other so that we lost no momentum at all. It sounds kind of incongruous now, but it worked. At five in the morning we would have a hot breakfast, and then both of us would begin to row. We'd take a break of five minutes every hour, but we'd alternate them so that one man was always pulling.

Our hands began to get sore, although we never raised serious blisters. We found that our hands were becoming so molded to the thick handles of the oars that we couldn't clench them. The rowing was tiring, of course, but it was not exhausting. The nonstop canoeing had been much harder.

We never felt that sense of aching loneliness that comes over some men in small boats on the sea. We talked incessantly; in fact, we could hardly wait for the morning to come so that we could begin talking again. We never argued. That would have been disastrous, of course. We knew each other so well that we didn't have to try *not* to argue. We just didn't. Nor were we ever bored. There never was enough time to do everything we needed to do, such as mending our clothes and keeping the cockpit shipshape.

In those early days we were gripped by a great sense of nostalgia for the pleasant experiences of our boyhoods. I'd tell Chay how it was at school, walking back after fishing on a winter's Sunday afternoon, strolling through quiet English villages, and the smoke going straight up from the chimneys. And Chay told me about going fishing with his uncle in Scotland, walking the river bank and then sitting down and brewing tea, and the scent of the smoke from the burning wood. You could smell that smoke right out there in the boat.

Although we had been at sea for more than 10 days, I still sometimes found it hard to believe that we were actually trying to row across the North Atlantic. On June 16th I noted in my log, "Only just beginning to reconcile myself to the fact that we are on this trip. Wake up and believe I am in a cart ambling through a farmyard."

On June 17th, after rowing through dense fog for three days, we began to hit great swells with wide valleys between them. This must have been the edge of the continental shelf. We were really on the deep sea then. And we thought, what in the world is this going to be like in a storm? We couldn't imagine surviving when those swells were driven by a wind.

It was on that same day, while rowing through this gray, gloomy thing, that we first saw some whales. Rather, we heard them first—great gushes like escaping steam. We heard one tremendous blast to our right, and there was a huge whale coming right for us. His back was as curved and as wide as a Quonset hut, and I could see his eyes low down in the gray water.

I freeze at times like that, but Chay leaped immediately for his lifeline. Then the whale dived without a sound, this immense power sinking silently into the sea, and we thought that surely he was going to come up under the boat and knock us into the air. By this point we had had a lot of discussions about the whaling accidents in *Moby Dick,* and we could imagine all too vividly what it would be like. But the whale passed beneath us harmlessly and surfaced again some distance off. He looked just like the whales you see in magazine cartoons, lolling on the surface, spouting steam and actually enjoying himself.

While we were shrouded by fog, we had one terrible fright. Softly at first, and then growing steadily louder, we could hear the thump-thump-thump of the Diesel engines of an enormous ship. As it drew closer, we could hear the great rush of it through the water. But we couldn't tell where the monster was coming from—there were no lights, and the sound enveloped us in the fog. I blew our pitifully small foghorn a couple of times, and then gave up. We just sat there, staring wildly around us at the gray fog and waiting to be destroyed. Then, suddenly, the thing roared past us, still without showing a single light, and the thump-thump-thump receded. We slumped back in relief as the swells from the wake began to lift our boat.

Even when we could see them—and they could see us—we were terrified of ships. They were so huge, they moved so fast, and we knew we were so helpless before them. The few ships that did stop would seem to absolutely race straight toward us, until we wondered if they would be able to stop in time. Then they would loom above us like cliffs rising out of the sea.

On June 19th the fog cleared, and we met the *Albatross IV* out of Woods Hole, Mass., which gave us the good news that my navigating was accurate and that we were dead on the course we had set for the last four days. They said if we went east-southeast for another 70 miles, we'd be right in the Gulf Stream, but they didn't suggest we do that. They suggested that we forget the whole thing, sink the boat, and come on board. "No, thank you very much indeed," we said. We didn't even go up on their deck.

When we set off again in pursuit of the Gulf Stream, sharks began to prowl around us for the first time. One began to chase its tail around and around, just like a puppy. Then we got another great fright on June 22nd. It was a day of blasting heat.

I noted in my log: "The first hot day—slowly it became like Lawrence of Arabia crossing the Nafud Desert, and our strength sapped away." We had just finished reorganizing the boat and were lying back in the sun when Chay said, "Why don't you go for a swim?"

I said that I guessed I really didn't want to, and slipped the oars in to start rowing again. Because I was tired, I began to pull gently. We sort of slid quietly away, and there it was. I have never seen a fin like that. It was so big that it kind of drooped over, and it was all battered and scarred. The front of it was curved like the conning tower of a submarine. As we moved away, the shark began to swim slowly to keep its head in the shade of the boat and out of the sun. It was so big that its fin was about 10 feet back in the water.

I suppose that shark would have finished me if I had gone in swimming. After that, we gave up any idea of taking a dip for the rest of the trip. From time to time, we'd see other sharks following us, great shapes of darkish brown in the gray water. They'd nose their heads under the boat—I guess because we were the only shadow on the sea, and we certainly were moving slowly enough for them. We could feel the vibrations when some of the sharks scratched their backs on the bottom of the boat. Chay grabbed one by the dorsal fin, but I doubt that the thing even felt it.

The next day was a bleak one for us. We discovered that Alma had done far more damage than we had thought, stoving in many of the polystyrene boxes that held our rations. We decided that we had to cut back our calories per day from 4,000 to 2,700 which raised the danger that we might begin to grow weaker gradually. I wrote in my log: "Still, as Field Marshal Slim said, 'Things are seldom as good or as bad as they are first reported.'"

Three days later the *Robertson II*, a Canadian fisherman, stopped to talk to us. I was shaving when we spotted her, and I thought I'd take these guys for a bit of a ride. I kept on shaving, sitting there in the middle of the Atlantic, while they came up at terrific speed. The captain asked, "Where's the engine? Have you had a blow yet?"

We told him we had no engine, but that we had had some wind. I kept on shaving all the time we talked. He asked where we were going.

We said, "England."

And he cried, "In *that?*"

Then he gave us the dreadful news that we were still 70 miles away from the main part of the Gulf Stream, by his calculations. When he pulled away, we stopped being nonchalant. We were deeply discouraged again. Our logs during this period show how the strain of the trip was beginning to get to us better than I am able to recollect the feeling now. Chay wrote: "We have been out three weeks now, and I am getting a bit depressed. Mainly I think because of lack of westerly winds. Goodness knows where Johnstone is. He's been out five weeks. He should be almost finished. . . . I think a great deal of my mother now and how much she really meant to me. My wife—and how I intend to spend the rest of my life with her.

"The food plays a large part in our lives. We try to alter the flavor by a series of concoctions. Jam into rice pudding, cheese and marmalade. The amount of beef cubes with the meat blocks. Rice with meat blocks. Mixed vegetables with curry. Our sole spice is pepper, and now even that is wet. Mashed potato—we used to cook it on its own, now goes into thickening the stews. Soup cooked with biscuits. Coffee—black and white, with and without sugar, and the same with cocoa. This cocoa is our luxury. We are beginning to feel the lack of sleep."

During this period I described a typical day in my log as follows:

0500. Started raining with good wind, force 4.

0900. One man rows. One man reorganizes the rations until 1400.

1500. Tanker passes very close to the south, but fails to see our signal on end of an oar.

1815. Hove to for night in force 5 easterly wind (which drove us backward toward the United States).

Wind becoming depressing. Patience above all else is the requirement.

Blyth and I wish we were at home. He could not row against the wind as the evening wore on. We went to bed with aching hands. Mine are breaking out in spots, and a boil behind my right ear is hurting. Blyth chopped it.

On other days I wrote, "Impressed by the way Blyth managed to sleep in bad weather whilst I hung on in terror. . . . This east wind is the steadiest we have had during the whole trip. How depressing it is to think we are going to have to row all this again. . . . A liner passed at 2230 to our north all lit up heading for Europe. A very different kind of sea voyage, I thought, and looked at Blyth's huddled shape under the tarpaulin in the stern. It drizzled all night. Thunderstorm in morning quite frightening. Lightning very clear and rain quickly rose above the floor boards. . . . When we can't row during a storm, I am nearest the pumps. I estimate about 7,000 strokes during the hours of darkness.

"Seabirds are becoming fewer and fewer. Now only Mother Carey's chickens and a large bird with brown wing tops and white underneath. Fatigue is painful, and waking up from under the wet blankets and tarpaulin is agony. Rowing into the gray dawn glassy-eyed day after day. We need sleep."

But the wind did switch to the west after a while, and then *Rosie* swept on like a surfboard. Five days after meeting the *Robertson,* a Liberian tanker hove to near us and gave us our position, which showed that we had made 150 miles in five days. And we were in the Gulf Stream, or as close to it as we ever got. I suppose this really was the turning point in the whole trip. We had proved to ourselves that we could make good progress even on shortened rations and with the wind sweeping around to the east time and again to blow us backward.

We had complete confidence in the boat and in each other, and we settled down for a six months' voyage, if necessary. This was our game, really, a contest of endurance. We knew we could win it.

And so we rowed on, one man at the oars all night long. Chay was rowing on the night of July 4th when the wind began to build steadily. I was sleeping—curled up miserably on the floorboards of *Rosie* when, suddenly, I was shocked awake. Cold sea water had flushed me out from under the canopy as though I had been hit by a stream of water from a hydrant.

"It's a 'white-out,' " Chay screamed, and that's just what the sea looked like, the same kind of absolute white in all directions that dazzles skiers. I was still fighting to get my bearings when a second monstrous wave hit us. *Rosie* was lifted by the sea and dashed along through the white spray as though we were shooting rapids. The fluorescence in the water sparkled like snow in the sun.

I took over the oars, and Chay went under cover. When our

heads were under the canopy, we somehow felt safe, no matter what kind of hell was breaking loose three feet away.

For the next two hours I sat there in absolute exaltation. It was one of the great moments in my life. Again my safety and my life had been taken out of my hands. There was nothing I could do except sit back and watch what was happening. *Rosie* would soar up on a great wave, and then we'd slide down the slope, and I could see the stern rise until the silhouette of the rudder would be clawing for the sky.

The sound of movement of the storm and the boat became something like an orchestra. It was wonderful. I'm sure I was sitting there with a great grin on my face. I thought if I was going to die, this was the way to do it—going right through the front door instead of being run over by a motorcar.

As the days went by, we discovered that the voyage was having a very moving effect on us. Three shifts a night, every night, you sat there on your own, and the sky and the sea couldn't help but impress you a bit more each time. The clarity of the air gave you a tremendous impression of the stars and the enormity of space, and then there was the vast power of the sea. There are incredible forces out there that you never feel in a ship. You have to be within a few inches of the sea to come to know it.

As we went on, the sheer vastness of the Atlantic and the sky made us feel more and more humble. Many of the little things that used to worry us before the trip seemed so petty now. We talked of our wives and our parents, and how much we wanted to see them. Chay had two letters that he read often—one from his mother when he enlisted in the Army at the age of 17, and one written several years ago by Maureen, his wife.

The feeling of humility that came over us during the trip changed our views of Johnstone. Originally we had set out to beat him back to England. If we beat him, I thought that we might get a few hundred pounds from some publication. We hadn't begun the trip just to make money, but it was a subsidiary motive in my mind. As an Army man, I didn't think I'd have any other chance to make some capital.

But, as the trip went on, we lost any interest in getting money out of the trip. We wanted Johnstone to beat us back and get all the glory and money. We did want to make the passage in a shorter time than Johnstone, who had left two weeks before us. But that's all we wanted.

We were down to about 2,700 calories a day by now, and when we weren't talking about our wives, we were talking about food. We began to plan our celebration dinner with our wives in London with such elaborate care that the discussions went on for nearly 50 days. We assumed, of course, that there would be no publicity about our landing, since Johnstone would have beaten us in, and that we would be confronted with all the problems that we had always faced, including the lack of money.

We decided that the whole thing must not cost more than 20 pounds. For cocktails, I thought we might pop into a place called Jules Bar on Jermyn Street in London, but I was afraid we couldn't because I'd be unable to find a place in which to park my car. The actual dinner would be at the River Club, which is a rather elite sort of place, dinner jackets and so on, down on the Thames. Marie-Christine and I were taken there by my parents just after we became engaged.

We were going to start off with avocado pears, and then go on to lobster with Rhine wine, but lobster, we thought, might be too filling. Should we have lobster cocktail? Or should we in fact have some kind of lobster salad?

Then we'd go on to Aylesbury duckling, which would mean more wine, and we began to worry if the girls would be able to get through both courses, the lobster *and* the duckling. We never got beyond the duckling—the trip wasn't long enough.

As we discussed food and sang every song we could remember and talked incessantly, we were slowly moving deeper into the Atlantic, and we got the feeling, really, that we belonged there, and that the ships that passed on the horizon were only hurrying strangers. We were actually living on the ocean. We discovered that the birds all seemed to league up at nighttime, resting on the water by the hundreds. When we came poking along, we seemed so much a part of the sea that the birds wouldn't move until we were about five yards away. Then they'd flutter off, leaving feathers floating in the water, and settle again a few yards away.

The dolphins and porpoises would come up at sunset and move in among us and the birds. They'd come up very lazily under the birds, which would go up on their heels and flap their wings a bit, and then settle right down again. Two whales joined us one evening and played ring-around-*Rosie* so close to us that Chay could have reached out an oar and tapped one.

We were part of this life of the Atlantic. The jet trails streaking across the sky seemed to belong to a different world. "Ah," Chay would say, "there goes a jet-setter hurrying back to New York. He must have forgotten his comic books."

All through the trip we had looked forward to reaching 40 degrees west, because that was the spot at which we took our final course for home. We were making good progress toward the 40th, clipping off about 30 miles a day, and then the wind began to blow from the east. It was just as though the 40th were a great fence in the sea—we'd approach it, and be blown back, approach it again and be blown back again. We contented ourselves by reasoning that the longer the wind blew from the east the less time we had to wait until it blew from the west. It was a curious philosophy.

We had calculated that we had just enough rations to make England, but the easterly winds caused an agonizing reappraisal. It would have been an interesting experience, running right down like that, but we felt we must not risk other people's lives by making them search for us. We decided to accept rations from the next ship that stopped. Was it a mature decision? Or was it chicken?

This was also the time when the strain of the voyage really began to tell on us. I wrote in my log: "I have known fear many times in my life, and indeed I have often striven to develop a situation that provided fear in both boxing and parachuting. I have never known anything like this—this cannot be over tomorrow, or for many tomorrows. Somehow it is like being rubbed down with sandpaper. I honestly do not know how many storms there have been now, and each leaves us progressively weaker.

"Tonight we lie and wait. Nothing could save us if we get into difficulties. No ship could get us off these seas even if it arrived in time. We are completely in God's hands, at the mercy of the weather. All night the wind screams louder and louder, and the sound of the sea grows. We talk of many things—the night train to Scotland, the many things we've done, and slowly we are overtaken by an enormous feeling of humility and a desire to return to try and live a better life. The weather reached a climax at 0300 and then declined rapidly. Thank goodness we could not see the sea."

At another point I noted: "Today I was sick of the whole business. Time to play this malaise like a fish on the end of a line, and let it take some line off the reel. I shall cheer up no doubt as the westerly wind returns."

Chay was writing much the same thing. "The wind changed all right—to the northeast and not the west. God, this is a thing which will get us. Knowing each day we get hardly any miles east. The food still has to be eaten. We may have to cut down further. How I don't know. . . .

"I feel very tired. I'm beginning to itch a bit with the damp. It would drive you up the wall. The blankets are soaking through regularly and have been torn quite a bit by now. They seem to tear easily when soaked.

"There's only one word for it—nightmare. We often think of Johnstone and where he is. How fortunate for him he has a cabin. If both boats make it, I'll shake his hand. . . .

"At 0300 we were awakened by the storm. You could hear the waves roar like an aircraft coming toward you—crash into you, then roar off into the night. Then the next one. The only thing for it is sleep and prayer. God comes close to you out here. You have three feet on each side of you, then death. I had never been so frightened before as I have here. I pray tomorrow it will change."

We began to hate the sea water as though it were acid. After a while we tried to do everything we could to keep it from getting on us, and of course we couldn't. The feeling was something like the unpleasant sensation you have when you get a noseful while swimming—only it lasted all the time, and the feeling was all over our bodies. We hated the stuff.

Because we couldn't stretch out when we slept, our knees began to ache so badly that tears came to our eyes. Initially the man rowing at night gave the sleeper five minutes' notice before the changeover. But we found that was too long; the sleeper was always so tired that he would doze right off again. So we shortened the warning to two minutes. Then you really had to get up fast and force your hands onto the oars. For the first few minutes it was like trying to grab them with clumsy steel hooks. You couldn't control your hands at all; you couldn't even close them tightly around the handles.

During this period we also cut down to about 1,000 calories a day, and food became an obsession with us. I used to cut up my ration of cheese into little bits and let each one literally melt in my mouth. Chay for a while would put a candy in his mouth with its wrapper on, and then take the paper off with his tongue to make the sweet last longer.

Then, finally, on July 23rd we crossed 40 degrees. Six days later we were hit by our second hurricane, which was far stronger than Alma but never had a name, as far as we could determine. It is impossible to say how big the seas were. They were at least as high as a house, but a house doesn't seem very high when it is a mile long. The really impressive thing about the waves was their thickness. To go from one side to another might be as far as 100 yards. When you were on top of one of those monsters, it was like standing on a hill and looking down into a valley.

I wrote in my diary on July 29th: "Today would appear to be the nadir. All day long we lay together in a huddle in the stern in a space about 5 ft. by 4 ft. The boat is unbelievably sea-worthy—the waves are like mountains now and bigger than we have ever seen during the day, yet she ships very little water. The waves have the tops sliced off by the wind, and we can hear their express-train approach louder than ever, but somehow the train always races under the bridge that is *English Rose III.*"

The wind howled so that we had to raise our voices to be heard. Each of us began to pray silently. Early in the voyage I refused to pray because I thought it was an unworthy thing to do. Never having prayed in the good times, I was damned if I was going to pray in the bad times. But after a while I began to swing the other way.

After two days of screaming, the nameless hurricane departed, having torn away a plaque attached to the stern by one of our Cape Cod friends. The plaque had said: THREE THOUSAND MILES—WHAT HAVE I DONE? It was a question asked in despair by Chay one day while trying to learn how to row on Cape Cod.

Then, as our rations ran lower, the easterly winds came back.

I wrote in my log: "It is hard to describe how depressing it is to row all day, head into the wind when you are a thousand miles from home, knowing full well that at the end of the day, after all the toil, you will still be a thousand miles from home."

As the days went on, we found that we were beginning to fade, that 1,000 calories were not enough for us to keep going. "This depression and self-pity is an interesting and anticipated phase of this experience," I noted. "The shortage of rations and slowness of progress is not. Depression seems to tie my stomach in knots. We are both filled with remorse over the worry we are causing our wives."

On August 5th a wedge-tailed gull fluttered down and landed on my head, resting there for about 45 seconds. I wrote a theatrical passage in my log: "Was that seabird on my head the clutch of doom, I wonder? There are so many things I want to do, to try to make those around me a little happier. Surely this cannot be the end so soon?"

One week after the visit of the bird, I wrote: "Certainly an interesting situation is now developing:

(1) We have 800 miles to go.

(2) We have 30 days' rations.

(3) I have a pain in the groin indicating a serious infection."

Some tetracycline took care of my infection, and the next day, August 13th, a British tanker stopped and graciously offered us the stores that we needed so desperately. We felt we were disgracing ourselves by getting out of *Rosie,* but get out we did and went aboard the tanker for some magnificent scrambled eggs. We found that we were unable to walk straight. An hour later we pushed off for England with our stomachs full and our spirits high. "It is uncanny how fortune has guided us across the ocean," I wrote in my log. "It is almost as if some Divine hand had provided the conditions to test us and then to guide us home."

At the time, we were too far south to hit the British Isles. In fact, we were about opposite Finisterre in Spain. We turned north, and in a few days a terrific storm hit us from the south, driving us on like a speedboat. In a week's time we moved from a spot opposite the coast of France to a spot opposite the middle of Ireland. Suddenly the cold became a severe problem—the cold and the rain and, once again, the depressing easterly wind that held us in place like a huge hand, row as we might. Our clothes and blankets were now beginning to disintegrate, and I started to suffer from more boils and an irritating rash that spread over my body. Both of us had saltwater sores on our hands and wrists.

During this period Chay was writing in his log: "My hands are very sore, and the calluses are forming double heads. I thanked the Lord for his help. I've been thinking of Maureen and church. I'll step ashore a more humble, wiser and appreciative man. . . . I think the sleep I had last night was the best I had in the whole trip. It was really quite comfortable. At least by animal standards. . . . At 1200 hours it started to rain, and did it rain! The rain flattened the sea, and then bounced up and formed a kind of mist. This happened twice while I was rowing. I was delighted I couldn't get any more wet."

When the winds blew out of the east too strongly for us to row, we would put out our sea anchor and huddle under our canopy, which leaked a constant, cold stream on our heads, and watch *Rosie* slowly slip backward toward the United States. It was utterly depressing. We'd wrap the wet plastic blanket about our bent knees, and the pain of our strained position would become excruciating. We tried to take comfort from Chay's philosophy. "It will soon be a memory."

One night I had a vivid dream of a girl carrying a whole pile of Army clothes. I said, "Whose clothes are they?" And she turned her head as if afraid to answer. And then I saw a flash of Marie-Christine's head lying on a pillow. She was crying.

I never told Chay about my dream. Then, during one storm as we pushed toward Ireland, I became fairly certain that I was going to die. There was a chance that one of us would get killed, and I was fairly sure it would be me. It seemed so unlikely that it would be that it *would* be me, if you see what I mean.

So then I began to work out—am I afraid of dying, do I really mind? Chay had always impressed me with his hatred of death. I thought, well, I've had a pretty good time, really. I don't mind dying. If one of us is going to die, it had better be me.

On August 26th, massive seas rolled in from the southeast all day, making it impossible for us to row and pushing us slowly away from our goal. We talked over all the plots of every cowboy movie we had ever seen. At 9:30 in the morning I gave

Chay a chance to call it a day, if he wanted to. We could pull the handle on one of our search-and-rescue radios and have someone come out to take us in. He said immediately, "We'll go on."

I wrote in my log: "If he wants to go on, I shall go on—why, I can't tell you, but I must, and I will just go on and on and on."

We were aiming at the center of Galway Bay, which is about the midpoint of the cost of Ireland. And then, suddenly, after all the days of easterly winds, a storm began to blow out of the west and hurled us at Ireland. We covered 250 miles in a week. Seaweed and cork and other signs of land began appearing in the ocean.

We knew that the west coast of Ireland was very rugged, with cliffs coming straight down into the water in many places. We decided, quite matter-of-factly, that if we hit the cliffs, at least one of us might drown. To serve as floats, we put together two water-tight containers holding everything we thought we would need, including rations and flares.

Then on the morning of Saturday, September 3rd, the wind suddenly shifted from the west to the south, and I saw a thin line above the horizon. "That's it over there," I said very quietly. We tried to keep our emotions understated throughout the trip.

Chay said, "Are you sure?"

And I said, "Yes, I'm quite certain."

But Chay still refused to look. He said he'd wait until we got closer before he'd risk a look. A gale was beginning to build up, and the land disappeared for another hour and a half. When it reappeared again, there was no mistaking it. I persuaded Chay to turn on his seat and look. "Oh, yes," he said. "That's definite."

Neither of us felt any real elation at that point—just a relaxed feeling that we were nearing the end of our very long voyage. As we drew closer to Ireland, it became more and more apparent what a horrifying landing we were going to make. The gale was building up steadily, dashing waves halfway up the great cliffs that rose out of the water. We were headed directly for the island of Aran, which had two smaller islands off its northwestern tip. I decided to get into the lee of the third island, which had a lighthouse on it.

By now the gale was so strong that we could see spray blowing over both of the small islands. As we drew nearer, we had to go in broadside, rather like a crab. If we turned our stern to the sea, we absolutely raced along. We were afraid that we'd miss the sound altogether and go crashing into the cliffs.

Dashing before the storm, pulling for home, was the second great moment of the trip for me, equaling the elation I felt during the "white-out." Once again our fates had been taken out of our hands; we could simply enjoy watching to see what would happen next. We were both singing at the tops of our lungs against the howl of the wind, singing not because we were going to make our fortune, because we were certain we weren't, or even that we were going to land, but just for the pure joy of it.

We sang one of Chay's favorite Scots songs:

> The cold wind was howling o'er moor and o'er mountain,
> And wild was the search for wha' the lassie might be.
> She appeared like an angel in feature and form.
> As she asked me the road and the miles to Dundee.

And then we sang:

> At hush of eventide, o'er the hills beyond the Clyde,
> I'll go roving to my haven down in the glen.
> The sheep are in the fold, and there's peace worth more
>   than gold,
> In my haven, with my lassie, down in the glen.

We did make it to the lee of the lighthouse, but the gale was blowing so hard by then that the waves were coming around both sides of the island and meeting just about where we were. In an hour's time, sprinting as hard as we could, we made only about 100 yards. By then we were absolutely certain we weren't going to die. We had come all that way, and it just wasn't going to happen.

Finally two men from the lighthouse waved us over toward the other island. We started to head that way, when we saw a lifeboat with seven or eight men coming out after us. Neither of us wanted to be helped even the last little part of the way. Chay said, "Ignore them—keep rowing."

So we kept on rowing in embarrassment, and the lifeboat crew circled around us in embarrassment. The men kept asking us if we wanted a rope, and we decided after a while that we couldn't just tell them to push off. It was Saturday, and those fellows had left their families to come out to rescue us. So finally we took a rope and transferred to the lifeboat for the last short row to land.

I gave up writing in my log after we spotted land, but Chay managed with his usual tenacity to keep making notes right down to the end. I think they're a good record of the last few hours of the trip:

Cliffs looked like jaws waiting.
Life jackets on. Lift harness.
Kit ready for landing.
Morale high.
Zigzagging.
Pouring rain.
Quick prayer.
Discussion—I relied on John.
Middle of sound—howling wind.
No place to land on island.
Lighthouse keeper waved us away.
Energy expended.
Made for Aran.
Very heavy rain and wind.
Almost to island.
Hard work.
Almost to island.
Lifeboat.
Embarrassment.
Good talk.
Father McMann (who met us on the dock).
Wonderful people.
It's all over.
I'm not getting in that boat again for nobody.

Some of the newspaper posters in England said, THE BOYS WHO BEAT THE ATLANTIC. We didn't beat the Atlantic. We were lucky to get away with it. We got the feeling that the Atlantic had decided that we really were giving it a try, and that we should be allowed to go free. We didn't beat the Atlantic. It let us go.

Down
the Colorado

BY ROBERT ORMOND CASE

Great adventures seldom have a press agent. The thing is done first; the world hears of it later. It was so in the fall of 1937 when a 28-year-old filling-station employee, Haldane (Buzz) Holmstrom, took a vacation from his gas pump and, in his home-made boat, did what no man had ever done before—ran the Colorado River alone from Wyoming to Boulder Dam.

Classed by white-water veterans as the world's most dangerous long river, the Colorado and its no less savage tributary, the Green, fall 5,000 feet in these canyon-imprisoned 1,100 miles, with 365 great rapids and nearly twice that number of smaller ones.

The tremendous gorge had been threaded but seven times throughout its length, never by one man, sometimes with more than a dozen, and always with elaborate equipment. Powell's original party in 1869 required months for the passage; they were forced to line or portage their boats past something like a hundred rapids. With none to help him with his quarter-ton boat, Holmstrom rode down all but five.

Buzz had dreamed and prepared for the attempt for months. He had already run the rapids of the Salmon and Rogue Rivers solo; the mastery of these formidable chutes had won him his chevrons in the white-water guild. Only the Colorado, ultimate in roaring rapids, was left.

Buying a rattletrap car for $10 and building a trailer to haul his boat, he left his home in Coquille, Oregon, on September 29, 1937, headed for Green River, Wyoming. A little more than $100 was in his pocket, the last of his savings. Only his mother, his boss, and a few friends knew where he was going. Five days later, on October 4, without publicity of any kind and only a handful to watch him go, he shoved off from Green River. Fifty-two days later he bumped the concrete wall of Boulder Dam. This is the story of those 52 days.

FIRST I built my boat. I'd studied boat design, of course, the specialized types created for running rapids. Mine was made out of Port Orford cedar, very light but very strong. There are only two stands of this cedar in the world, one in the Holy Land and one down here in Southwestern Oregon. It's expensive, and if I'd had to buy it on the open market I'd have been sunk. But I went out in the woods and found me a windfall that was sound and had a close interlocking grain—the type I wanted—and had been naturally seasoned where it lay. I hewed out a cant about two feet square and fifteen feet long, and worked this by hand down a half-mile slope. Then I got a couple of the boys to help me load it on a trailer and brought it to town and had it sawed up.

It took six months of careful planning and building, but when it was done I knew every joint and rib and watertight seam; and I knew it was a good boat. You've got to know that when you run rapids. When the grip of the rapids closes on you and you know there's no way out except to ride 'er down, your mind has to be absolutely free of worry about what's under you. You can't say to yourself: "Is the boat sound? Will she stand up? Will the oars crack?" You've got to be able to say: "Everything is tough and tested. The rest of it's up to you, Holmstrom."

She was a good boat. A man at Green River liked her looks before I started down, and I almost promised to sell her, when and if I made it through. More than forty days later and close to 1000 miles downriver, when she took me safely through Deu-bendorf Rapids—more about that later—I would just as soon have sold myself.

She was fifteen feet long and five-foot beam, decked over,

except for a small cockpit; flat-bottomed, except for an inch and a half of arc for strength; ten inches of rake fore and aft; weight, empty, 450 pounds. All equipment was stored in watertight compartments fore and aft, the spare oars lashed securely aft. Nothing was in the cockpit except me and my life preserver. The cockpit could be brimming and she would still be buoyant, capable of supporting tons. She could turn end for end and roll completely over, and as long as I stayed with her I would have a chance. The stern, which was always to be downstream in rough going—for better visibility, control, and to reduce speed—had to be broad and doubly strong to stand up under the impact of solid water.

I was ready to go on September twenty-ninth. I had read and studied every book published on the Colorado—particularly E. L. Kolb's *Through the Grand Canyon From Wyoming to Mexico,* which was priceless in its detailed description of each rapid and eddy—and the best Government maps. I had thought, slept, and dreamed nothing but the Colorado for months.

The jump-off, for me, was not Green River, Wyoming, but Coquille, Oregon, where I was raised and where, when I die, I hope to be buried. I had all my stuff loaded that night. The last of my capital—a little better than $100—was in my pocket. I had said good-by, ready to get an early start in the morning.

But I knew, as twilight deepened along the Coquille, that I couldn't sleep that night. There was no use waiting. So I said good-by to my mother again and headed east. At sunup, I was across McKenzie Pass and in the Oregon "high desert."

A blizzard was threatening and a biting wind was blowing when I got to Green River, Wyoming, on October third. I spent the balance of that day and most of the next getting my stuff ready. I didn't tell anybody there what I was up to except a friendly couple who lived down by the river. I had to tell them because I wanted some place to park my car and trailer while I was gone.

I didn't want any publicity, and I'll tell you why. I didn't have much money; I looked like a tramp. I had a good boat, but the rest of it didn't look so good. No balloon-silk tents or fancy camp kits. I was afraid some official might stop me. He wouldn't know my experience. He wouldn't know how husky I was, nor that I'd studied and dreamed about the Colorado until I felt I knew each rapid and rock and eddy. All he'd see would be a wild-eyed Swede with a shoestring outfit, tackling the longest stretch of bad water in the world.

So I shoved off at dusk on October fourth. This couple at whose place I left my car and trailer—I told them I'd be back for it in six weeks or so—were down at the river to see me off. Several other folks were standing around, and the usual group of small boys. I don't think they ever expected to see me again. I wasn't so sure they would, either. It was twilight—I was getting under way at night again, because I knew I wouldn't sleep—and a gray, biting twilight it was. I could hear the boys yelling to me long after I was out of sight, and I yelled back. I wouldn't hear many voices again, after that. Only four stops to Boulder Dam, 1100 miles away.

Shooting the Colorado divides itself into two stages. The first stretch is the Green River to the junction with the Colorado below Greenriver, Utah. This is about 500 miles and includes the upper rapids and canyons. From the junction to Boulder is around 600 miles, the last 250 of which is the Grand Canyon proper. The farther downstream you go, generally speaking, the rougher the water is, the last and toughest, just above Lake Mead, being Lava Cliff Rapids. So the first stretch, to the junction, might be called the breaking-in period, where you learn what it's all about.

There are four possible stops for supplies: At Jensen and Greenriver, Utah, above the junction, and at Lee's Ferry and Grand Canyon below. In between, once embarked, there are stretches of hundreds of miles where you can't get out of the canyon, if your boat's smashed beyond repair and you're afoot. You can't follow down the banks, because there are oftentimes no banks in the sense of an ordinary river; the walls go straight up. There are timber and game in the upper stretch; below the junction you're soon rolling through desolation where there isn't much living except lizards. Every expedition that goes through finds traces of some unfortunates, individuals or parties, who have started down and never been heard of again.

My hands were benumbed with cold, dropping down from Green River, Wyoming, which is flat country. Each morning I had to thaw out my clothes before I could get them on. Wherever my breath touched on my sleeping bag during the night would be stiff with ice. We don't have cold like that in Oregon, and it seemed to bite into my bones.

The mountains were ahead. They looked friendly, and I knew that if I could beat the blizzard to the canyon, I'd get along. I could see the cleft coming for miles ahead, where the whole terrain tipped upward and the river began to dip down into its gorge, the first of its 5000-foot fall to Boulder. From a distance it looked as if the river was running down into a bottomless crack.

I thought of those ancient words, "Abandon hope, all ye who enter here," but didn't believe them.

Flaming Gorge, Horseshoe and Kingfisher canyons were short and rapids-free, filled with sunshine and songs of countless birds, and with the call of geese and ducks high overhead. Many deer and beaver could be seen along the tree-lined shores.

It didn't last long. I was soon into the first of the rapids, in Red Canyon, where I shoved, rather than shot, the shallow, rocky stream for three days; past Ashley Falls, the scene of many earlier disasters, and where inexperienced parties usually come to grief. It didn't seem very tough, at low water and with a good boat—not much tougher than the Rogue—and soon I came to Red Creek, where it was necessary to make the first portage. Here I started to throw away equipment that I didn't need, in order to shorten the ordeal of moving the boat and duffel over the rocks. I was learning. I threw away the heavy tent and slept after that in my sleeping bag alone. Out went the heavy iron pulley, which was useless; even extra cakes of soap. That helped, because moving the boat was bad enough.

I didn't figure to portage the boat more than I had to. That was one spot where previous expeditions had it on me. There'd always been two or more in previous parties—sometimes ten or a dozen—and you need plenty of help to move a boat over some of those places. When you figure what it means to move a 450-pound boat single-handed over shoulder-high boulders and knife-edged fragments and down cliffs, you can see why I planned to ride everything down that was short of suicide. I portaged only five times—three above the Colorado junction and two below. At each bad rapids I tied the boat and went ahead to study the lay of the land. If there was a way through, I went on through.

Nights were swell. Like that night after my first portage below Red Creek Rapids. I ate a good meal, and stretched out in my sleeping bag beside the dying fire. I was tired, but couldn't sleep right away; I just lay for a while, comfortable, watching the fading glow of the flames in the branches of the mountain cedar overhead, and after that looking up at the stars—I had never seen them bigger and brighter—high above the black, jagged silhouette of the canyon rim. The slapping of the waves against the drumlike compartments of the boat mingled with the roar from distant Red Creek. The peace and friendliness and physical relaxation wiped out the hardship of the day.

In some ways I was lucky to be by myself. In most expeditions there was always an unfortunate or two who couldn't stand the constant strain of it. Three of Major Powell's party balked on the lower stretch, climbed the canyon wall at about the only place along there where it could be climbed, and pushed out on foot across the desert, only to be killed by hostile Indians. Every large party since has had somebody that cracked. I loved it.

I was learning fast. Remember, this is still the first stretch, above the junction—the preinitiation. Beginning where my education had left off at the Salmon, I was being prepared for the Colorado. Two more days of hard rowing—the current was too slow—took me through the wide, beautiful valley of Brown's Park, long uninhabited, except for thousands of beaver, to the gateway of Lodore Canyon, only twelve miles long, but packed with vicious water. The first bad rapid, Disaster Falls, had claimed a boat from Major Powell's 1869 expedition, and just last year Tony Backus left his boat wedged there. Biting off a chew of tobacco, in accordance with the advice of old rivermen, I was soon through and on and through Triplet Falls.

At the bottom of Triplet, I found jammed against a pile of drift the punctured stern compartment of a wrecked boat and two broken oars. There was no way to tell whose finish was written there. When I asked about it later, nobody knew. Just another voyager who had started down the one-way route and had guessed wrong.

Hell's Half-Mile came next, where I almost guessed wrong myself. Major Powell's expedition gave it its name, in '69, and it's a good one. The river drops thirty feet here in less than a half mile, and the roar of it warns you for miles in advance that the horseplay is over and the rough work begins. From above, its twisted channel appears to grin, its fangs bared and dripping. Having looked it over carefully and charted my mental course down that tossing mane, I went over the brink quickly, knowing that I dared not hesitate.

I went over stern first, facing the rapids, rowing as hard as I could uphill to check the speed. That's where the early boats, like Major Powell's, made their mistake; they went down bow first and so had to row faster than the current to keep control, which, in turn, made it far more difficult to avoid the rocks. When you understand that the speed of the current here is better than twenty-five miles an hour—it seems much faster, but that's how the Government experts measured it—and that the full force of the river rolls down at that speed, you can imagine how fast the rocks seem to be leaping toward you and how exact must be your control on the oars to dodge in and out.

Halfway down the boiling chute, we struck a submerged boulder. You can't see such things in advance in such water. Had we been going head-on, the boat would have been done for, right there, but at retarded speed the reinforced stern held. We hung for a split second, head-on in the current, then swung into the full grip of the heaped-up channel, out of control and speeding down upon the big rocks that must be avoided.

I gave the oars all I had, whirled the boat and pulled for my life. The instant we were in the clear we struck again, and this time the river seized my left oar and tore it from its socket. We hurtled sideways toward a huge boulder, and it was there that the boat itself did the trick. It slid upon the rock instead of crashing—I was thankful then for the rake I'd given her bow—spun, and slid off. By now I had the oar in place, and we eased between the remaining rocks to a safe landing below. It seemed like the boat almost chuckled out loud at me there, when we were in the clear. "Happy to oblige. But next time don't depend so much on me."

We came to my second portage, where I stumbled and sweated with heavy loads over boulders, through deep sand, up a rough mountainside, through thickets and then down to the river again. Never again, I decided; so I discarded some extra flashlight batteries, 150 feet of heavy rope that I saw would be useless now, alone as I was; a half gallon of dry beans, two cans of coffee, an assortment of nails, a vacuum bottle and several cans of canned heat. I might tighten my belt thereafter, but I'd get through faster.

The next day we went through Split Mountain, one of the most unusual channels of the trip. The river runs parallel, then turns suddenly and, for no reason apparent to the eyes, knifes into the heart of a mountain. But instead of going through, it doubles back and for six miles has cut a meandering, stately gorge before returning to what would appear to have been its natural course. This was the last tree-covered canyon, and not far below Jensen, Utah, where I restocked with provisions, the vegetation disappeared almost entirely.

The name of the next canyon, Desolation, describes the whole country. The illusion was of sinking deeper into the heart of the earth, into giant dimensions. I was approaching the junction of the Colorado.

At Greenriver, Utah, just above the junction, I heard about the last expedition before me. A daring young Idaho river runner named Hyde had started there, in 1928, with his bride, to "honeymoon" through the canyon. Women have their place in the world, but they do not belong in the Canyon of the Colorado. The amazing part of it is that they got beyond Grand Canyon—the town—which is a long way down. A relief expedition went in later and found their boat. I was later to see Hyde's name painted on a cliff. I painted my name below his—mine is now the last—wondering, as I did so, if my name, like Hyde's, would also appear on the long and lengthening list of those who failed to make it through.

And so we came to the Colorado, where it swings in from the east to join the Green. I had covered 500 miles; 600 of the Colorado were ahead. Here, where you start down the deceptively easy-going first stretch of Cataract Rapids, is your final chance to turn back, though the early explorers, prospectors and trappers didn't know it. It is probably the world's most deceptive and fatal river trap.

You begin by easy stages—you're an early explorer now, with no previous records to guide you—and you tell yourself that this isn't bad; you'll see what's around the next bend. From the bend it still doesn't look bad—if you've come down the comparatively smooth Colorado above the junction, you've forgotten, or overlooked, how much more water has been added to the stream—and you go on to the next. Suddenly it doesn't look so good. It isn't bad, but the walls are speeding by faster than before; there's a strengthening roar ahead, deep-toned and reverberating; and, altogether, on second thought, you tell yourself you'll turn back.

But it's already too late for second thought. You're in the canyon now—the most wonderful and beautiful and pitiless canyon in the world. The walls are sheer, their crests are rising, seeming to stretch higher and higher toward the blue sky right while you're looking at them, and the speeding water joins wall to wall. There isn't any bank. No boat or living man can backtrail now, upstream. Well, you say—being a hardy adventurer who's seen plenty tough rivers—we'll have to make the best of it and go on through.

So you do, and not having the proper boat—a boat for the specific purpose, a good boat—that's the end of you. If you crack up in midstream, the river claims your body and doesn't give it up. If you make it to the shore, your bleaching bones will join the others scattered along a 100-mile stretch. Your equipment will litter the banks and swirl to the outer edges of the great eddies, and so come to rest among the mute records of other parties who have passed that way. How many have perished there will never be known.

Toward the middle of Cataract Canyon, the river was kind to me, a neophyte knocking at the door. I had tied up on the edge of a comparatively quiet eddy and had gone ahead to study this particular rapid. I decided to run it, but just as I was turning away, a whim of a receding wave showed a great submerged rock in the only possible channel. Had I turned back two seconds sooner, I would not have seen it.

There was nothing to do but portage, a 100-yard, backbreaking, man-killing overland trip that took all afternoon. I had to get poles and small logs from the drift to use for skids over the great rocks. I would bridge gaps and slide the boat over. Sometimes they would roll, letting the boat drop down. At other times I would work the boat up a steep pitch, grunting and straining, get it near the top, and then it would slide back to the bottom again. I wished I had had a partner. As twilight fell, I had it back in the river.

That night I had my greatest fright in the Colorado. The only strip of sand wide enough for a bed was above the rapids, so I went back up over the man-killing rocks to it to sleep.

Tired as I was from the portage, I couldn't fall asleep. I lay there half dreaming, thinking of the rapids ahead, rechecking my mental data on them, and most of all trying to visualize Deubendorf, the greatest test of all. Presently the moon rose above the canyon wall—and a friendly moon it was to me, down there in the bottom of the great fissure, insectlike. Suddenly I remembered the boat. I had left it tied in such a way that the rope lay across a sharp rock. Had the constant stress of the water frayed the rope through?

I reared on an elbow and looked down over the rapids, and there in the moonlight I saw the boat, the broken rope trailing, just swinging out and into the grip of the current.

Leaping up in a cold sweat, I ran down over the rocks, stumbling and falling. With the boat gone, I was done for. The main channel tossed and glistened in the path of moonlight, empty and lifeless, but in the shadow where the boat had been, a gray shape loomed. It was not until I could get my hands on the canvas-covered hull that I knew that I had only dreamed it. The rope was sound and good, and the boat was still there.

I changed the rope—you can bet on that. For a long time I sat there in the shadow with my hand on the boat, drawing reassurance from it. I was tempted to stay there till sunup, but I went back up over the rapids and crawled into my sleeping bag, half ashamed. If I could get that scared about a dream, what about Deubendorf?

While toting the equipment over the rocks to the boat, I found that I still had too much duffel, so overboard went the poleax, side of bacon, three cans of chili, three cans of corned beef and a pup tent that I'd held out before. It was like burning my bridges behind me; and, on the other hand, it was just another bet that I was right. If the boat cracked up and I made it to the bank, a hundred tons of food wouldn't have been enough. In the end, having eaten it, I'd starve just the same.

That day I ran through Dark Canyon Rapids, the last bad

one in Cataract, and it made me feel better. I had got farther than those who had perished in Cataract, and that was something. At the same time, I knew from my maps that Glen Canyon began a few miles below, and after that there would be 165 miles of relatively still water to row.

Just below Cataract were the names of travelers who had made it this far, and I added mine, glad that I'd kept the can of paint: Buzz Holmstrom, 11–1–37. Few would see my name painted there, but those few would understand. Eight miles below, I saw the name of the Eddy Expedition on the cliff, and as I approached I saw below it carved the one name and date: Hyde, 11–1–28—nine years earlier to the day.

Four days of rowing took me through the 165 miles of Glen Canyon. It was beautiful here, and I stopped to take photographs of abandoned mining operations and cliff dwellings of a forgotten race. These were lazy days, and though I did not know it, I was storing up stamina for Marble Gorge and Grand Canyon below. Particularly Deubendorf, which was never far from my thoughts.

Probably the place of most interest in this stretch—Glen Canyon—is Hole-in-the-Rock Creek, where the early Mormon pioneers, who could not be stopped even by a barrier like the Colorado, performed the incredible feat of lowering horses and wagons down the almost perpendicular wall of the side canyon. The horses were then forced to swim across and the wagons ferried. Not far below is Father Escalante's Crossing, where steps were hewn in the canyon wall to get the horses down to the water. It was hard to believe, yet the record is there, carved in rock.

I made the mistake of passing Lee's Ferry, formerly operated by John Lee, Mormon pioneer, later executed for his alleged part in the Mountain Meadows Massacre. Five miles below, at Navajo Bridge, the river has started its plunge into Marble Gorge and leaves but one exit, a perilous climb over the walls of a side canyon. Two days were spent in overhauling the outfit and worming my way up and down the walls with fresh supplies obtained from the proprietor of Marble Canyon Lodge.

There were touches of civilization here, glimpses of people and life. I had a momentary rebellion against saying good-by to that bright upper world and imprisoning myself again in the somber depths of ever-deepening Marble Gorge. But the challenge of Badger Creek Rapids was in the air. Waving good-by to antlike figures on the bridge 500 feet overhead, I shoved off.

Badger Creek wasn't so bad, and I went on to Soap Creek, whose reputation wasn't so good. I was sure, from my data on it, that it would have to be portaged, but when I looked at the jump-off, I could see that portaging would be a back-breaking job. Since the river and I understood each other better by now, I walked on down to study it.

Sure enough, the message was there: "Unload your boat and start near the right shore, cutting across below this first rock, where this big eddy will swing you out of the main channel, and then you will slip past the other rocks and on through. But don't miss a single stroke of the oars, or you'll answer to me."

The river having been honest with me so far, I did as directed and the boat took me through without shipping a drop of water.

That gave me my first sense of false confidence. Late in the afternoon, when I came to North Canyon Rapids, the river put me in my place again. I hadn't studied the currents carefully enough, and, as a result, the boat was tossed crosswise into the largest wave I had yet seen. Its trough was so deep that the boat was held on its bottom, while the wave shook it so roughly that I had to let go the oars and hang on with both hands to keep from being catapulted out. Then, when I was helpless, the river contemptuously kicked the boat free, as much as to say: "Let that be a lesson to you."

I went on, head up, with violent drops coming so close together that I had no time to relax after one before I was into the next, and on to Cave Rapid, whose rough voice fills the great cavern from whence it takes its name. It was at this point that the Government survey expedition of 1923 found the equipment of some unknown party.

From this point I traveled rapidly past gloomy caves and beautiful hanging gardens that were ten times more beautiful in the midst of all this desolation, down a wider canyon and on to the mouth of the Little Colorado. It was low and clear at this season, bringing in some drinking water that was surely welcome after the silt-laden currents of the main river.

While eating lunch there—consisting of one large, cold hot cake and one can of sausage—I caught the sun on the wings of an airplane far above. To the pilot, the river must have looked like a pencil scrawl. But I was close to the river, close to its irresistible power, and could well believe that it alone had done the incredible job of carving such a canyon.

One day's run brought me to Granite Gorge, where the river, using its silt as an abrasive and cutting tool, has cut through what the geologists say is the oldest rock known to man, and on to Bright Angel Trail, where I tied up and went after supplies sufficient to last me to Boulder Dam, 275 miles away.

At Grand Canyon village I was told of a party of geologists representing the Carnegie Institution and California Institute of Technology, who were studying the old Archean rock found in the Granite Gorge, and who were at that time about sixty miles downstream at Kanab Creek. I hoped to overtake them there, as they were traveling slowly, but there were famous rapids in between. Walthenberg was particularly bad. And finally—after close to 1000 miles of expectation—Deubendorf.

The lesser rapids above Walthenberg bent both oarlocks and cracked an oar. When I came to Walthenberg itself—I was ready to portage, but it couldn't be portaged alone, and there was nothing to be done but run it. So I looked it over and then shoved off. I bumped rocks twice—both glancing blows that made the boat groan accusingly, but I came safely through.

Camp that night was fireless, since the only driftwood was that caught in clefts fully seventy-five feet above the present surface of the river—proof enough of the mighty cataract that is there in flood stage.

The next afternoon, I came to Deubendorf, named after a member of Julius Stone's party whose boat cracked up there, but who successfully and miraculously survived the last half without a boat. Stone says that anyone who runs these rapids, at any stage of the water, will know he has tackled a real job; and I can vouch for the truth of that.

The more I looked at it, the worse it seemed. And the worse it seemed, the more I wanted to run it, even though it could be portaged and I didn't have that excuse. For forty days in the canyon and for months before, I had dreamed of this moment.

The smooth current curved swiftly at the start, then reared up in huge waves that crashed and thundered over half-buried rocks below. These were the rocks upon which Deubendorf himself had crashed. Yonder, on the left, were the rocks that had taken one of Clyde Eddy's boats when they were attempting to line it down, in 1927. On the right were other rocks and islands that thrust the channel in.

But there was a way. There was no channel, true, but there below the jump-off, before the force of water built up in those tremendous waves, there was a space—time for a half dozen strokes on the oar—and two rocks at the right. Couldn't I shoot through there, dodge that submerged one below, and so pass on safely into the farther eddies?

I wasn't sure but that I was kidding myself. The line of rocks on the right threw back a big curling wave toward the heaped-up mountains in the main channel. At times this big wave wasn't so high; again, its curling crest was fifteen feet overhead. The first problem was to get by that backwash, hugging close to the rocks on the right, because if it ever slapped me back into the grip of the main channel, I was done for. That's what happened to Deubendorf; it's probably what happened to everyone else that tried it. But I had a good boat; I could move fast in a pinch. The wave could throw me back toward that towering mid-channel, and still there would be time for five or six quick strokes. Maybe. And if I got out of the clutches of the main channel, hard forward on one oar, hard backward with the other, should see me between the rocks on the right, and so into easier water.

Understand me about this "easier" water. A month before, it would have looked plenty tough, that stretch halfway down Deubendorf. To get the proper slant on it, you should remember that the Government experts figure 8000 second feet at that point. In other words, there's 8000 cubic feet of water rolling down at every tick of the clock.

Well, I looked it over for fifteen minutes and then turned back to the boat. There was no use waiting; when you've got 'er figured, it's time to go. I could feel my heart beating. It seemed like it was beating down lower than usual, down in my stomach. I remembered that British officer at Waterloo, when he climbed into the saddle and found that his knees were shaking. "Shake, damn you," he said. "You'd shake worse than that if you knew where you were really going."

Sure I was scared. I saw to it that the spare oars were properly lashed down, the proper side of the blades up. Those oars, lashed aft on each side of the deck, were always within my range of vision, because I was facing the stern, downstream. Then I felt of my sheath knife to see that it was hanging at the proper place on my belt. If an oar broke, I'd have no time in the rapids to unlash a spare; I'd have to cut it loose—fast. Like the fellow said about the gas attack at the front, there's only two kinds of folks left in the rapids when an oar breaks: the quick and the dead.

Then I shifted my life preserver so it fitted comfortably, was just tight enough and still left my arms absolute freedom, tilted my hat, braced my feet exactly right in each corner of the cockpit and took a big chew of tobacco. In the rapids you've got to have something to sink your teeth into. Then I spit on my hands, took hold of the oars and shoved off.

How long do you think it takes to run rapids like Deubendorf, once you're over the brink? About as long as it takes to say that old tongue-twister: "The ragged rascal ran around the rugged rock." And that's about the way it went too.

I was over, crowding as close as I dared to the right. The water in the main channel was a heaped-up muddy mountain at my left; my eyes were fixed on the big, curling wave that would tell the story. We came to it and the boat rode up it. We were standing on end; we were thrown in toward the main channel; we were halfway up to the crest. In mid-air, so it seemed, I was waiting, the oars free; when we struck, the oars dug in.

I didn't count the strokes, but I think there were about five. On the second I thought I was done for; it seemed that the channel had me. On the third I was sure of it. I said to myself: "Well, Holmstrom, you came this far, anyway." On the fourth we rode up a twenty-foot wave in the channel, but on the right-hand side of the crest; we were sliding down. The boat had had that extra margin that it takes. On the fifth, the two rocks I'd aimed at were alongside. Hard back on one oar, hard forward on the other; and we were through, scuttling down between the rocks in the easier water below.

It was that simple and that fast. I rode on through the eddies, the danger past, looking up toward the sky. To my amazement, I found I was singing, bellowing, like I was trying to outdo the roaring of Deubendorf behind me. More than that, I'd remembered four lines of Barnacle Bill that I'd tried to recall for 1000 miles back. I had 'em now, and I'll never forget them again.

Two days' traveling took me down past Havasu Creek, a quiet little stream that enters the Colorado through a narrow slit in the walls, but which opens up, in the interior, into a fertile, hidden, rock-walled valley, inhabited by the shy Havasu Indians. Toward evening of the second day, the roar of Lava Falls strengthened. Its vicious waters, twisting down between great blocks of lava, have never been run, and for a while I played with the idea of trying it rather than portaging.

But I decided not to crowd my luck—you get that way while the memory of Deubendorf is fresh—and portaged over. The scientific party had portaged here, and it was plain that they weren't far ahead. I could even tell a lot about their boats. White paint scraped off on sharp rocks told their color; slivers of wood gouged out by the jagged lava showed that they were planked with mahogany.

I put on speed, anxious to overhaul them; and when night brought me to a camp site in Granite Park, I came upon a tripod made of driftwood and bearing a single sign. Two words. I read it, blinking, "Hello Buzz" and the date: "11–17–37." They knew I was coming; they were expecting me down below. They had also left a can of cocoa, the most welcome imaginable addition to my limited fare. That cocoa warmed my stomach and the greeting warmed my heart.

Next morning I entered lower Granite Gorge, and at noon came to Diamond Creek, where the geological party were eating lunch. I hadn't realized before how lonely I'd been. With so much in common to talk about, we practically drowned out the noise of the river, and it was hard to tear myself away the next morning. But they had plenty of time; I had to get on. Lava Cliff Rapids—last, and classed by some as the toughest on the Colorado—was ahead. I was close to Boulder.

As I was ready to pull out the next morning, Frank Dodge, head boatman of the party, and one of the greatest living river runners, followed me over to my boat. He was a heavy-boned, towering, silent man who'd been running rapids before I was born. He hadn't said anything to me the night before, nor that morning. After he'd looked the boat over, he stood there looking hard at me. He said, suddenly: "Buzz, you're all right." Then he walked away.

Separation Rapids were the next hurdle, so named because it was here that the three men left the Powell Expedition of 1869–70, choosing to go out overland rather than face the last stretch. But instead of life, they met death at the hands of the Indians. Some authorities on the Colorado believe that a quarrel with Powell, rather than fear, was responsible for their desertion. It sounds reasonable to me. After all, they'd come through close to 1000 miles of the Colorado. They should have been used to rapids by that time.

The tragic part of it, of course, was that they were almost through, though they didn't know it. Only Lava Cliff Rapids were ahead. After that, the last great barrier, the home stretch. To tell the truth, though I had maps whose reliability I had proved beyond doubt, that showed how close it was to Boulder, it didn't seem possible. You'd never know it to look at the canyon or the river.

I shouldn't use the words "only Lava Cliff Rapids." They are supposed to be as bad as Deubendorf and are classed by some as worse. But from the first they had loomed in my mind as something to think about after Deubendorf, and it didn't seem likely that they could be as tough. I'd known all along that they couldn't be lined by one man, or portaged; so they had to be run, and that was that.

It was a jolt when I came to them. I've never seen anything like them, and unless I run the Colorado again I never will. A delta had pushed in from the left, at the very brink. On the right a tremendous lava cliff, from which the rapids take their name, thrusts out into the channel. The full force of the current roars through and down directly upon bristling rocks. Because it is narrowed by these inthrusting escarpments, the heaped-up flood, bursting through, has a peculiarly sinister and savage appearance; and there is absolutely no chance to ride the main current directly down, because the rocks are waiting.

But there was a back eddy at the left, below the delta, and I soon saw that if I hit the jump-off at an angle and rowed hard to the left, I'd have a chance to miss the main channel and the rocks and ease down alongside the wall. A chance being all I could hope for, I made ready and shoved off.

It came off as I had planned; I made it in and through and down, hard to the left and so into the swirling but easy eddies that wheeled along the wall.

A few minor rapids were left, so the maps said; and I proceeded cautiously. No use taking chances now, this close to the tape.

In the morning I ate a big breakfast, filling my stomach for a hard day. Shoving off, I eased past the corner of the wall, and was surprised to find myself in quiet and deepening water. It lapped gently against the walls on either side. The great waves smoothed out. For the first time in forty-four days on the river, the grip of the current relaxed, changed from steel to velvet, and from velvet to a last, lingering touch, and was gone. My momentum carried me on, but it was momentum alone.

It couldn't be. No still water like this was recorded below Lava Cliff. The maps said so, and I had proved their honesty a thousand times.

Then I saw it. Since the maps had been made, Boulder Dam had been built. The impounded water had crept back this far into the canyon—much farther than I had dreamed. This was Lake Mead, created by the dam. There were no more rapids.

Already the roar of the river was a whisper in the canyon. Ahead, the lake was widening, becoming more brilliant. Sunlight was beyond, flashing on the water.

I drifted on for a while, head resting on my arms. Don't ask me how I felt at that point; not many would understand. It wasn't exultance. It was a kind of all-gone feeling. The rapids were behind me now—Deubendorf and Lava Cliff and Walthenberg and two hundred others—and I would probably never run them again. I would never be so young again, nor so fit.

I rowed around in circles for a while, within sound of the river. Once again there was no way out but ahead. So I spit on my hands and headed out into the open, through the widening canyon.

It was warm here; the sunlight was dazzling. The silt had vanished from the water like mist at morning; it was crystal-clear. They had heard at the dam that I was coming, and a speedboat had been sent out to tow me in. But my goal was the dam, and I wouldn't take the tow.

It's a big lake, and it took me three and a half days to row it. When I got to the landing, there was quite a crowd there—photographers and tourists and the like. After I did an errand that was on my mind, I posed for pictures and put the boat through her paces to show what she could do; though I know she felt self-conscious, like I did, out there in the open quiet water. I was wearing close to two months' whiskers; my undershirt was ragged; I looked like a tramp. She was battered and bruised by the rapids. Her original paint was almost gone. But she was a good boat still.

It was Thanksgiving Day—November 25, 1937—and I knew my mother would be glad to hear from me. So I wired her:

> OKAY AT BOULDER DAM.
> HALDANE.

Scouting Party

BY HASSOLDT DAVIS

The French Foreign Legion has a long and honorable history dating back to its founding in 1831. When Hitler's troops occupied France in 1940, General de Gaulle formed the Free French movement, which continued to fight in Africa; units of the Foreign Legion swelled the ranks of the Free French forces. Their professional skill and courage added immeasurably to the spirit of the Allied army that hounded and finally destroyed Rommel's forces.

Hassoldt Davis, an American writer, joined the Foreign Legion as a volunteer in 1942. Before that, he had traveled through the Near East, Africa, China, and much of Southeast Asia, including India and Nepal, and spent four years in the South Pacific, where his writings ran the gamut from ethnological studies of the Polynesians to a movie script. The night patrol which he describes in this story took place in the Qattara Depression in Egypt, not far from the Libyan border and only a few hundred miles from El Alamein. It was one of many small links in the chain that led to Allied victory in North Africa.

IT WAS night at last, the bright day ended, the dust settled, the flies sleeping, and an hour of peace before the flying carpet of mosquitoes from Lake Maghra would fall upon us. We could see at last without squinting, without sand and sunglasses. We could lie still without continually shuffling our hands over our desert sores to keep away the insects that squat and poison them. We were at rest in preparation for a long night, with perhaps no morning for some of us.

"Me, I'll drink a dream to Mamma Death," said a youngster of the Foreign Legion, draining his cup and falling asleep at once. That appealed to the Legion, the legend of Mamma Death dressed in clotted blood and sand, waiting on the cliffs we were to explore some twenty miles behind the enemy lines. They slept like bearded babies, confident that they were the pets of Mamma Death. My own Spahis turned over occasionally for a drink of salty water, the best we had, and I stayed wide awake, probably popeyed in anticipation of my first night patrol. I was a second lieutenant of Spahis, in the first flying column of the Fighting French, an American volunteer, an amateur in war.

I looked along the sand to Capt. Morell Deville, blessedly stocking the energy of sleep, propped against the tire of an armored car. As a soldier of France, Morocco, Eritrea and Syria, he, too, knew how to drop into sleep at will.

Lieutenant General Montgomery had taken command of the British desert army and we were excited by a handout which came from him: "There will be no withdrawal and no surrender." Forces were on the march which were to send Rommel scurrying across the desert for a last desperate stand in Tunisia.

What the British wanted was firsthand news of the lost world behind Himeimat, of those escarpments edging the Qattara Depression which were occupied by the enemy. The mystery of the depression was gradually being pared away. Our own French troops had come from the Siwa Oasis across it, proving for the first time that it was traversable by a motorized army, but most of it was still unknown. It was a colossal rift where nothing lived, a wound in the desert 200 miles long and 200 feet below sea level. The enemy were thickly camped along its northern edge and might well descend into it in an attempt to break through our southern defenses.

Our specific duty was to cross the depression, climb the escarpment and make the first patrol about twenty miles inside the enemy lines, a task that looked to me like the most exhilarating suicide. But it seemed that always the French were to accept eagerly the suicidal actions. In October, still to come, two small battalions of our Foreign Legion were to hurl themselves up the cliffs at the Italian Folgore Division of 11,000. It was in preparation for this that twelve of us were assigned to reconnoiter routes, locate mine fields and discourage the enemy observation posts.

Maghra was not properly a lake, but an incredible swamp in the sand, with harsh tufts of green sprouting from sodden dunes, and it lay in what might be called paradoxically a heavily forested desert. For miles around, this desert was crisscrossed with petrified trees like giant jackstraws, trees two feet in diameter, their branches crumbled to flints that tinkled musically beneath your feet, their leaves become dust. This was a wasteland dedicated to death, the corpse beneath the skin of Egypt.

Every day we made tentative patrols for the eventual reconnaissance on the cliffs, setting out at dawn in our armored cars to skirt the escarpment that rose sheer from the Qattara Depression like the lost world of Conan Doyle. In my "blindee" I had a theological student and a physiologist, both in their early twenties, the fightingest men I ever knew. It seemed quite obvious to them that, since the purpose of this armored patrol was to find a way up the cliffs for our foot patrol later, the logical thing was to approach the cliffs as closely as possible.

The fact that they were teeming with Italians was incidental.

Grayay, the physiologist, had his head poked, like a jack-in-the-box, from the turret of our car. "Men moving up there," he said, pointing. "That's the path, all right."

We swung quickly back to camp, chased a gazelle, shot it with the 25-mm. and served it with our report to Captain Deville for supper.

He ripped at the joint held in his long fingers and nodded his round blond head. "Good. We'll make them dance, those Eytie chorus boys. Get to sleep at once. We'll leave at nine."

The Eytie chorus boys were the 11,000 Folgores. We were an even dozen.

We woke a few minutes before nine. The dullest of us must have dreamed the whine of bullets in the screaming of mosquitoes which pierced even the Bedouin head cloths with which we had tried to protect our faces. We were scarcely recognizable. My nose pulsed like an elephant's feverish trunk. My lips felt numb as fungus.

All Morell Deville's sociability had left him now. This bitten, bloated man was no longer the one who had banged a petrol tin

at the mess and sung advice to "La Salope" who wasn't "prop'e."
He tied the end of his pistol holster to his leg, put a tommy
gun on his shoulder.

"Grenades for you, Davis," he said. *"Allons!"*

We drove as quietly as possible in the armored cars toward
the spot on the southern edge of the depression from which we
would start on foot. We didn't talk very much. We could
scarcely doubt that some of us would die that night.

I began to wonder if I would be afraid. Sitting on the turret
of the car, my legs swinging, my arms aching with the effort to
hold on, I watched the full moon come up. Half an hour later it
was so bright that I could distinguish the Fighting French cross
of Lorraine and the Moroccan star of the Spahis painted on the
car 500 feet away, and I knew that the enemy must be watching
our approach.

They were. A white light rocketed from the escarpment to
our right. A mile ahead, another went up, drifted slowly toward
a third that exploded a mile farther on. All three went out
almost simultaneously. Then two lights only appeared, from
behind, and far ahead of us. This continued for the next half
hour. We were seen, all right, and the Italians were probably
signaling funny stories about us as we drove straight toward
them.

Deville, beside me on the turret, was chuckling over his chart.
As each new light went up, he jumped off the car to get away
from its magnetic pull and write down a compass bearing.
"That's nice of them," he said, "to give us their exact positions."

It didn't seem to bother him that the moon had given them
ours. We were as obvious as flies on a windowpane. We ground
out the last cigarettes we were to have till morning and drew up
at the edge of the depression. It was a strange-looking band that
assembled there. We had left our helmets behind, for we would
have to travel far and probably fast, and though the wind blew
cold from the cliffs we were dressed in our lightest clothes,
sleeves rolled up, pants legs tucked into boots. Some of us had
tommy guns, some rifles, some hand grenades. We stood around
our captain, waiting for instructions. On my right was Picoux, a
gangling man of fifty who looked more like a Kentucky farmer
than a professional soldier. On my left was little Vallin, brown

and neat and murderous, who had come to the Legion from China to fight for the France he had never seen. It occurred to me that I probably didn't look very fierce among these veterans.

Captain Deville spoke quietly. "Make sure that you haven't any marks on your charts that would indicate our own troops' positions, and that you're carrying no papers but identity cards. We are going to explore Point D. Now get this straight: our main job is to bring back information, so don't provoke a fight. If we do have trouble, try to take prisoners and leave no wounded to talk. If anyone approaches you to surrender with a cloth covering his hand, kill him outright. I buried the legs of one of our men a short while ago; he had been too eager to take a prisoner with a grenade hidden in his flag of truce."

Gaunt Picoux looked disgruntled at this slim chance of fighting. He mumbled that he was a soldier, not a secret-service man.

Morell Deville spun on him. "Shut your jaw! . . . While crossing the depression we'll spread out in three lines, fifty feet apart. Men on the right keep eyes right; on the left, eyes left. Don't forget they know we're coming, and they may try for us from any direction. If we get separated on the escarpment during the night, try to reach Point Three, where the cars will be waiting. If you can't get down before daylight, hide until night before attempting it. Understand? Let's go."

The cars swung away from us, and it was like having a wall pulled suddenly from your back. The men looked tiny, separated. The lights were still going up gaily from the cliff we were headed for. I followed fifty feet behind Deville in the center column, conscious of the din I was making in my Himalayan boots. The others wore crepe-soled shoes lent by the British army to night patrols, but there had been none to fit me.

Most of this dead earth far below sea level was marked on the charts as impassable for cars. At each step we broke through the crust of gravel into the sucking powder underneath, and my boots seemed to clack like castanets. From time to time a man would turn toward me, making a gesture of silence, and I would try to walk more quietly, following on tiptoe in Deville's footprints, balancing each step carefully. I still clacked.

For three hours we plodded through the depression, crouched as low as we could, inching our way around ridges of sand that might conceal snipers. Occasionally Deville would stop. We would sink to the ground and stare tensely at the shadow ahead. The three men leading would crawl toward it, identify it as a bush, a rotting camel, and beckon us on. It was like cops and robbers, which we played as children, but now we were playing with Mamma Death. We were in the open; the enemy was hidden, holding every advantage, and I could feel my nerves jangling like piano wires as we sought him through the glaring moonlight while he waited for us in the shadows of his own cliffs and canyons. I couldn't help thinking of what one glancing bullet would do if it struck one of the grenades with which each of my pockets was loaded. We had taken them from the Italians, and I didn't trust them much.

Again Morell Deville stopped. I caught up with him, hoping he hadn't heard my boots. He pointed to the tracks of a large tank and beside it those of a German jeep. The depression was certainly traversable.

He turned to me, shifting the tommy gun to his other shoulder. The smile was kindly in that hard fighter's face. "I'm sorry, Davis," he whispered, "but you're making a hell of a racket with those General Grants you're walking in. Tear up your scarf and wrap them, and if that does't work, you'd better follow us some distance behind. Once the shooting starts, you can run up and have your fun."

I felt pretty sick at the thought that I might be sent to the end of the class on my first patrol, but I wrapped the scarf around my feet and trudged on like a flamingo, making almost as much noise as before. We followed the tank tracks into the thin blue shadow at the base of the cliffs, and into the gully we had found on reconnaissance the day before. The flints were sharper here, and the bandages on my boots kept tearing and slipping. I would have to stop to rewrap them, then rush to catch up with the others. I was beginning to feel very foolish, thinking what a fine thing it would be if I scuttled this patrol, upon which so much depended.

Up and up we went, following the tracks, till we came cautiously to level ground, but the tracks ran straight north from here, so we abandoned them to look for the observation posts. It seemed incredible that we should have got this far without drawing their fire. Ominously, there were no flares any more. The moon was almost directly overhead, for it was two o'clock and we had been walking four hours. Clouds chased furiously across it, thick, tremendous, abnormally fast, like clouds in a Russian film. The whole scene was theatrical—the gray plateau, the hunched men, the spotlight effect of the moon flashing off and on between clouds, sweeping the canyons on each side of us, four or five hundred feet deep. Niched in those walls somewhere were the posts of the enemy, watching for the patrol that their rockets had signaled. We took a bearing here and had a small sip from our canteens of the salty water of Lake Maghra. It still wasn't Chianti.

"Point D," whispered Capt. Morell Deville, pointing.

We followed him on hands and knees to the edge of the plateau. Directly opposite and a hundred feet higher was a horn of a cliff, Point D. We went down quickly from shadow to shadow to the bottom of the wadi. The signs of the Italians were everywhere—boot and tire tracks, empty tins, paper caught on bushes. The light at this depth was the purple of underseas, and we moved through it heavily, feeling our way like divers.

I craned my neck to look up at the new cliff, our objective, towering high above us, and wondered what sort of fighting we would be in if we ever reached it. I thought, *Holy Moses, I'd love a cigarette.* Then a strange thing happened as I realized with astonishment that I wouldn't at all. There was the hankering in my chest which usually smoke allayed, but it wasn't now for a smoke. I realized with a shock that made me dizzy that nothing could assuage this hunger but the killing of men up there. It was a terrible and heartening discovery, and I felt suddenly healed of my weariness.

Captain Deville raised his hand, grinned. In single file, but widely separated, we began to ascend out of the shadow and into blue moonlight again. Flattened against the cliffs, we climbed hand over hand, and every handhold crumbled into little avalanches which I was sure could be heard for a quarter of a mile. To make things worse, the rags had ripped loose from my boots, and now I was making more noise than ever. There were only two alternative solutions to this: go to the end of the patrol or continue barefooted. I chose the latter, my feet wincing at the cold, sharp edges of the rock.

The whole cliff was pocked with caves like the eye sockets of skulls, and we wriggled past them with guns ready and grenades balanced, for any one of them would have been excellent for an enemy post. The sergeant of the Legion ahead of me passed back a message from the captain; three of our men were missing, he said, two Legionnaires and a Spahi, but it was impossible to look for them now. We must be going.

We did, straight up. The edge of the cliff hung over us. Our hands reached it, and at the moment when our eyes came level the sky burst open with a vomit of flame. I saw black shades humped over me and fire hurtling out of them. An Italian with feathers on his helmet deliberately took aim with a machine gun as I tore at my breast pocket for a grenade. I ducked, flung it, ecstatic with the realization that I was loving this, though it scared me silly. The earth heaved and the rocks splintered around us. The Italians were screeching. Our men, old desert rats, made not a sound as they triggered their tommy guns, flung their grenades, then spun to toboggan down on their backsides along the wadis where the cliff had crumbled to dust.

I spilled down headforemost, praying I wouldn't rip the rings off the grenades in my pockets, trying to keep an eye on the spurts of sand where the bullets struck.

We gathered finally in the shelter of a cave, panting and scratched, but without a wound.

There was still a wild chattering from the garrulous Italians above us, but they made no attempt to follow. They probably assumed that we were much more numerous than we were, but we knew by the din they made that we were outnumbered by hundreds. Some one of us laughed, and I heard the slap as his mouth was shut for him. I washed the cuts on my feet with spit.

"That takes care of Point D," Morrell Deville said. "Get going. You can rest tomorrow."

We spread-eagled against the cliff again, rounded it slowly and wormed our way into the darkness of the canyon. With our luminous compasses we took the azimuth of each important point and marked it on our charts. There were more footprints here—of a camel, a Bedouin and a small child. The child's were pathetic in this brutal arena of war. A little farther on, we entered a sort of crater where a tank had been playing; some idle Hun seemed to have attempted to cut a huge swastika in the sand with his treads. It seemed appropriate that that naïve emblem should be written in moving sand.

Deville whispered, "There's something funny here."

We distributed ourselves around the edge of the crater and squatted motionless while he examined those curious tank tracks on hands and knees. He passed his discovery around the circle; the whole crater was sown with antipersonnel mines—the kind with three little whiskers protruding aboveground. The slightest contact causes the whole mine to jump a yard out of its hole before exploding. Then a shrapnel of ball bearings flies horizontally over an area of a hundred yards.

Deville beckoned to two of the Spahis, indicated the passage by which the tank had entered. They buried three of our own heavy mines there.

We had cautiously started down again when a fusillade of shots rang out beyond the ridge on our left. We distinguished the bark of machine-gun fire, the great cough of mortars, the harsher yapping of tommy guns.

"There are our three lost men with the tommies," said the shadow beside me.

The valley echoed from cliff to cliff, and flat on our bellies we watched the flashes of the fight.

Hell's door might have been suddenly opened. The tall shadow of Deville was framed in it.

"We've got to get to them." He spoke evenly. There was no need of silence now. We pushed hard at the ground, pried our weary bodies up. Then the shots, the flashes withered, and the tommy guns of our own men spoke last.

"*Bien*," said our captain. "Good job." He passed a flask of whisky among us, and we toasted those soldiers fighting alone in the dark.

We had nearly reached the floor of the depression when three blobs of black challenged us over a ridge: "*Qui va là?*"

"France!" we replied.

There, grinning, were our three lost men. They had wiped out the post and taken a wealth of documents.

Slowly we trudged back across the depression, in three columns again, slogging through the mush of sand, alive to nothing but the lust for sleep. We had already done thirty miles, most of it vertical, in the past nine hours, and we couldn't have ducked very fast if the Eyties on the cliff had seen us in the brightening dawn.

The sun came up through the morning fog and we found our cars faithfully waiting for us, among them Deville's staff car, a blessed vehicle with sponge-rubber seats. We got into it with awkward dignity, joking at the night behind us, and dizzily, suddenly conscious of the boast, admitting that the bedroll among the flies would be wonderful. *Now,* I thought, *we'll drain the dream to Mamma Death.*

We spilled our grenades upon the floor, loosened our belts and slid the pistols from them, leaned back each in his corner and went to sleep.

I surged up, nauseated, from sleep again, clawing my way through oily billows of sleep to reach a voice shouting, *"Avions! Avions!"* Our car was still moving, but we pitched headfirst out of it. There were four planes plunging straight at us. I tried to run away from the cars, but my legs had stiffened and I fell on my chin. I lurched on frantically, seeing the planes bloat as they dived toward us, at the same time searching for anything in that polished desert that would shelter me. The planes filled the sky and I fell flat with my arms crossed behind my ears. *This is for me,* I thought. The machine-gun bullets raked toward me with a hundred prongs, over me and on to the cars. I heaved up to make another run for it while the four Messerschmitts were circling back. The car I had left was gushing flame.

I saw a little rock ahead of me, a cordial little rock, and jammed my head under it, curled my body around it tight. The planes were returning, their motors roaring. And there was another sound. There under the rock, less than a foot from my eyes, hissing at me, was one of the horned, brown-spotted desert vipers.

It was a ludicrous situation. I didn't know whether to go in with the snake or out with the jerries, who were diving again, but I decided on the snake, though I knew this sort to be deadly poisonous. I hardly dared to move, but I did manage to flick a little sand at him, and he backed away a bit, shaking his head in rather a reproachful way, for we were in this thing together. Down zoomed the planes to within a few yards of us, and I felt my buttocks quivering as they used to at the swing of my father's razor strop.

You feel totally impotent under the lash of an air attack. Shattering thoughts like bullets strike through your mind. *They'll get my legs,* you think, your toes burrowing. *Maybe my lungs,* and you tear your nipples on the rock. *Now it's coming, now, now.*

The bullets spat over us like a mouthful of rice and I felt the shock as my little rock was hit. My companion, the viper, hissed, and I heard the yell of Captain Deville and saw him flattened but grinning at me a few yards away, his pillbox hat still tilted jauntily. I leered, one eye on the snake.

Four times the planes came at us, seeking us individually. Each of us, dead, was treasure. On the planes' last circuit, Deville wove to his feet, bounded to an armored car and swung the Bren gun up. The planes screamed down at it, barely over the top, then off like bats into the sun with a long mist of petrol trailing from the last. If its tank was hit, it would probably land within our lines. Our men came up, cheering, from the sand, and for the first time, with their eyes wide open, saw the holocaust that had been our car three minutes ago, that might well have been ourselves.

I nodded good-by to the snake, which ignored me pointedly, and wavered over to my captain. He cocked a snoot at the four vicious little planes. He spoke appropriately. "They're asking for it," he added. "They're based on the cliffs, and we'll be back."

I looked at those eleven Fighting Frenchmen, ragged, crusted with blood and dirt, but excited anew at Morell Deville's promise of sport with a few thousand enemies. They'd be back, on their way to France again.

Only God Knew the Way

BY FLIGHT CAPTAIN C. J. ROSBERT, AS TOLD TO WILLIAM CLEMENS

During World War II, while the famous Burma Road into southern China was in enemy hands, thousands of American transport pilots regularly flew the "hump" over the Himalayas from India with supplies for the beleaguered Chinese. Lumbering and overloaded, the unarmed transports faced constant danger in the form of Japanese fighter planes.

But the "hump" pilots faced an even more remorseless foe: Himalayan weather. Once forced down among the forbidding and inaccessible peaks, few returned. But here is a story of two of those gallant men who lost their fight with nature but won their fight with death.

ON OUR last flight from India we took off into a pea-soup fog, and a few minutes out of our base the monsoon rain was flooding down the windshield in torrents. At 12,000 feet the rain turned to snow. We couldn't see our wing tips. That meant we were safe. As well as the enemy liked to take pot shots at us, no self-respecting combat pilot would fly in weather like that. With another few thousand feet, we'd be over the hump and the worst would be over.

My copilot, Charles (Ridge) Hammel, was a veteran of Pan American's famed "Africa Corps." A past master at desert flying, he distrusted this land of three-mile-high peaks. With seventeen other Flying Tigers, I had enlisted with Pan American Airways in the China National Aviation Corporation when the U.S. Army took over General Chennault's little squadrons. As our Douglas C-47 kept climbing with her heavy load, Ridge's face broke into a grin and he reached back to pat our Chinese radio operator, Li Wong, on the head.

"We're okay now," he reported. "Another thousand feet and we'll be clear of the hump. Another hour and you'll be home!"

But we couldn't get that last thousand feet. Even while Ridge had his back turned, I could see a thin layer of ice spreading over the windshield, then over the wings. In less time than it takes to tell it, that thin film grew into a layer six inches thick. We started to drop, not in a dive, but slowly. Then we lost the last slit of visibility. All the windows were frozen over solid from the inside. I pressed the palm of my bare hand up against the glass until I could feel the skin stick, then I switched palms. Just before both hands turned numb, I had managed to melt a little two-inch hole. I saw that we were passing through a cloud. Suddenly it opened and dead ahead loomed a jagged peak.

"Look out!" I yelled. "There's a mountain!" Grabbing the controls, with my eye still glued to the tiny opening, I swung the ship violently over into a bank. We missed the face of that cliff by inches. Then my heart stopped. A huge dark object swept by. A terrible scraping noise tore under the cabin; an explosive crash struck right behind me; the engines raced into a violent roar. Something stabbed my ankle, an intense pain shot through my left leg. Then, suddenly, we were not moving. Only the falling snow broke the silence.

I don't know how long I sat there before I heard Ridge's voice. It seemed to come from far away. "Get out of that thing before it catches fire!"

I heard my own voice answer, "Come on back in. You'll freeze to death out there."

My shocked brain told me the ship wouldn't burn. Both engines had been torn off when we hit. The cabin was intact, except for the radio station, which was crumpled like tissue paper. Wong lay sprawled in the aisle behind the cockpit. I struggled out of my seat to reach him. I held his wrist; there was no pulse. I put my arm under him, and a broken neck dropped his head back between his shoulders.

Ridge huddled against the rear bulkhead. He was badly cut about the face and hands. Little rivers of blood dripped down on his flying jacket, and he was holding his left ankle. His right eye was closed and the swollen flesh around it was already discolored.

I struggled to stay conscious. Nothing seemed very real. I tried a step, but my left ankle turned under me. The pain almost took my breath away. I looked down. I seemed to be standing on my leg bone, and my foot was lying at a right angle to it. Holding on to the roof supports, I swung myself down beside Ridge. For several minutes we just lay there looking at each other.

Finally he spoke. "What happened?"

"We hit a mountain."

This is certainly a crazy conversation, I thought. *Things like this don't happen. You hit a mountain at 180 miles an hour, and that's that.* Together, we thanked God for being alive, and all my life I will make deep and humble acknowledgment to God that I do not take any credit for our rescue. The fact that we were the first white men to come out of that unknown section of the Himalayas has little to do with it; it is partly the knowledge that in any one of a hundred different instances death awaited a wrong decision, when we had neither the knowledge nor experience for our choice; and partly the marvelous chain of coincidences—or "miracles," as Ridge and I called them —that led us through forty-seven days and nights, into and out of another world and back to civilization again.

We took stock of our situation. The plane was lying at a thirty-degree angle. Outside, a zero wind drove the snow in swirling gusts, but, by huddling close together, we could keep from freezing at night. The first rule of a crash is to stay by the ship. It's much easier for searching parties to spot a plane than it is to sight a person. In our case, we were both in such bad shape that we had no other choice. My leg was continually throbbing and even the slightest movement would send shocks of sickening pain through my whole body.

Ridge was only slightly better off. His left ankle pained him—

it proved to be badly sprained—but he managed to move about. Dragging himself over and about a jumbled cargo of machinery, he found our parachutes, which we spread out to lie on. He also found six tins of emergency rations, equivalent to three meals apiece. We figured we could stretch these out for six days, possibly longer. Because of his condition, the steep angle of the plane and the high altitude, the quickest trip Ridge was able to make over the twenty-five feet to the forward part of the ship and back again took nearly an hour. Just locating our parachutes and the rations took up the whole day, and we fell asleep from exhaustion—a sleep broken frequently by the pain from our injuries or a nightmarish awakening to our predicament.

By daylight, the snow had stopped. The scene almost took my breath away. Glistening, ice-encrusted peaks darted up all round us. Then I looked in the direction in which the plane had been headed, and yelled to Ridge. Together, we stared at the ugly, jagged peak. If we had gone another fifty feet we should have been crushed against it like an eggshell. Our steep bank away from the peak had miraculously paralleled the slope angle of the mountain, so that, when we hit, the plane simply slid along the face of the cliff. One outcropping of dark rock, 100 feet back, had caught the left engine, forcing us to a stop. Had it not been for that one rock we should have catapulted directly into a second peak another fifty feet ahead.

We were perched 16,000 feet high, up against one of the peaks of the Himalayas somewhere in the Mishmi Mountains, on the frontier of Tibet. We did not know in what direction we should head to get out, what we should look for, how we should plan. The slim chance of our being sighted by searching planes was buried under the two feet of snow which had covered the plane in the night. That meant we'd have to manage our own escape. We studied the topography of the mountain, debated various courses and finally picked the side which we felt offered the best chance. Five thousand feet below, possibly five miles away, was the edge of timber line. A sharp crease in the mountain and a junction with another ridge suggested that there might be water there. If there was water, it might lead to a river, and a river might run beside a house or a village. It wasn't much of a promise, but it gave us hope.

In five days, we estimated, our ankles would have improved

enough to allow us to move without blacking out every few steps. We considered for hours what we would take with us. We could afford to carry only what we absolutely had to have. In Wong's clothing we found a deck of cards. We would play gin rummy until we were exhausted, would sleep for a few hours, then start all over again. We discovered a gallon jar of soft-drink sirup, which we mixed with snow to drink. We recited navigation lessons, talked over our kid days, compared fighting in Burma with flying in Africa—anything to keep from thinking of the overwhelming odds against our ever getting out of this alive. By the end of the third day, we couldn't stand waiting any longer.

At dawn we started out. We knew we had to make it down to timber line before dark, because we could never live through a night on that unprotected slope. Our injured ankles turned under at every step, and we began to flounder. The slope was so steep that we kept falling, and the struggle to get on our feet again would sap every ounce of strength we could muster. In four hours of almost superhuman effort we had covered scarcely 200 yards. It was hopeless. We just managed to get back to the shelter of the plane with the last streaks of daylight.

Gripped with despair, we lay awake most of that night. We had only one full emergency meal left between us. We had to get down the mountain. But how? Finally, from sheer fatigue, we dozed off. I was awakened by Ridge, who was prying up one of the extra boards used to reinforce the floor. A sled! Now we were riding the crest of hopefulness again. Why hadn't we thought of that before? While it was still dark we pried braces off the side of the cabin and made splints. We tore our parachutes into strips, bandaged our ankles, then set the splints and wrapped yards of the silk around them until our injured legs were fairly stiff. What was left we wrapped around our hands and feet for protection from the cold, except for two long runners which we used to strap ourselves to the sleds. By daylight we were on our way.

We literally flew for the first 100 yards, but when the slope flattened out, the ends of the boards plowed deep into the soft snow. The struggle to get off, pull them out, set them flat, pile on and get started again was almost as difficult as our walking had been. We threw away everything we could possibly get along without. Even that didn't help enough. Finally, Ridge got his board sliding, only to have it hit a rock and send him sprawling down the slope. He rolled fifty yards before he was able to stop. Inspired, I started rolling after him. I rolled fifty yards too. Then we hit upon a technique. Lying on our backs, holding our injured feet in the air, we slid on the seat of our pants, rolled over on our sides—sometimes on our heads—ten, twenty, fifty yards at a time.

The slides grew steeper and steeper until, finally, within sight of timber line, we struck a slope that was almost 500 feet straight down. If getting out of the plane alive was a miracle, we both felt it would take another miracle to get down to the bottom alive. Because Ridge had a little better control with his sprained ankle than I had with my broken leg, he took the risk first. I watched him hurtle downward in a cloud of snow and suddenly disappear. I heard him scream. The most welcome sound I ever knew in my life was Ridge's voice, breaking that awful silence. It sounded weak and far away. "It's okay, but it's rough. Come on down." I slid over to the edge, took a deep breath and shoved with my good foot. Finally, I hit solid earth with a crunching jolt. As I lay there, afraid my back was broken, I heard the sound of rushing water. Just before darkness settled, we reached a stream in a steep-walled gorge.

Soaking wet and so weary that we could scarcely move, we found a cave, so small that the two of us could only half fit into it. We tried to make a fire by kindling some twigs with what papers we had with us—our passports, photographs of my wife Marianne, my license cards, address book. In our anxiety to get a tiny bit of warmth, we destroyed every tangible bit of evidence we possessed to prove that we had a home, a family, a country. But the wood was soaked through and we gave up. We took off our wet outer clothes and hung them up, hoping they might dry during the night, and, with our arms around each other, we tried to get some rest.

Looking back on that ordeal now, I cannot see how we could have made it. With our bad ankles, the best we could manage was a painful hobble. We could not follow along the bank because, for the most part, the river flowed through walls of sheer solid rock. We could not use the river itself because it raced through boulder-strewn rapids and over deep falls. Our only chance was to climb over the rough, jungle-covered mountains, keeping the river in sight as best we could.

For three days we crawled up and down those tortuous hills, taking one half bite of our last remaining ration at daylight and dusk, huddling together on the ground at night. Near the end of the eighth day we had to turn back to the river. The peaks were too steep to climb. We struggled over and around the boulders, half in, half out of the water, until, suddenly, the river dropped off into a series of steep falls. It was impossible to go forward. On both sides the walls of the canyon were almost vertical. We were at the end of our strength. We had spread one day's normal emergency minimum over eight days, but had swallowed the last bit of it that morning.

Numb, unable to think it out, we sat down beside each other and stared at that solid rock wall. Suddenly, Ridge leaned forward. A long heavy wire or vine was hanging down the side of the cliff. We tried it for strength. It held. Someone had at least been up the river this far. Foot by foot, we pulled and clambered our way up the wall. At the top, we found another sign. Saplings had been notched as if to mark a trail. With lighter spirits than we had had in many days, we hobbled on, and for three days more we drove ourselves through the brush, over boulders, up and down the hills, looking for those all but indistinct marks.

Our first day without even a bite of food left us with an intense empty feeling. After twenty-four hours, the emptiness turned into a steady dull ache and a feeling of intense weakness which left us wondering, each night, how we could recover enough strength for the next day's march. We searched continually for anything we could get into our mouths. We tried most growing things with stalks or stems.

At the very peak of our hunger, however, another miracle befell us. I fished from the stream a piece of fruit which looked and smelled like a mango. The taste was indescribably vile; it seemed as if someone had struck me a blow in the mouth. I retched horribly and rolled on the ground in agony. But on the verge of starvation you will try anything. Ridge had to try a bite, too, and he went through the same torture. But there is some good in everything. Our stomachs were numb for the next three days. Even starving as we were, we could not bear the thought of food.

On the thirteenth day we reached the practical end of our endurance. The stream divided and went down two valleys, exactly opposite. Which way should we turn? Because we were facing east, we took that direction. Had we had the strength to think, we would have chosen the westward valley, since in that direction lay Burma and our course from India. To the east, we realized afterward, lay only the wild mountain frontier of Tibet.

That turn to the east was the fourth in our chain of miracles. After an hour, we broke into a clearing. The hut had been burned to the ground, but it was a sign that human beings had lived here. Somehow, we found new strength. Later in the afternoon we we found the prints of a child's bare feet in the mud, and then, in the last few minutes of daylight, we dragged ourselves over a hill, and there was a thatched roof. The hut, made entirely of bamboo, stood on stilts about four feet above the ground. The door nearest us was securely latched. So was the center door. When we got no reply to our knock at the last door, Ridge threw himself against it and we sprawled inside. It was so dark and the air was so thick with smoke that we could scarcely see. A big pot was boiling over an open fire in the center of the room. Then we made out the huddled forms of two very old women to whom six nude, wild-looking children were clinging. At the sound of our voices, they appeared to be even more frightened. We tried our few words of Chinese. Finally, by gestures, we tried to tell them that we were fliers and only wanted food, but the children kept pointing to the old ladies' eyes. One, we learned, was totally blind, the other almost so.

The children later gave us each a gourd. But instead of ladling out the food, one of the old women simply picked up the boiling-hot cooking pot in her bare hands and passed it around while each of us, and then the six children, scooped out a gourdful of the food. Ridge and I were so impressed with this witchery that, starving as we were, we momentarily forgot all about eating—until our gourds got so hot we had to set them on the floor. Almost immediately, with hot food inside and the hot fire outside, we rolled over on the hard bamboo floor and went sound asleep.

Eighteen hours later the hundreds of wood ticks we had attracted in our wanderings chewed us awake. Sunlight was streaming through the open door and some of the smoke had cleared. The faces and bodies of the women—such as showed outside the aged, ragged blanketlike cloth they wore draped over one shoulder and around their middles—appeared to be encrusted with a lifetime's exposure to dirt and wood smoke. Their hair was long and coarse, and around their heads each wore a wide metal band.

It was on our third day there that the two oldest children disappeared. Late in the afternoon they returned with three men who stepped right out of the Stone Age. They had broad flat foreheads, cheekbones and noses, and mops of long shaggy hair. They did not even have sandals on their wide, strong feet, and their legs were bare to the thigh. Each wore a sleeveless leather jerkin that reached to a small loincloth, and carried a long swordlike knife on one hip and a fur-covered pouch on the other. These costumes were typical of all the Mishmi people we saw until we walked out of this strange world nearly a month later. Their long matted hair hung down over their shoulders, from each ear dangled an ornament made from silver coins, and chains of beads, animal teeth and coins were draped about their necks. They were cheerful, hospitable, interested little men.

By a carefully thought out sign language, we explained as best we could that we were flying men who had crashed into one of their mountains, and who very much wanted to return to the white man's country. They smiled continuously, nodding their heads in what appeared to be perfect understanding, but which we knew was complete bewilderment. Finally, they could resist no longer. They had to feel our clothes, try our shoes, run the zippers up and down the front of our flying jackets amid roars of gleeful laughter, blink their eyes in childlike amazement when we let them turn on our flashlight, listen with ever-widening eyes to the ticking of our watches.

After a while they left us, but our act must have made a hit. That same night two others arrived, one a young boy. From their pouch they offered us two eggs, a sweet potato and a handful of boiled rice, and then invited us to come with them. Because their food was better, and thinking they might be from a village from which we could send word to the outside, we decided to follow them. Apparently elated, they simply took off their knives, swung their fur-covered pouches around until they rested on their stomachs, and rolled over beside us to spend the night.

Next day, after eight hours of struggling with tortured and bleeding feet over a primitive mountain trail that would have been covered in two hours by our native friends alone, we managed to reach the door of another hut, a bigger one. We fell onto the floor, exhausted.

When we woke, we discovered that friendly hands had carried us inside to a pallet in one corner of the big room. The three men who had brought us were here, and four others, apparently all of the same family. Fifteen women also lived in the house. In the two weeks we were there, Ridge and I never did get all the children counted.

There, in that primitive smoke-filled hut, deep in the heart of the Himalayas, Ridge and I held court for two incredible weeks, receiving scores of these long-haired, leather-jerkined, bare-legged men of the Stone Age. Their implements were cut from wood or stone and, from what we could learn, they had never heard of Chinese or Indians, let alone Americans. After days on the trail and in their smoke-filled huts, we were as dark-skinned as they. It was not until Ridge felt strong enough to walk and had gone out in the rain that the natives discovered we were white. It produced some awe, at first, and then a curiosity which expressed itself in sly, quizzical looks from all except the children.

To entertain them, Ridge and I repeated, over and over again, our gestured description of our flight, our crash and the display of our clothing and equipment. Not knowing how long we might have to stay in this strange land, we had tried to learn the language. We learned to count up to twenty and mastered, altogether, about 200 words of their dialect. They had many peculiar customs, but their one characteristic which never ceased to startle us was their imperviousness to certain kinds of pain. The men would sort through the red-hot coals with their bare hands to find a tinder with which to light their pipes. One of them, trying to get us to unwrap the bandages from our ankles to see what was under them, rubbed his hand over his own ankle in a gesture. For the first time, apparently, he discovered a large round bump, like a cyst, on his ankle bone. He simply drew his knife, sliced off the bump with one deft blow and, with the blood streaming down his foot, returned the knife to the scabbard and kept right on talking to us as though he had simply brushed away a fly.

What work was done was managed by the women. The men, for the most part, sat about the fire, which the women tended, conversing with much raucous laughter, smoking their long bamboo pipes, into which they would stuff dark, stringy, home-cured tobacco. I had never smoked before, but I became an inveterate tobacco fiend with the pipe they made for me. We began to smoke opium, not only because it was expected of us but because we thought it might help us to sleep. It did not have the slightest effect on us. Later, we were told that, had we stopped smoking and then started again, we might have become addicts.

Late one evening an elderly trader from the Tibetan hills, wearing a great wide bamboo hat and carrying an ancient flint-lock musket over his shoulder, appeared. Two bearers lugged huge bags of lumpy red sand, which, we learned, was salt. We told him our story, which by this time had become a mechanical routine. The trader, who told us he had known a white man once and had seen others in his lifetime, wanted us to go with him. We explained that in about five days more our ankles would be strong enough, and then we would follow him. He seemed disappointed, and several times that evening came back to us, motioned for our pencil, which we used for one of our stock demonstrations. We did not want to part with what might be our only means of getting word back to civilization, so we shook our heads. Finally he gave up, signaled to his porters and disappeared into the night.

A few days later his son appeared, a fine-looking youngster wearing earrings and a necklace of large silver coins. With elaborate gestures he presented us with a chicken, a pinch of tea and a bowl of rice from his bag, and then he, too, evidenced a peculiar interest in the pencil. To keep in his good graces, since his father might be the one to get word to the outside, I tore off a corner of my flying map and wrote this note:

We are two American pilots. We crashed into the mountain.
We will come to your camp in five days.

He snatched the slip of paper from my hand and disappeared. We concluded that he wanted the note for a souvenir, and that in five days he would return to lead us to his father's hut. By noon on the fourth day he was back. Although obviously tired from a long, hurried march, he was beaming. He first sat cross-legged before us, took four eggs out of his pouch and presented them to us, then left the hut and returned with an envelope. It was a standard India state telegraph form sealed with wax. With hearts beating like trip hammers, Ridge and I clawed the envelope open. It contained a message from Lt. W. Hutchings, the commanding officer of a British scouting column then about four days' march away. He was sending rations by the messenger, and a medical officer with aid would follow shortly.

Ridge and I were delirious at the good news. We hugged each other and cried like a couple of babies. The boy explained to our houseful of hosts and hostesses, and they, too, joined in our jubilation, heaping more wood on the fire, breaking out bamboo stocks of some alcoholic corn drink and dancing and shouting about the room. In an hour or so, the porters arrived with the supplies, and we shared cigarettes, matches, salt and tea with everyone in the hut. The matches and white salt they put in their personal treasure pouches, the tea they brewed, and the cigarettes they smoked with a religious ritual, deeply inhaling each little puff. It was daylight before any of us in the hut slept. It was a night to celebrate.

It took Capt. C. E. Lax, the British medical officer, two days longer to make the trip than the native messengers had required —days that seemed hundreds of hours long—but never was anyone made more welcome. He told us that no white man had ever set foot in this country before and, had it not been that the British column, because of the war, had penetrated even as close as four days' march, we might never have been found. It was one chance in a million, and we had hit it. Another of our miracles.

Tired as he was, he got our clothes off immediately, gave us a thorough going-over and patched up more than twenty cuts and bruises and bumps on each of us. Ridge's ankle had been badly sprained, but was now in pretty good condition. Mine was fractured, but it had healed over, and this was no place to try to put it back in place. In the morning we would start for their nearest camp, with his native boys to help us over the roughest spots. From that camp possibly they could get a plane in to pick us up.

Long before dawn, Ridge and I were urging the doctor to start. Such a swift change of fortune had unsettled us a bit, and we both confessed to a heavy tug at leaving these strange people who had been so kind and so hospitable to a couple of strangers who, dropping suddenly out of another world, had been taken into their family and treated as brothers through these many days. We divided among them everything we had—the pencil, the flashlight, everything out of our pockets, and then borrowed all the silver coins the captain had, in an effort to express our appreciation. They, too, seemed to regret our going, and accompanied us to the edge of the clearing as Ridge and I, leaning on the shoulders of the two native messengers, followed the doctor down the rocky trail.

It took sixteen more days of hiking to get out of the mountains, but hiking on a full stomach, resting at night in shelters on grass pallets, swathed in blankets. Over the tough places, our little native helpers, who weighed fifty pounds less than either Ridge or I, carried us, resting in a sling swung from their foreheads. Up the sides of cliffs, along boulder-strewn river beds, on cable-slung bridges that Gurkha engineers built ahead of us over monsoon-fed raging torrents, these little men led or carried us until, finally, we reached the crest of the last mountain range. There, below us, in a lovely green valley on the banks of a great river, lay a little British frontier station, a sight as welcome as the sky line of New York.

A truck hurried us back to our India base to our friends. Ridge would be ready to fly again in a month. They wouldn't let me stay. Pan American had a plane waiting, and in five days I was home, and in the hands of a Seattle specialist who was to re-make my ankle. I found that my wife, Marianne, had never lost hope of my return. She was singing with a hotel orchestra a song written in her honor—"I'll be Waiting."

Before we left, they traced our course. The strange world we had come from was only ninety minutes—flying time—from our base. The doctor could not understand how, with one broken ankle and one badly sprained, we had lived through the hundreds of miles we walked. He called it a miracle.

One Man Against the Sea

BY WILLIAM WILLIS

Many brave men are adventurous through necessity. When hazard or duty challenges them, they respond with courage and resourcefulness. But sometimes, a more than usually daring man will undertake adventure by choice, pitting his wits and strength against the vast forces of nature for the sheer joy of the fray.

William Willis is such a man. An experienced seaman and writer, he had always led a life "in search of experience." Then, at the age of 69, he posed himself his greatest challenge: to sail a small raft, alone, across the South Pacific. His destination: Australia, 10,500 miles away. This is his own story of how he met that challenge.

THE SEA TREMBLES and I can hear the three young sailors on the raft with me chattering above the whine of the wind. In 50 years and more at sea, I have never experienced anything like this before. The water shudders under my raft's three pontoons; the world seems to be shaking itself to pieces. I have been dozing, leaning against the little hut on the deck, vaguely aware of the steady powerful pull of the towline and calculating my tasks for the voyage ahead.

But now the peace has been shaken out from under me, and I rise and walk forward over the quivering planks toward where the young Peruvians are babbling into their walkie-talkie. The lights of the big tug *Rios* that is towing us, 300 yards away, rise and fall, sometimes disappear behind a wave, sometimes are sliced by foam that rips through the blustering night. I intend to ask the sailors what they have heard from the tug over their radio, but suddenly a new force envelops the sea and us, and we are going skyward, high and higher, 20 feet, 50, then even 70, so that we look far down at the tug's lights, as if we have been lifted to a hilltop and the *Rios* is in a valley.

Then we start coming down, and it is the tug that is being lifted. And again we are caught in a shuddering sea, and then again it is our turn to be thrust up by an astonishing wave we can feel but cannot see—it is that dark. I brace myself and strain to discover how the raft is taking the stress. I would hate to lose this raft on the tow out of Callao, before I have had my chance to do some sailing.

Five or six times we are carried aloft and slide down the walls of the huge waves, and then at last the sea drops and dies and the normal ugliness of the night resumes. The raft is safe. Morning is near. It comes, gray, blowing, dank, sullenly flinging its winds and waves. The pontoons pound like drums played by madmen. Finally, 50 miles off the Peruvian coast, the tug stops, and circles. A small boat is put out. The three sailors shake hands with me, wish me well and leave me alone. For a moment I think they look at me with something like awe, but then I had been given a tumultuous send-off from the Peruvian naval base at Callao the morning before; and, too, they are young men, and young men tend to look oddly at people of my age. It is 8:15 on the morning of July 5, 1963.

The sailors have explained what their walkie-talkie told them —that there has been an earthquake. It centered under our raft and shook up the coast of Peru, but I did not learn the details for months; now I have work to do. I must sail this raft across the Pacific; I must prove that I can, just as Alpinists feel compulsions to climb their mountains. I must go from South America, across the Pacific, past the islands, past the solitude and the reefs and storms and whatever else intervenes, and on to Australia.

My raft, square-rigged like the ships I sailed from Germany as a boy, is 32 feet long, 20 feet wide—a fleck on the Pacific, but it is enough. My little house holds plenty of food. I am sure that I have enough fresh water—three barrels—to last 250 days, and I reckon my voyage at no more than 180. My steel mast, with its mainsail, jib and mizzen, is 34 feet high. I can steer in the familiar way, at a wheel rigged to the rudder with cables.

I want to prove that a man can sail anywhere on earth aboard a craft no bigger or fancier than this, and at any age. In 1954, when I was 61, I sailed another raft from Peru to Samoa, covering 6,700 miles in 115 days, and alone. Now, nine years later, I have expanded my ambitions, and set my sights on Australia, 10,000 miles away. In a sense, this voyage is to be the climax of a life in which I've roamed in search of experience: as a seaman, a prospector, a fisherman, a longshoreman, an oilfield worker, a writer—among other things. To try the world, to test myself—those are my ways.

I have waited long for this moment and worn myself lean arranging for it. Yet no matter how hard I tried, I could never have completed the arrangements without my wife Teddy, who is back in Lima. She gave me all her strength and energy. I am a fortunate man. Teddy has complete confidence I will make out against any obstacles I meet on the sea. Now I am ready to sail, and content.

Naturally I pushed westerly as directly as possible. But my course must be north and then northwest, for the Humboldt Current sweeps up this coast from its Antarctic origins, until Cabo Blanco bends it westward as the South Equatorial Current. To ride the Humboldt but escape from it when I could—this was my first project.

Day after day the weather snarled, as it was to do throughout the journey. Captains who travel to Australia were to tell me this season brought the worst weather they could remember. And the raft itself brought problems.

The pontoons, being steel and therefore rigid, made the deck bounce and tilt constantly; it was difficult even to drink a cup of coffee. The tug had hardly vanished when I discovered that this was really a five-man raft, and I would have to work very hard all the time to sail it. I also knew that one should take a year to test a square-rigger like this, but I had not taken the time. Once I had decided to make the voyage, I wanted to go immediately.

The letters on the mainsail, AGE UNLIMITED, looked good to me even against the gray sky, and I felt good as I began the adjustment to solitude.

My two cats, Aussie and Kiki, would not eat for the first three days, and Kiki, a gentle tortoise-colored New York City cat, cried a great deal. Aussie, a Peruvian ranch cat, only four months old, was tougher. But soon they were at home on the deck, with perfect sea legs, although I kept them tied for a month so they would not become too bold and wash overboard.

For me, adjustment took longer, as I had known it would. Solitude has an impact that benumbs a man. It is like being dropped into space, into a new environment altogether. One feels odd at first, and there is uncertainty, as if one's skin doesn't quite fit, and then little by little it comes to fit better. Many people had asked to go along with me—I think most people dream of having a great adventure. But I *had* to go alone; a man is most challenged when he is alone.

I fished every day as was part of my plan. In my hut I had stored staples—beans, lentils, rice and flour, canned milk, fruit and dried potatoes, onions, potatoes, cabbage, lemons and, of course, coffee and tea, but I counted on the sea to supply me with protein. Yet, after only 11 or 12 days out, I could not fish so much because I had a new and unexpected chore.

One morning I was checking the gear, something one must do constantly on a sailing craft, when I came to the rudder. What I saw here startled me. The rudder was turned by two hollow steel rods welded to its sides, controlled by cables leading to the wheel. Both these rods, I saw, were beginning to crack near the waterline. The metal was too thin. Twelve days out and 118 more to go, and already gear was giving way.

I fought down the anger and went over the stern and splinted pieces of wood to the rods, lashing them with a very strong fishing line. This held for a while, but I would have to do the job many, many times more, and eventually the flaw in the steel was to cause a tragedy.

The foul weather would not cure. This meant I had to stay close to the wheel at all times, alert to the creaks of the rigging and the flap of the sails. Naturally I wanted to keep the big sail up as much as possible, to the last possible moment before a storm attacked with full force. One carries the big sail and then decides in a split second when it must come down. At that instant I must leap forward and lower the canvas and dive into it to get the gaskets on before the wind can destroy it. Then I must set up the jib, crawling out on the jibboom—knowing at some undetermined moment the wind would drop and the big sail would have to go up again. It was an unending fight.

This was a damn hard raft to sail, I reflected. If I can make this—as I shall—it should prove that a person of my age can do a great many hard things. How I loathe the expression *senior citizen*. These two words alone make older people outcasts, even lepers. On the other hand, back in California I had seen many older people who had given up. We must never let society thrust us aside, as it will try to do.

I may have a catastrophe, I thought, but fear is simply not in my nature. Death is only a phase of life, and life has many glories.

There were glories there on the raft. The life cycle of the sea can be seen best from a craft that moves without sound. You watch in awe at first, but finally you are one with the sea. Several families of dolphins had moved under my raft to escape the sharks, and they were to accompany me for thousands of miles. Some of their babies were only four inches long. It got to the point where I gave some of the dolphins names—for instance, Jack and Jill.

The dolphins went fishing in the morning. Unbelievably fast, they dashed after their favorite prey, the flying fish. But these little fish could seek safety in the air. Then the heavy-winged frigate birds from the Galápagos, whose ancestors supplied the world with guano, would come marauding, and for the flying fish there would be no more landing.

Meanwhile the sharks were always around, blending into the shadows. The sharks were patient and pretended not to care about their favorite food, the dolphins. But once in a while a shark would see an opening and flash in, and the water would boil. The dolphin families united in counterattack. I had to keep my fishing handline short—no more than 40 feet—or else I could never get a dolphin to my deck past the sharks' teeth. I would get a bloody head while the shark got the rest. At night my cats prowled the deck, waiting for a meal of flying fish to land. In the morning the flying fish leftovers went on my hook to lure a delicious dolphin for my belly.

Gradually routines established themselves. Dejection is not in my makeup, nor is fear of catastrophe. Yet in evening, energy drains from all living things—even plants droop, and I would want to do so too, but I did my chores. In earliest morning—that is the glorious time. I felt exaltation. The mind opens, the body comes alive. The water coursed through the colors, from black to gray to pink to gold. In the great sea, surrounded by life and power and death, I found it fantastic, and yet I was at home with it.

Slowly and fitfully, with more and more constant struggle but about on schedule, I was bearing northwesterly on a course that brought me 100 miles south of the Galápagos—the islands 600 miles west of the mainland, where Darwin did many of his studies. To keep my mind exercised and alert, I forced it to work. A man must do this in solitude. Otherwise he will go dumb and inert and be helpless when a decision is needed.

As I sailed, I sang old sea songs, because singing makes you feel good.

I memorized whatever printed words were at hand, particularly lines from Bowditch's great textbook on navigation.

I recited lines from *Hell, Hail and Hurricanes,* a book of poetry of my own:

> She stood between the palm trees, swaying, like a shaft of
>   light,
> Her flesh and soul all shaped by wind and sea;
> A thousand storms wept in her eyes and a thousand waiting
>   nights
> As they called for love before the hours flee.

I forced my mind to confront problems I hadn't thought of in years—a better way to raise a square sail, an improved design for a gasket—and I worked out solutions in my mind in the finest detail.

I summoned and explored details of incidents that had happened to me many years before. I made my mind hunt and find the exact colors, the sounds, the faces and even the spoken words—everything. The statues of the Greek gods in Hamburg's

Kunsthalle, which I had seen as a boy, I saw again. And there was the first time I had sailed these waters. It was 1908, on the square-rigger *Henriette*, 168 days carrying coke from Hamburg round Cape Horn to the Gulf of California and the copper smelters at Santa Rosalie.

We are westing south of the Cape. The wind has been battering us incredibly. It is the forefringe of an Antarctic hurricane. I ask the sailmaker if we will make it; he has made 11 Cape Horn voyages before; he is a fussy man with curtains at his bunk, made from cloth given him by a girl he is sure waits for him. He declines to answer me. A little after four bells on the twelve-to-four watch: shouts, stomping of boots, and the mate's howl, "All hands!" The mizzen and main royals have blown out of their boltropes, I go up the rigging, and I am alternately smashed against the mast and almost torn loose from it. It is long after daylight before we are done. Then breakfast, a tasteless blueish-gray cereal I cannot identify. But perhaps later we will have the soup we love, made of prunes and molasses and dumplings.

Sweep the forecastle, polish the brass lamps. And turn into the bunk beneath the sailmaker's. How cold and awesome is the sea. How it boils. The escape into sleep is fitful. Again all hands, again the running. The captain gives the first order I have ever heard him give: "Lee braces!" A white mass is about to engulf us. The mate shrieks: "Clew up the upper topsails." The full hurricane is on us. I claw aloft. A man goes berserk in the rigging. He says he will throw me to the deck. Finally the gaskets are on. Now we get the beautiful soup!

That night the men in their bunks are talking about other nights, other storms, when suddenly the house is buried in water. It is a long time before the *Henriette* comes up again, and then the talk goes on. That was the way it was and I make myself recall it all very clearly. I remembered how the berserk man was straitjacketed and put in the lazaret.

I encountered my first calms in the 3,000 miles between the Galápagos and the Marquesas. About a month had passed when I entered this leg of the voyage. Until that time the winds had been powerful, but then they turned spotty, veering from easterly to northerly, southeasterly—occasionally westerly, head winds that pushed me back. Or they vanished, and the raft rolled hideously and hopelessly for days at a time.

During the calms I made repairs. Every piece of rope had to be checked and checked again. For a sailing ship, a calm is the time of greatest danger. You are without power and steering. The sails flap—the stitches come out. The mast yanks at its legs and rips at its rigging.

The calm is a time that edges into the sockets of your teeth and seeps into your skin and finds your nerves with barbed hooks. In the old days the mate kept the men working hardest during calms—not because he was brutal but because he knew the calm was the time when men would get desperate to go to some port. But there would be no port within 1,000 miles, and so men went mad.

When even a little wind would come, I grasped for it with a sail as if it were food and I were starving. Then it would die away.

Well, what did I expect? These were the horse latitudes, so named because they were the place old ships that carried horses to Australia would be becalmed. The rolling would fling the animals to the deck, their legs were broken and they would have to be thrown overboard.

Naturally the calms brought the squalls. The horizon would be clear, the sun harshly glittering, the temperature around 90—and then a hill of clouds would begin to build out of the sultry heat.

There it would stand, rising and sucking in power from the heat. To the southeast a rainspout anchored in the sea. As always, I watched alert, and with awe. Even as I watched, another mountain formed, this time to the north. Then yet another one, to the west, and another and another, until I was surrounded by these black windy cliffs.

The raft rolled on a windless sea, and the electric tensions grew until it seemed the air itself must catch fire.

Hours passed. Squalls form in day and strike at night. In early evening one squall began to move—a little one, moving slowly away from me. This one will pass, you figure, but that other one you will have to fight. The cloud masses towered gray and squirming against the sky. The main job was to be ready, and keep the raft directly before the wind when a squall finally swept on me. The raft always steered worst before the wind. On the square-riggers we sometimes had three men at the wheel at such times.

For weeks it was like this, for thousands of miles. Later, as I got deeper into the hurricane season, the weather got much worse.

Though I was keeping pretty close to my schedule, I did not like the way many things were going. My raft was too heavy; the mast was unnecessarily high. The sail was very hard to raise, even with a winch. All my life I've been able to say that I can work alongside any man and outwork him, but this was too much, and it was draining me.

The rudder kept getting worse. I used rope and finally wire cable to lash the cracking parts. Sometimes the repair would last a week, sometimes an hour.

My body was wearing now—not just my fingers and arms, which were torn in dozens of places from going over the stern among the eroding steel edges to repair the rudder. I was also weakened by the lack of proper food. I was in a part of the sea which has few fish—not even flying fish—a desert in the sea. I had counted on the sea to supply me with protein, and now the sea was failing me. And the sleeplessness. With such a poor rudder I always slept near the wheel, leaning against the side of the house. I dozed and woke to find myself groping for the flashlight so I could check the needle again.

I was heading southwesterly toward the region where the islands begin to crowd the Pacific—the Marquesas, the Societies, the Tongas. By now the raft was making strange noises that I had never heard before—shrieks and screams and bumps. My ears as well as my eyes had become fantastically acute. However, I began to recognize that my body itself was going wrong. The food was not sufficient; I have experimented enough with diet, even growing my own food in the California hills, to realize I had to do something. And I knew what to do. Each morning, in the dawn hours, I knelt by the side and daubed salt water on my eyes, for that, I knew, would relieve the burning from the sun; and inhaled it into my nostrils, for it cleaned all the passages and kept them healed; and splashed it on my face; and gargled it, and then I drank one mug of the sea. I drank a mug every day thereafter. Believe me, sea water has medicinal power, and my body cured almost at once.

One can also learn a lot about keeping physically fit from watching dogs and especially cats—almost everything there is to know. Aussie and Kiki were superb sailors by now. They prowled everywhere on the raft, even the very edge of the deck, and always managed to leap out of the way of the waves. They were experts at taking care of their bodies. Throughout the voyage they kept perfect health and offered me perfect companionship, since their morale was always superb.

About this time a foreign object appeared on the horizon and bore down on me from the northeast. It was the *Whakatane*, a freighter from Panama to New Zealand, and I was directly on its course in the only shipping lane I was to pass. It was 3:24 in the afternoon of a fairly bright day—August 16—and too noisy with winds for us to shout back and forth. I raised the American flag and she raised the British, and she came up to me and circled once. The officers and passengers waved and I waved back, indicating I was well and needed no help. I thought briefly of asking for help to fix my rudders, but the raft was too low in the water to do the work; nothing permanent could be done until the raft was on land and in the hands of mechanics with a machine shop. Then the *Whakatane* went on her course and that was all.

That was the only occasion on which I saw a human during the whole voyage, though I came close a second time. The following night, the mutter of an engine came out of the wind and a ship's lights slipped by to starboard, only 100 yards or so away. If they had run me down, I briefly wondered, would they have even noticed in that roaring night?

This was perhaps not an ideal time to observe a birthday, as I did, my 70th, on August 19.

I had just one regular contact with the world, via a transistor receiver. I had brought along a radio sender with a crank on the generator, but after several weeks of trying to send the message "*Age Unlimited*—on schedule and well," I concluded that I was not being heard, and I gave it up. Teddy, my wife, wouldn't really expect to hear about me anyway. But the transistor had to work. It brought me the time signals essential for navigation, broadcast from WWV in Washington, the world's best station for navigators, and then later on relayed from Hawaii. I knelt on the deck with my chronometer before me, and clicked on the radio, and a deep, clean voice came out of it: *"When the tone begins again, it is exactly . . ."*

It was the only voice I heard during all 130 days. To use the radio indiscriminately would have worn the batteries; who knew how long I would need them? Besides, what would I hear on my radio?—music, propaganda and silly talk. What good would storm warnings do me? Where could I hide? If a great world event had happened while I was on the raft, I would not have known. Only the one voice: *"When the tone begins again . . ."*

But there are two other voices. I had heard them on my first raft trip, and so I am neither frightened nor surprised now. I accept them. They are part of my experience, and part of me. I believe they come from an unconscious area from which the safeguards and barriers have been stripped by the solitude.

They have started early in this voyage—after about two weeks. They come perhaps six times a day. For a man who likes to study the mind, as I do, they are interesting. My wife Teddy speaks. Or my mother. I am perfectly confident of myself, and now something has gone awry. That is when they speak.

I am aware of their presence, and even of their faces, though there are no personalities. They are 10 or 15 feet from me. They always have the same message. They agree with me and approve of me. "That's right, you're doing just right," or something like that. They never give advice. They bring confirmation. It is very pleasant. I can hear them so clearly. I met my wife on a ship in the Caribbean in 1938, and when we got back to New York we married at once and have been together ever since, except when I have had a call to take one of these voyages. Though she does not want me to go, Teddy does not oppose me, because she knows I must. Before the first raft voyage, it took me two years to get her blessing. Then finally she said, you must do what you must, and then she helped me.

My mother was a woman who could make a decision. She came from Germany, but she was Czech. She taught me that, above all else, each person must make his own destiny; a human must do everything alone eventually. She did not oppose me, either, when I had to go journeying from her house to the salmon fishing and prospecting in the Klondike or to the oil fields or the Texas docks, or to be an acrobat or a wrestler or a sailor. Or, for that matter, when I did nothing for seven years but read the books in New York's big library, supporting myself in any way that would not interfere with what I wanted to do. My mother died in California in 1947. I am reminded of her teaching when I see small American children pout, "What can I do now? I have no one to play with."

And now I hear them both, these two who have been closest to me. It is wish fulfillment, if you please. Sometimes their voices waken me. I wake with a feeling of disappointment, even anger against them. Why are they not there? Why have they abandoned me?

At more than 5,000 miles and 75 days out of Callao, I had yet to have one good sailing day. Then, south of Penrhyn Island, I came into a region of incessant squalls. I had to go overboard almost every day now to lash the rudders. I would put a line around my waist, and slip into the water with a pair of pliers or some other tool between my teeth. I had to work submerged half the time, and somehow hold on. When the raft wrenched upward as the waves beat down, the strain seemed sure to pull my arms out of the sockets, and sockets out of my shoulders. My whole body was becoming more and more battered.

The sharks of these waters were naturally attracted to white things, such as human flesh. Some of the sharks swam with me for 1,000 miles at a stretch. They came in families, including young ones of two and one half and three feet, or sometimes just a male and female.

The sharks filled these waters as I approached the region where the Pacific sprouts islands and coral reefs by the thousands. Sharks became part of my daily life. My eyes could spot their gray shapes in the blue water even at a great distance. They were always around me in a hungry pack, eight or nine at a time. The sharks have a wonderful way of blending into the shadows until, suddenly, they are there. The rudder continually threatened to break, and I had to keep going over the stern. What I feared most was losing the rudder in a storm. Because I had to keep going into the water, I had to find some defenses against the sharks.

Fortunately I had taken some split bamboo along, and put it on deck to keep the waves from spraying up between the planks. I lashed some of these strips together and tied them to the stern and slipped into the water with them as a shield against my back. The sharks came so close I could hear them thrashing—I suppose they might even have nudged the bamboo. But they could not get at me, and I could labor on the rudder until the bamboo shield finally washed off in a heavy sea.

Later, I found still another method. I caught a big shark on my fishing line, dragged it to the raft, lashed it, shot it with my Enfield rifle and let the carcass hang at the stern, in the water near where I wanted to work. Seeing a dead shark, the other sharks of the same family steered clear of the area. All in all, I caught and killed a good many sharks—not that I really minded them so much, but because they deprived me of so much food by devouring the hooked dolphins before I could haul them to my deck.

One day I was trying to fix the rudder from a kayak-lifeboat I'd taken along in case I should be driven helplessly onto a reef. Suddenly my line to the raft gave way. The nylon line had sawed on a sharp steel edge. For a few minutes the raft sailed away from me, looking as if it thought it could do just as well without me. I had to paddle hard to catch up to it, and if the mainsail had been raised I never would have caught up.

One gray, windy afternoon, as I worked in the water on the rudder, I sensed something unusual. I looked around me and saw the most astonishing creature I have ever seen at sea. It was 18 to 20 feet long, and enormously thick. It had the pectorals and tapered body of a shark, but a head that was four feet across the front, and flat. I am not much for estimates—ordinarily I will not even guess at the height of waves—but I knew this monster weighed several tons.

At the time I was passing south of the Rakahanga group of islands. The monster stayed several feet under water, so my rifle bullets couldn't reach it. I shot at it for good reason: It kept nosing around my rudder. I guess it thought my raft was a giant fish and it wanted to make friends. If it had tried to play with the rudder, I would have been in real trouble. I shot several times, but it ignored me and finally gave up hope of having a romance with a raft, and disappeared. Later, back in New York, I learned that it was a *Rhineodon typus*—the so-called whale shark—a prehistoric creature that rarely comes up from the ocean depths.

One day, in this region, I went over the stern in a particularly heavy sea, my rope around my waist and my anger against the faulty rudder rushing through my head. I had to ignore the sharks. As I always did, I lashed the rudder, which was about three feet by four, and of heavy steel. But it soon worked loose and swung back and forth and battered me. My hands were cut anew as they moved along the rudder's upper edge, fighting to work and keep their hold. I was constantly being plunged underwater. I had put new cables on and was tightening them with a marlin spike when a particularly heavy wall of water came down just as the raft was rising. An agonizing pain stabbed my groin on the left side. I felt as if I'd been pierced or torn open. I almost screamed. I could not hold on, and I dangled on the rope until the pain had subsided and my strength returned enough for me to move.

When I was able, I climbed to the deck, crawled to the cabin and lay there. By now I knew what had happened to me. Ten years earlier I had had a hernia, on the right side, just before my first raft voyage. I'd made the first voyage without much trouble, but this one was much worse. The pain was horrible. I remembered the doctor who'd examined me before I left New York. My wife had insisted I go. He'd found my condition perfect, but he had given me some morphine tablets, just in case.

The morphine eased me. I explored my abdomen and found that the intestines had not come through the tear in the wall. I knew there would be special danger if the tear was small, since then an intestinal loop might be caught and strangulated. But this tear seemed like a good big one, or, at any event, there was no strangulation.

I wrapped myself in a large rubberized bandage the doctor had given me. That same evening I went back over the stern to go on making repairs. Gradually the pain lessened. After that it did not cut down noticeably on my ability to work, except in the evenings after a particularly long, straining day. Then I would feel so weak I could not lift five pounds.

Thirty feet over the raft's deck, where I am standing as I work on the yard, the steel mast whips fearfully and the salt-coated rungs of the ladder are slippery as ice. It takes legs as well as arms and hands to hold on. The ladder is a single steel pole with rungs welded to it. The rung at my temple line is always plunging at me, and I do not duck in time. It hits me like a club. Through the pain I force myself to think that I must not surrender. I hang on and, when I can, climb down slowly. To bring down the bump, which is rising to egg size, I use an ancient method that I know works: I press a steel knife against the skin to restore circulation. A few days later I see in a mirror that my hair, which had still been brown, has turned white. I don't know why. I would like to know. I have always wanted to know the why of things.

Why am I here? Well, I want to show what I can do. For me, solitude is a self-expression. I want to prove many things—that my way of life has been good for me; that age can be coped with; that the small signs of physical deterioration I had noticed in the preceding 10 years can be largely obliterated.

Why is the number of a man's years on earth so important? Mankind is only at a doorstep, I believe, beyond which he will make advancements, physical and intellectual, that exceed anything he can now even dream.

Why have the powers of my eyes and ears and nose increased to such an astonishing degree?

Why? And why again? And again—why has my hair turned white?

The worst weather came in the final third of the voyage, as I got deeper into the winter and farther south on a fretful course. My most serious problem came in this area. I had been having constant squalls for weeks, and they were becoming more and more intense. On this particular day squalls started building early in the afternoon. I stood at the wheel, watching the clouds mount up on the sea, eyes on sail as well as sky—and, of course, also on the rudder.

The squalls began to reach me about nine o'clock. The first

one swept on me and I brought the big sail down. Fifteen minutes later, to take advantage of the wind, I winched it up again.

The next blow came quickly, and as I always did, I waited until the last possible moment, to draw every possible bit of power from the wind, before taking down the canvas. Again the wind slacked, again the heavy sail had to go back up. Again and again, as the night wore on, I was attacked by squalls. The raft pushed on, and the foam streamed from my face and the seas sloshed over the deck, and I kept sailing. Then, at about midnight, a particular squall arrived and I smelled it and listened to it and felt it out, and decided that I could keep the sail up a little longer. Perhaps I was influenced by a desire to avoid another struggle with the sail. Anyway, I made a mistake. It was the most powerful storm of the night, of full-gale force. It came from the southeast. It crashed on me, and now I really had a fight on my hands, just to handle the wheel. The seas thundered on my pontoons. Then all at once the raft swung off violently and the mainsail was aback and beginning to rip, dashing and shattering against the mast. I worked the wheel hard, but it was no go this time. My rudder had broken completely at the height of a storm, and with more storms coming behind this one.

The raft was in the wind and I knew I had to get the mainsail down before I lost it, to put up the jib, set a reefed mizzen and ride things out.

My hands on the useless wheel, I felt the acid of irritation, the heat of anger, even an instant of self-pity. But then a little later: *I* was all right. It was this raft that was the wreck. And because my raft was wrecked—I had to face this fact—so was I.

All that night the storms battered me. Only my six centerboards, two-by-ten-inch planks that could be lowered through brackets on the pontoons and extended six feet into the water, gave the raft any stability. How it did wallow and wash around. It was flotsam with a passenger. There was little chance I would capsize—not on a raft this size—or sink, for my pontoons were filled with a corklike chemical so they wouldn't take water even if they were punctured. But I could lose my mast, for I was pitching horribly. As my wreck staggered around the Pacific, I sometimes dozed. Morning came. Sometimes I sang as loudly as

I could, because that always helps. I recited some love poetry—mine—the pages strangely gray under the malicious sky.

> O, the kissing and the holding—
> The mingling of the earth and of the sky—
> The mingling mad of time and space
> While gazing on the loved one's face,
> The mingling of the cry.

I had many pleasant words with Aussie and Kiki, and wondered what Kiki's friends at the New York Humane Society would say if they could see her now. And Aussie's friends on the Peruvian ranch.

To keep my mind alert, I exercised it by planning repairs in the greatest possible detail. As I did this, frustration tried to invade me. How could I really fix the rudder? I fought these feelings off, of course, and they proved corrective in a way. A look at despair can be its cure. I would make it. I was going to make it to Australia. Having thought all this, I had a big meal, and felt better. Nervous tension makes one hungry.

At last, on the second morning after the night the rudder broke, the sea was peaceful enough for me to tackle the repair job. I took turn buckles and other gear and went over the stern and gave that rudder hell. It took two hours of struggling to get it working again, and it still worked only very poorly. I patched the big sail along a seam 17 feet long. By the time I was finished, it was afternoon, and squalls were building up again on the horizon.

It comes like a flash. A specter. An impression. I look at the solitude in the ocean, and see it, and grope for the word. There is no right word.

It does not come at a time of struggle—oh, never then, for then I dig in and fight and come through. It comes at easier times. There is no depression before or afterward. And I can examine it and learn from it. The principal cause is the excessive work—of that I am sure. I am not going mad, but I am learning how a man goes mad. It—the specter—comes from inside, but it seems to come from space. It is a flash without light or color. It is very real as it invades me and gives its message and then goes.

I do not have to go on. Why haven't I seen this before? I can get away! Not harm myself—no—simply escape. Escape this raft that will not sail and the rudder that will not stay repaired and the winds that will not ease and the work that will not stop. In that flash that fills the mind with the specter, escape seems attractive. Over the side.

The mind is able to observe itself while all this is happening. I see a part of my mind I had not known about. I learn something about why people commit suicide and how the idea comes to them. I am glad I am an old sea dog and have ways to adjust myself to problems.

The specter finally disappears as it came, without warning or notice. That was a few weeks before my journey was to end in a way that, for me, was so tragic.

On the 120th day, more or less—it is hard to pinpoint some things—I came to the realization that Australia would probably not be mine, not until I had the rudder repaired. To sail there would take another 60 days at least. And there were too many things against me. I would have to pick a new destination—a place with some sort of shipyard. I could go on to the Fijis, 900 miles ahead, and try to put into Suva, or to the Tongas. At either island group, I'd take stock and calculate the chances of continuing.

My hope still hung on to the Australian vision, but my mind and experience said no. To make the raft work at all, I had to steer continually, and I simply could not steer day and night.

On the morning of Nov. 11, at about seven o'clock, as the raft wallowed and struggled after one of the worst storms of all, I had my first sight of land since Peru. It was the Samoan island of Upolu, a mountain rising out of the sea. My navigation had been just right, which pleased me. I was about 20 miles north of the island, and I looked at it through my glasses, though the day was too muddy for me to see much more than the outline. I knew the island, as I'd been there before—the mountainsides green with the mangroves and palms, the shores fronted by a coral reef on which waves pounded themselves endlessly.

I set about the day's work—a bath, daubs of sea water on the eyes, a mug of the sea for my stomach, food for my pets and then for myself, and then repairs to the mainsail, which had been torn again.

Meanwhile the raft was behaving miserably and I could not avoid the reason: Three of my centerboards had been broken in the last storm. Despite the unceasing wind and a sky that told me there was no letup in sight, I wanted to sail on past this island, on to the Fijis, and maybe much farther.

When the mainsail was mended I put it up, but I had to lower it at once. The rudder would not take the strain. The steel rods had given way altogether, and my lashings did little good.

I went over the stern to make new repairs. It was useless. I tried it with just the mizzen and the jib. The rudder did not make enough pressure on the water to keep me on course.

The night before, helpless in the gale, I was not particularly upset. But now to be this helpless was, for me, tragedy. I wanted to keep sailing. But I also thought ahead to the miles studded with reefs without a harbor anywhere. On a crippled raft, there was the possibility that I'd be cast up on some pile of coral and bleach there.

I said to myself that either I put into this island for repairs, or I would never get ashore anywhere. I hated the decision.

By now it was about 11:30 in the morning and I had drifted closer to the island. I could see the sea breaking on the reef. I had gone 7,450 miles; it was my 130th day at sea. Having little power to steer, I hoped to summon a towboat. I began sending S O S's. A gadget on my radio sender let me send the S O S just by pushing a lever, and then winding the generator. I put on my earphones and waited for a response; none came. I put my flag upside down, a distress signal known to all sailors. Meanwhile I maneuvered toward the shore as best I could.

Through the day I edged toward the shore. I sent the S O S's every 15 minutes, and then oftener, and then almost constantly. I scanned the mountainside and the sea with my glass. At any moment I expected to see some sign of life; I was only about six miles down from the town of Apia. Yard by yard, lucky to make any course at all, I edged toward the coral line. By now I would have been happy to see a small boat which would show me where there was an opening through the reef into the lagoon.

Then I gave that up. I would have to make my own way to the end of this trip. I set about the task. I climbed up the mast and, through the binoculars, studied the coral wall, peering for a likely-looking place to try a crossing. Finally I made my decision and headed toward that spot. In most places the coral stuck a foot or two into the air; I could see its black, jagged face when the sea would go back. Three hundred yards beyond the reef, across the lagoon's smooth face, the mountain wall was intensely green. I could hear the breaking of the waves on the reef. Naturally one must expect to tear the bottom out of his boat on a reef like this, but now the choice had been taken out of my hands and I was going to go over the reef or get stuck on it, or be capsized by it. My raft seemed to halt just before the coral. I had lashed everything down and stowed my instruments. Naturally everything was shipshape, as it had been during the whole voyage.

I stood at the wheel and braced myself. A wave came from behind. We bumped and scraped and stuttered, and then another wave came and we went over. Somehow the pontoons held together. I sailed over the calm waters and anchored among boulders 20 feet offshore. It was early evening by now. It had taken me an entire day to make those few miles. I had seen a few houses as I came in, but now there was no sign of life at all.

I anchored, lest a tide sweep in, lowered the sails. I fed my cats and opened a can of beans for myself. After a while, a skiff appeared, with a man and a woman aboard. I called to them and they came over. Perhaps it took courage on their part, since my beard was so heavy and my hair so wild and my skin so black from the sun. I imagine I looked somewhat like an old man out of the sea.

But as I'd known would happen, the process of readjusting back to life with people was as quick as the descent into solitude had been slow. I asked the couple if they spoke English. The man was the Rev. Russell J. Maddox, chairman of the Methodist Church in Western Samoa, and the woman was his wife.

I identified myself and asked them if they would notify authorities of my arrival so my wife could hear. They went away in their boat to do what I'd asked.

Later in the evening a native policeman came with some other men and asked if I needed help. I told them no, and they stayed for a while, talking, and then they left. I spent that night on the raft. I was perfectly at home there. I could not desert the raft. If a sailor loses his ship—and if I left mine I could not say what would happen to it—he has nothing.

Next day I had more visitors, and was driven to Apia by Police Superintendent Leo Schmidt and introduced to many of the leading people of Western Samoa including the government leaders. In the evening I returned to my raft and slept aboard it. The next day the raft was towed to a dock to be repaired. This time, to the rudder we attached solid steel pipe three inches thick, and we improved all the steering gear, and I was eager to resume the voyage. While waiting for the work to get finished, I visited a hospital, just to have my hernia checked. The chief doctor there said that while my condition was otherwise fine, the abdominal tear should have attention before I sailed farther, and I decided that if I were to be delayed at all, I'd best get the job done back in New York where I could be with Teddy.

But I was not through with this voyage yet. During the long months when I was getting myself back into shape, the raft was undergoing repairs of its own. By April, it was lying on an Apia dock fully repaired, its rudder now strong enough to withstand any sea. Soon I would get aboard that raft and head west once more. I had set out for Australia, and I would get to Australia. I might be delayed, but I would not be defeated.

I set out at three o'clock in the morning on June 26, 1964, heading due north at the end of a tug's towline. It was black, stormy, rainy, and my pontoons thundered and trembled as we pitched past Apia's coral reef and into the open sea, but I had picked this as the time to sail, and on the sea one goes through with a plan, for who can guarantee that the morning will not be calm or the next night will be less fierce? As the newspaper *Samoa Bulletin* later reported: "There were very few people on the rainswept wharf when the raft hitched up to the harbor-project tug. Captain Willis had let it be known that he was merely shifting his anchorage, but under cover of darkness he headed out to sea." So I went off like a fugitive, for a reason I find both real and absurd.

My mistake was to forget that for several months, while waiting back in New York for the raft to be repaired, I had not done any work. Hauling on a rope, I felt a sharp pain. An abdominal rupture—suffered while struggling to fix the rudders on the first leg of the voyage—was opening up again, and the intestine was herniating through. This one was a small tear, but this can be at least as dangerous as a big one. At such a time you feel intense pain, and perhaps you howl, although this feels foolish since there is no one to hear you, and you try to fix yourself, to put the strangulated intestine back in, acting very systematically and methodically. If you can't eliminate the hernia, you know the trouble is serious, and it might come to be a matter of life or death.

I tried every trick I had used before—exercises, massages, muscle movements, pressing and relaxing and pushing. I worked like this for hours. But everything failed. I heated water, applying hot packs in order to soften the muscles and make them flexible. This failed too.

The next morning I was beginning to get feverish and desperate. In two voyages I had sailed over 14,000 miles alone and never encountered such difficulty with my body. And this voyage had hardly begun. The current kept pushing south and the shore of Savaii was looming nearer. I lay very still and made my mind attack the problem, made it think in terms of the way the body is made. For a while I tried propping my legs up over my head, leaning them against the cabin to lessen the strain on the abdomen. This seemed to help, but it didn't solve anything, and the fever was becoming more intense. I made my mind work more. I calculated. Very carefully. Finally I thought: I must take all the strain off those muscles. I'll tie a strap around my feet, reeve a rope through a block overhead and then down through a block on the deck, so that I can raise my feet high in the air. That way, little by little, I was able to raise my legs higher and higher until all my weight was on my shoulders. I found that in that position I could rest sometimes and then continue with the hot packs and massages. For hours I did this. Then, all at once, the strangulated intestine went back inside.

By now I had drifted to within 20 miles of Savaii. Still the wind failed. To the east I could see, vague and misty, the outline of Upolu. For a sailor this is a time for swearing or weeping: barely at sea, and driven back toward the island from which I had embarked. How much I would have given for another tow, enough so I could clear the western tip of Savaii and be in open water again. Time after time, perhaps 20 times in all, I sent an S O S, pushing down the lever which automatically sends the signal, and grinding on the generator to supply the power. Nobody came. It was noontime, warm, moist, tropical. In the haze Savaii was a huge, lumpy smudge protruding out of the sea. Finally the sails made a rustling sound, a beautiful sound to hear: A wind had come up, increasing quickly. One moment I had been drifting on glass, and the next I was being tossed about and fighting with the sails and taking spray in the face. It was pleasant to be drenched again.

For about three weeks I sailed west and then southwest with little to do except contest with the incessant squalls and make sure I kept far enough away from the Fijis—50 miles and more—in case the wind should fail me again and surrender me to a southerly current. But then in mid-July the wind began to get worse and worse, until it developed into an unrelenting gale, so that it took all my strength to keep anywhere near my intended course. As the storm built slowly, the waves rose around me like foothills, and then hills, and then white-topped mountains. The wind roared at the canvas; the raft pitched like a toy. The spray pelted my face, blew over the top of the mast. Night and day I struggled with the wheel and the sails, and still I lost ground. Piece by piece the wind tattered my plans and blew them into the sea. The plan to pass New Caledonia to the south went first, of course. So I set out to try to slip through the passage between New Caledonia and the New Hebrides; that way, even though many miles off my course and getting into reef-dotted waters, I still hoped to have a chance to keep heading for Sydney. The wind continued from the south and south-southeast, and one morning about a month out of Apia my hernia bulged out again, and I couldn't get it back in. In the heavy seaway it was harder to fix, but this time I knew what to do. Working with my feet hauled high in the air and my shoulders on the pitching deck, I finally succeeded. But for hours I had drifted north, and now my last hope of holding my course was gone, and I was in danger of being driven onto the New Hebrides.

In this part of the world all the east coasts, facing the prevailing wind as they do, are deadly. The soil has been stripped away, and bare, steep mountains drop down to boulder-strewn beaches where no vessel can survive. The wind had become even stronger, from the south-southeast. I had to run north and escape while I still had a chance.

As the hours went by, it seemed that I had waited too long to turn north, that I would smash up on the rocks no matter what I did. For the second time on this voyage I sent an S O S. Sending the message was like howling into the wind, hoping the sound might be heard somewhere.

The South Pacific is like few other places on earth. It is so huge, so abandoned, so full of reefs. And fragments of stone rise like spires thousands of feet from the ocean floor to catch a sailor and give his bones a place to bleach. An S O S sent by a man off the New Hebrides is like a stone tossed in the air on the chance it will hit the moon. I think now, why did I bother? I would have liked a tow, of course, but there was no one to tow me. And I would have been pleased to have someone know my position, so they would know where to search later on. But above all, I would have wanted my wife Teddy, back in New York, to know, if I was driven on the rocks, where it had happened. In any case after about 15 minutes the transmitter broke down.

My mood was far from grim, however. My raft was seaworthy, though the mainsail tore repeatedly. My body was strong though worn down by the long spells of work, and my diet was meager for lack of the fish I'd counted on catching. Though I trailed a line constantly, I did not catch one fish, not even a shark—the weather was that foul.

The New Hebrides with their sheer rocks and polyglot names —Ambrym, Pentecost, Maewo—kept looking over my shoulder from the west. For now I was running for my life, running as near to dead north as I could—running away from my destination. Twice I saw mountaintops through holes in the storm—I was that close to the islands. Then finally a sight with my sextant showed me I was as far north as I needed to go—north of Maewo and of Espiritu Santo Island, the main island of the group. I turned west now, for the wind had dropped almost to a calm. Utterly exhausted, I slept for the first time in days. I did not count the sleepless days, but I could feel in my bones that there had been many of them.

Ordinarily I could nap by the wheel and count on my senses to awaken me if the sails flapped or the rigging creaked in some unusual way. But now I fell deep into sleep, lying on the deck with the wind pressing my raft forward, slept and then awoke abruptly at two in the morning, feeling strange for no reason I could name. For a few moments I lay still and listened to the water beat on the pontoons and to the sounds of the rigging—and they were all right. I rose and looked about. I was on a port tack, with the boom to starboard, and I looked left and behind me, and at first my eyes seemed to say that I was moving through a shadow. A black shape, like an enormous monster, seemed to look over me. It was an island, perhaps two miles away, smoothed by the darkness into an ominous hump, a monster's back sticking out of the sea. I watched the black creature slip by, and I seemed to come out of its shadow at last, and I felt a certain strangeness. I cannot be sure to this day what island it was, but I think it was Mera Lava, the easternmost of the Banks Islands. I can only be sure that its shore would have wrecked me, and that I did not sleep so deeply on any night thereafter until the voyage was over.

It all fitted into the voyage's hardening, developing pattern. On the previous trips, even with the rudders smashed, even in the worst storms, I faced no great danger to my life so long as I could stay clear of reefs—and in the eastern Pacific there is much water and few stones. But this time was different—this time death was plainly possible, and a sense of this came to life in the gloom of the island which cast a shadow even at night. The sense took shape there, and in time it grew, and I had the feeling of a man sitting on a mountaintop and watching a car racing toward danger in the valley. I was both on the mountain and in the car. That was the way it came to seem.

Around the New Hebrides at last, and north of them, I made a course that was southwest, as close to a straight line to Sydney as I could manage. Then the weather became bad again, but by now I accepted such things with equanimity, and observed with interest the way the mind adjusts to the conditions in which it finds itself, no matter how unpleasant. In time it can even come to welcome and enjoy what would seem harsh and hostile in another circumstance. For instance, a lashing storm that drove me in the direction I wanted to go was a splendid event to me now. An uninterrupted half hour of napping, with no need to work the raft, was worthy of a celebration.

So I came south and west, passing to the west of Espiritu Santo, on a diagonal crossing of the Coral Sea, through crashing water that reached to a floor 2,000 fathoms and more beneath my feet. For some days all went well, and I pieced together the fabric of a new plan. Now it would have to be north of New Caledonia, then weave through many shoals and reefs and finally down to Brisbane, where I would catch the coastal current to Sydney, altogether a journey of about 1,500 miles. I remember in great detail the moment this plan was tattered as the previous plans had been. I remember because, the way it happened, I had reason to observe every detail as closely as if a great light had been shone on them and me.

I had a block made fast to the deck with six strands of half-inch rope, at the edge of the raft on the port side in the wash of the sea. The rope in the block pulled the jib over when the tack needed changing—heavy work in a strong wind.

That night the wind was near gale force, and when it veered, I thought the raft would lie easier on the other tack. Slackening off to starboard, I began pulling the jib over to port. I hauled on the rope with all my strength, my rubber-soled shoes barely keeping traction on the planks of the deck. It was a routine maneuver, one I had performed many hundreds of times, though a great strain on my body. For a while it seemed the wind was too much. The jib simply would not come over, and I saw that I would have to get to the wheel. I braced myself once more and pulled with all my strength—once, twice, and again and again. Without warning the block on the deck gave way, its rope lashings eaten up by the bite of the sea water. As I was falling, I thought, *if I hit the jibboom*—the iron girders anchored to the deck—*I will be hurt.*

My back struck the iron, and I crumpled to the deck, not feeling any pain, for my nerves were stunned. As I lay on the deck, I felt nothing, but I realized that my legs would not move, that they seemed lifeless. I used my arms to pull myself to the cabin, and I lay beside it for a long while. It was the middle of the night and very dark. I lay still and analyzed my situation— that is my way at such a time. I had to reckon with the possibility that I would not get over this injury at all.

In my mind, as the days passed, I examined the pattern of the voyage and the possibility of death and the pain which slowly emerged as if from inside me and slowly spread over my lower back and hips. From time to time I pulled myself into the cabin and opened a can of beans and ate it. And I drifted, and the wind drove me north.

I drifted and thought of the possibilities, and that the Solomons were ahead. I thought of the chances that I would come ashore at a mission station, and decided that that was unlikely, and that the natives might have a pot for stewing a broken-down old man whom the Pacific tossed up to them. I thought of the chances of my getting back to my feet, and decided that I could only wait and see. In all I drifted helplessly under jib and mizzen for six days and nights, until I was little more than 200 miles from the Solomons, many miles off the course toward Brisbane.

Then one afternoon I felt something in a toe—found I could feel my toes. Soon afterward I could move my legs a little. The feeling came up to my knees. I massaged furiously and exercised, though at first this meant merely moving an ankle.

After the sixth day I could manage to stand if I lifted myself to my feet with my arms, and then I could make some sort of course. The pain began to bloom. An X ray later showed, the doctors told me, that the lower spine, the sacrum, had been fractured, and that somehow it had managed to fuse itself at least partly. But I have my own view—I believe that the damage had been done to the spinal cord by a damaged vertebra. Only this could explain the paralysis. Whatever the fact, the pain did not let me alone again. I am not one to make much of pain, but there were many times after this when I was ready to shout out loud for the mere fear that I would bang my back against a rail or the deckhouse or perhaps the water barrels. I could not sleep much at all after that. I could not lie down except on my belly. I did not manage to recover thoroughly from that accident, not through the rest of the voyage.

But that was not important. What counted was that I could sail again, and the wind permitted me at least to make a course to the west and sometimes the southwest. My plans, made so recently, had washed away. I would now have little chance of making Brisbane, though of course I would try. But it seemed too far, the wind was too wrong, and I had come too far west by now. I could head due west, but that way lay the Great Barrier Reef. I had no charts of the north section of the reef and northeast Australia, nothing to show passages through that formidable barrier—if there were passages that a raft could cross.

At last I made the new plan. I would set my course toward a little group of islands called the Chesterfields, in latitude 20 south and longitude 159 east, approximately 650 miles from Brisbane. If I could clear the Chesterfields, I hoped to get past the reefs to the south, then head for shore and land on Australia wherever it would have me. I came southwest, carrying my pain and making my way yard by yard. The weather had taken on a pattern that had first developed near the Banks Islands: four or five days of heavy winds, then a brief period of moderation, then another extended attack by a storm.

On the night of August 18, in latitude 16°4′ south and longitude 160°6′ east, a most extraordinary thing happened. I was steering southwest, having an easterly wind for once and in the center of the Coral Sea. It was a quarter to twelve. I have reason to remember the time and date very well. I had celebrated my 70th birthday rather quietly while sailing my raft between Peru and Samoa. Now, in 15 minutes, I would celebrate my 71st. I was at the wheel, and I happened to look toward the stern, and there, a good distance off, were the lights of a ship. It was coming toward me.

I took my flashlight and shined it on my mainsail so they could see me. I imagine that to the people on shipboard the sight was quite a surprise. The ship was bearing straight at me, and when it came closer, I used the flashlight to signal an S O S. They blinked an answer.

The ship came closer and closer, coming so fast I had to scramble to get the American flag up, and they caught it with their searchlights, flooding the raft with illumination. They came within 50 feet of me, and I saw it was a good-sized steamer, the British freighter *Baron Jedburgh*, on the Hong-Kong-to-Sydney run, and I saw men on the bridge leaning over the side toward me. One called out:

"What do you want? Who are you?"

"I'm Willis, Captain Willis, bound from Apia to Sydney," I replied.

"What do you want?" the voice insisted.

"I want you to report me." I remember my precise thought of the moment—and who can predict what details will cling to the mind, and which will slip away? On the wall of our apartment in New York, Teddy kept a chart on which I had drawn the course I planned to follow. The freighter would report me hundreds of miles off that course, and Teddy would not believe the report at first, but I wanted her to know where I was, all the same. For that reason alone I had signaled the ship.

By this time the ship was so close it took the wind out of my sails, and it still drifted down on me, and it looked as if it would run me down and wreck me right there. I bellowed, "Get away! Get away! You're smashing my raft!" She swung around heavily, leaving hardly 20 feet of water between us, and sailed off into the night.

But of course it was not precisely like that, there was more to it. I did not have much time to think, but I had to think hard in the time I had—think about whether I should go aboard the freighter and sail to Sydney in comfort. I thought, I would not have to be ashamed if I asked for assistance. I thought, they would probably tell me that the raft would have to be left where it lay, to be driven to pieces on some reef. That influenced me somewhat, as a sailor will understand. I thought, I must judge whether my body will hold together against the acids of exhaustion, and the pain along the spine, and the rent in my abdomen, and most of all, against the storms that seemed unwilling to permit me any respite. I thought all this very quickly, and also that I was on my feet, and strong enough still, and most of all, sailing. Then I knew that I couldn't abandon the voyage and comfortably face the world or myself afterward. Any old sailor or mountaineer or explorer will see this point immediately. Having thought all that, I watched the steamer's lights vanish, and wondered whether anyone can be sure whether such a grave and difficult decision is the proper one, and then I celebrated my birthday as quietly as I had the one before.

After a few days of fierce southerly winds it became clear that the new plan would have to go the way of the old plans. The current and winds made it impossible to get south to the Chesterfields and pick up the current that might take me through to the coast. Now I had to steer west through a maze of reefs and then tackle the Great Barrier Reef itself. I could not really expect to get my raft through the Great Barrier, but I might get through myself, lashing my kayak and canoe into a catamaran. Without detailed charts of the reef, I would have to go about this venture almost as if I were a 15th-century sailor for whom the known world reached only to the horizon. To go to the reef was the kind of decision one must hope he will never be obliged to make. But once made, or so it is my nature to think, such a decision must be carried out very calmly and with as much care as possible.

I have since read about the reef. It is 1,250 miles long and 10 to 35 miles wide. It is quite incredible. At low tide it mostly sticks a little way out of the water, and at high tide it is barely awash, built to that height by tiny creatures called polyps which live and die on the shells of their ancestors.

But then I knew nothing about the reef except that it was to the west. I headed toward it, with little I could do except keep very alert and listen for breaking waves and watch for a white line on the face of the sea. I spent much time on the mast, using my binoculars, and at night I always took down the mainsail, sailing with only jib and mizzen set, so that I would not crash too hard on the barrier in the dark.

For 12 days I sailed west. I put stores in my canoe and planned exactly how I would lash it to the kayak, and how, if necessary, I would drag the catamaran, or at least the canoe, over much of the reef, as if it were a portage, and paddle over the deep water—20 or 30 miles of it, I calculated—that separated the reef from the inner passage which runs along the Australian coast.

It was evening when I sighted a white line of breakers, stretching away about 10 miles on my port bow. I knew it would have to be the reef. I reckoned it carefully: I might sail north or south of this reef, and then perhaps into reefs even more formidable, and find myself trapped and unable to escape. That's how a reef always is. You may find deep water for a little way, and think you have found a passage, and then discover you have been led into a trap. If I had any chance with the barrier, it would have to be taken with a whole day ahead of me, when I would not be overtaken by darkness. At least I knew the general outline of the barrier, which extends on a southeast-northwest line paralleling the Australian coast. I knew that I had to head due north during the night, keeping well clear of the coral, and then sail west and look for the reef in the morning.

From that evening on I had to give up sleep almost entirely and settle for a little nap now and then. It was about this time that I ran out of charts I could use for navigation. The ones I carried showed the Admiralties, more than 1,000 miles to the north, and even a place, several hundred miles north of me, called Willis Island. But they stopped short of the region I was now entering. Quite literally I was sailing off the edge.

The weather pattern of the area had by now asserted itself—in evening, the wind subsided, and morning, about nine o'clock, brought winds of near gale force—and so I had had a night that was easy enough. At first light I turned west again, climbed my mast and reconnoitered with my binoculars but saw no reef. I sailed west all day and found no reef.

Once more in the evening I reduced my sails to the mizzen and jib, taking no chances that I would pile on the reef in the darkness, and again I headed north and sailed that way all night long.

The morning came and I turned west and sailed all day, feeling now that it was I who was stalking the reef, but I found no reef.

That night it was the same, and the next day it was the same, and by the end of the third day I realized I would need a new plan. Going west for a while, then north for a while, I was making steps up the coastline, without ever nearing it. With this system I risked running through the narrow strait between Cape York, Australia's northeast tip, and New Guinea, and thus emerging into another part of the world altogether. The next morning I raised all my sails and pushed west as fast as the raft would go, and when night came I reduced the sails to the jib and mizzen but kept due west. I spent most of the night on the mast.

All that night I sailed west and a little northwest too, and when morning came I kept right on. Perhaps an hour after dawn I saw what I had been hunting, my quarry: a line of breakers that reached to the horizon both to the north and south. I edged toward it. Or it seemed that way, though one cannot be too delicate with a square-rigged raft. I steered with the greatest care, moving along the reef, looking for an opening of some kind. Time after time I saw a place that seemed to promise a passage, and I moved toward it, only to see that I was sailing into a trap with one wall of breaking seas behind another one.

But I could not reconnoiter forever. The west, at least, was the direction in which I wished to go. I slipped toward the reef, moving toward it and yet reluctant to close with it; as long as I was sailing, I would have a chance, and I was slow to give up that chance. I moved toward the white wall, staring for a passage. And then I looked around, thinking I had an opening behind, but now there was a white wall of boiling reef behind.

Now the reef was just ahead of me. The raft hit it hard, shaking as if coming apart. Then the pontoons slid up on it a little way, grinding over coral boulders. It had happened. I was on the reef and pounded by the seas breaking over it. All I could do was sit there, a tiny speck in a huge and desolate sea—sit there and look about me as if I were some sort of misguided tourist, look about me and watch the seas break over me, and just wait. Seas broke solid over the deck, and spray swept over into the cabin with such force it was flooded inside. How long could raft and cabin hold together? The pontoons were grinding on the coral, and I had my kayak and canoe ready. . . .

And then the tide came in. It *had* been low tide; I had thought so, but I could hardly be sure. The raft began to wobble, to shift, and finally I was floating. It was about midday. I went back to the wheel, and found I could make headway westward.

I sailed over the reef with a sense of incredulity. Only a foot or two beneath my feet was a fantastic array of reds and yellows and purples, with many "foul patches" of green marking shallow water. Here and there narrow channels of deep water would appear, and the currents rushed in every direction as the tide forced its way through.

I sailed half the day like this, through this incredible place, different from anything I had ever seen in all the years since I first went to sea as a boy, around Cape Horn on a square-rigger.

Then all at once I was in deep water again. I was clear of the reef, I felt sure. It was just starting to get dark. By my reckoning I was in the inner passage, and I steered northwest, thinking to take my chances with crossing the passage to the coast in the morning. I knew a little of the passage, for Captain Cook had banged a hole in the hull of his ship when he hit a huge rock there. The passage has deep water but is a nightmare of rocks.

During the night a storm came up out of the south, and I had to struggle to keep westward at all. The wind flailed so that it seemed my arms must be torn out by the wheel. But by now that was routine. As I calculated it, I was no more than 30 miles from Australia, and could reach there the next day. I did not say to myself that I *would* reach there. One does not use such definite words so long as even one stretch of water separates your vessel from your destination.

I was at the wheel, at about midnight, when I heard breakers. I tried to turn a little away from the sound, but this could have little effect in such a storm. A moment later the waves were dead ahead of me, and the raft drove up on the reef and stuck there. It was coral again. The roaring of the wind was tremendous, and the seas have little pity on a craft that does not move with them. I cut the lashing to the kayak and canoe so that I could take them into the water with me and thus keep afloat. The raft was raked continuously; it seemed I must lose everything on board. Compared to this, my previous hardships seemed small.

I think I stuck there two hours, or perhaps three. It was near daybreak when the raft floated off, and by then the wind was beginning to let up, and I moved north and northwest. When dawn came it showed me I was over deep water, without any bottom. Surely I was in the inner passage *now*, and yet I was still making no bets. I sailed for a while, keeping mostly to the west, and then there it was again—a line of white marking a reef. This time I made straight for it as if I were an old Barrier Reef hand, but just before I reached the white line, I thought I saw a passage to the left, and I tried for it and found there was no passage, and I tried to escape and couldn't, and so went straight ahead and struck and went over the initial barrier. I cleared it, and bumped ahead, and struck again and stuck for a few moments and lurched ahead again, steering and struggling that way for hours. By nightfall I was in deep water again, and felt I had to be in the inner passage now, after wandering so long on the desert of the Barrier. It seemed to me certain that I had entered the passage once before, and perhaps twice, and been driven back onto the reef by the storm's southerly winds.

It was about six o'clock, and getting dark, when I came clear of the reef for the last time. Heavy weather was coming up from the south. The wind kept rising as the darkness came down, and I thought carefully about everything I had heard of the inner passage. The stories of huge rocks kept coming to my mind. The next morning I thought I would have a clear view of the coast, and I would run in, and that would be the end of it. I am not one to cheer and throw my hat into the air, but I looked forward to the next morning.

I dozed, at ease in the deep water and not paying undue attention to the storm. I had long since learned to rig this raft in a storm so that it would take care of itself unless there was a great emergency. I leaned against the cabin and felt the special powerful movement that deep water gives a sailing vessel, and let consciousness slip away.

Suddenly it was as if someone spoke to me, spoke of lights. A wheel in my mind took a small turn of its own accord, and the interpretation was that ships used this inner passage, that a light might well be there. Then I woke up, and knew without realizing that I knew, that I was heading northwest, that the raft sailed handsomely despite the storm, and I rose to my feet and looked for lights—not knowing why I looked—and on the port bow there was the light.

It was there for an instant, and then it disappeared. It sank behind a wave and then appeared again, and again vanished. At first I thought it was a ship underway, but when I had sailed toward it for an hour, I saw it did not bob—it disappeared when the raft sank and appeared again when the raft rose—and it did not move at all.

I sailed toward the light but kept away from it. A light, whether on a rock or an anchored ship, was a haven and a destroyer, and it could not see me, so the duty of defense was entirely mine, and a drizzle was falling steadily and visibility was poor. If this was a rock, I wanted to use it as a landmark but give it no chance to smash the raft and me. I had to go and see what it was and then escape from it. I thought, for a moment, that if it were a ship, there would be a pilot on board, and he would know all about these waters and tell me how to get to shore, but I knew it was almost surely not a ship at all.

After a long time I could see that the light had a rhythm. It flashed four times, each time for a second, and then for eight seconds it was dark, and then the flashing began again. That would be a lighthouse, of course. Those who sailed these waters would be able to distinguish this light from others by its pattern of alternating light and darkness.

I came closer to the light, working toward the decision. Either to the right or left—I had to choose. The water was boiling too hard to consider survival a serious possibility if I made the wrong choice.

I set out to pass the light to port, and then something seemed to warn me to change course, and I changed it, and went toward the other side. It was pure guesswork. One side, then the other—I knew nothing about either side. By now the light, as best I could judge from the pitching raft, was about five miles off, not a great distance in this wind and current that were sweeping northward around me. At two miles' distance I could see glints from the light reflecting off a gray, sleek, hard surface, and see that the light was quite high over the water. It was a lighthouse atop an island or an enormous reef. I steered to the left and saw that, as the light turned, its bottom rays came over the top of rocks. I could not turn northeast now, for the wind would not let me, nor due north, for then I would be on the light itself, and smashed on the rocks that supported it. Then without warning the light went out altogether. A light goes round, and it throws its beams in all directions except where there are rocks. In that direction the light is cut off. When the light goes out the sailor knows.

I flung the wheel over and lashed it and leaped forward to bring the jib over, and I was working at that when the raft crashed with an enormous sound. The water churned among the rocks and came upward like many cataracts. Over the side I could see nothing but rocks, huge ones. I was stuck on them, and the raft sat there and shook violently as the sail continued to pull, and then it began to heel over to starboard. The big crate that held my tools and rope and spare canvas tore loose from its lashings and went against the mast. The raft continued to go over into the rocks. It was as if I were being pounded by sledges. I got ready to jump, to get clear before the raft fell over on top of me, though there were only rocks to leap on. The port side was up now until it was almost straight overhead. The forces were tremendous. I held on to a line and braced my feet against the edge of the deck. Then she slipped down, stayed level on the rocks for a little while, and then began to heel over the other way. She went over until she was almost vertical, and I counted the seconds when I would have to take the canoe and go overboard with it. I did not seriously think I would last more than a minute among those rocks, in that water.

I thought it was the end of the raft, and then she straightened up again, the jib standing like a stone wall in the wind, and all at once she slid clear off and into deep water again. I am trying to describe what my mind will permit me. At such a time as that, you see the water rushing past, and hear the gale, and feel the pounding, but your mind is too bludgeoned to observe much more than what the instinct for survival demands. It is like a combat in which you cannot make any countermoves or maneuvers. There is helplessness.

Now I was sailing and keeping to the left as far as I could, and I could see the light again. I saw that mass of rocks later—actually it was an island, Brook Island—from a speedboat in daylight, and how I found my way among the rocks, I cannot even conjecture. That night the islands, of which the one with the light is the highest, seemed to be all around me, black and menacing. In daylight there did not seem to be a course among them at all.

I sailed in the open places. I thought I saw mountains as daylight came. I saw something that seemed to be one tremendous island, but the angle had deceived me, for there were five separate islands. I learned later that Cook had given them their name—The Family Group. About nine in the morning I saw a straight, low, level line—a line of trees, I thought—without a hill or promontory of any kind. I knew it had to be Australia.

I sailed toward the line for two hours, keeping as close to the wind as I could. I might, I kept reminding my mind, be wrecked 10 feet from the beach. Gradually the scene became clearer. I went up the mast with my binoculars and saw it was a sandy coast, with a short, steep beach—no rocks, no reef, no coral in the way at all. At about 11 o'clock I sailed up on the beach. I dropped my anchor and the jib and mizzen, then jumped overboard into waist-deep water and made sure my anchor was holding. The raft had swung broadside to. I saw I was about at the center of a long, very shallow bay girdled by a dense tropical forest. I had come a long way, 10,500 miles, and now I had reached this place. There had been times, both before and during this voyage, when I had thought that I would swing into Sydney Harbor with a naval escort, and bands, and planes, and crowds, and perhaps it would be a holiday too. It had not turned out exactly that way. I was on this coast, hemmed in by the jungle, with the sea at my feet and my raft rolling fiercely. I had reached Australia, but there were no crowds, no ships, not even a footprint. Indeed, I did not have the faintest idea in the world where I was.

I took my ship's papers in a little handbag, and a couple of flares, and walked a mile or two south to the end of the beach, and there was a river with a lagoon, and impenetrable mangroves all around, hemming it in. I turned about and trudged back past the raft and to the north, and again there was a river with a lagoon where it entered the ocean. As I approached the river, I saw the roofs of a few houses on the far side, but not a single person. At first I tried to walk around the lagoon, or to find a narrow place in the river, but there was no way. This was tropical, dense jungle. I began to strip to my shorts, planning to swim the 100 yards across the lagoon. Just as I was about ready, I saw a woman and a man.

I shouted, and they stared, but I couldn't tell if they understood what I said, and I was very eager to make contact, to make them understand. I fired a distress flare. It flew into the air and arched down. To the couple it must have been an eerie sight. The man came to the water's edge, and I shouted that he should send a boat if he had one. All right, I heard him say, I'll get the boat. He walked toward the houses and disappeared, and then I saw him coming back with a car and a boat on a trailer. The outboard motor churned, and the couple came toward me. I could not help but speculate what it was like through their eyes, and how they must wonder who this strange old man could be with his beard to his chest and the marks of the sea and the weather all over him.

The man was Hank Penning, a schoolteacher, a Dutchman from New Guinea, a heavyset man about 45. The woman was his wife, a nurse. "I'm Willis from New York," I said. It was all that occurred to me to say, it seemed the sensible, simple thing, all that I should say to this man and woman I did not even know. The Pennings came to me, and I got in their boat, and they told me, as kind people would do, about what I wanted to know. This was Queensland, the northeastern Australian province. The nearest town was called Tully. It was a good thing I hadn't gone swimming, because crocodiles infest the lagoon. Tully is a small sugar-refining town, with the plantations all around—a frontier town with a main street and friendly people.

We went to police headquarters, and I showed my papers and passport, and one of the officers came and looked at me quite severely and shrugged at all the answers I gave. I must be an escaped convict, he thought. I did look ragged and soggy, scorched by the sun, bearded, worn to tatters. He checked my papers again and again, and looked at me so carefully that I felt like a show horse, and he made it clear that within his analytical mind he could see through my ridiculous pretense. The joke was all over Tully soon afterward: I was a fugitive convict, and I had escaped in the days when Australia was England's penal colony, and I had been hiding out in the bush for the last century or so. Now I had been captured at last, and it was only fitting that a Tully police officer had been the one to bring me to account. An ordinary man could never have succeeded in doing something like that.

I do not ask others why they do what they do—why, for instance, they pretend to be ancient when they are only 50 or 60. If I be different in any way from any other man, then let it be accepted or ignored. I have never been, or sought to be, a person whose activities and thoughts would be agreeable to everyone else. I am sure that those with an ambition for popularity know many things I will never understand. I am sure they make peace with themselves, as I do with my friend Smith, when he asks, "Why did you do all that, Willis?" I can only smile, for there would not be much point in asking what he thinks he's up to in his life. Or remark that most of us have dreams, and only a few act on them, after all. I am momentarily content with the knowledge that the Pacific is mine. And I am sure that soon I will find the concept of another voyage which I will have to make or find no peace with myself.

The Unknown War

BY DAVID HOWARTH

In one of the most desolate regions on earth, a tiny fraction of World War II was fought and won. Here were no mighty armies, no imposing war machinery—just a handful of brave and desperate men pitting themselves against the Germans and against the frozen arctic wastes. Two conflicting ideals governed them: the patriotism of men whose country is at war, and the unwritten code of the North, according to which all men in the arctic—even Germans—are members of the same team. Which was the true victor? Was it the team that drove the Germans from Greenland? Or was it the serene, inscrutable arctic, which bred kindness and sympathy among enemies in the midst of battle?

ON THE northeast coast of Greenland, on a point of land called Eskimoness, about 600 miles beyond the Arctic Circle, there used to be a wooden house. It is burnt down now, and there is nothing left there except a small outbuilding which escaped the fire. The house was built as a scientific station, but in the early spring of 1943 it became the center of a fight—a fight which began near the house and then ranged for 400 miles up and down that beautiful desolate coast.

There were seven men using the house at the time, four Danes, one Norwegian and two Eskimos. They were cut off from the rest of the world except for the radio, and their nearest neighbors, so far as they knew, were in another house on an island called Ella, a 200-mile trip to the southward. North of them, there was nobody at all. But they were not oppressed by their isolation. Each of them, in his own way, was in love with the arctic. They were aware of its beauty and its peace and freedom, and they had all been happy there that winter, enjoying the primitive excitement of hunting dangerous animals, and their own mastery of the technique of living in the extreme of cold, and the peculiar exultation of driving dog teams on the sea ice in the arctic night.

In the arctic all men have a common enemy in the climate, and it has always been an unbroken tradition there that men are friends; and so it seemed incredible to the men at Eskimoness when they found themselves, at the end of that winter, suddenly faced with human enemies, forced to hunt men instead of polar bears and foxes, and to discover what it felt like to be hunted.

This is simply the story of the fight which began there on the afternoon of March 11, 1943, when one of the seven men, to his amazement, saw a human footprint in the snow.

Greenland is part of Denmark. When Germany invaded Denmark on April 9, 1940, the King of Denmark had ordered all Danes to submit to the German occupation, because it was obviously impossible to prevent it. In this royal order there was no reference to the colonies; on the face of it, it ordered Danish subjects in the colonies also to submit.

But luckily for Denmark, and for America and Britain, too, the two governors of Greenland—Aksel Svane and Eske Brun— and the Danish minister in Washington, Henrik Kauffmann, were men of independent character. They decided to carry out the orders of the government if they thought they were constitutional and, if they did not, to regard them as having been sent under duress. This stand was recognized by the United States. Since the United States soon became the main source of supply of goods for Greenland, and the major purchaser of Greenland's products, Mr. Svane spent most of the war in America. Thus, Eske Brun, for all practical purposes, became the administrator of 22,000 people and of the largest island in the world.

Since the tenth century, when it was discovered by Eric the Red, a Norwegian viking, civilization has touched only the fringe of the west coast of Greenland. The west coast is free of ice for several months each summer. There are several small towns there and all together over 20,000 people, a mixed race of Eskimo and Danish origin who call themselves Greenlanders.

The whole of the interior of the country is an enormous icecap which does not support life of any kind; and on the east coast, the nearest side to Europe, a sea current from the north brings polar ice right down to the Atlantic, so that ships can reach that side of Greenland for only six weeks or so in the autumn. This coast is 1600 miles long; its great fjords, which are frozen for ten months of every year, lead 200 miles inland; its mountains are nearly as high as the Alps. In this tremendous area there are only two villages. Four hundred miles up from its southern end is the Eskimo settlement of Angmagssalik, which has a population of 1500. Four hundred and fifty miles beyond Angmagssalik is Scoresby Sound, with a population of about 300. Beyond Scoresby Sound is the territory of Northeast Greenland, where nobody lives except a few solitary hunters and the radio operators in four weather stations. Three hundred and fifty miles north of Scoresby Sound is Eskimoness, distinguished from tens of thousands of other projecting rocks only by having a name and the ruins of a house on it.

When Eske Brun surveyed his domain from his capital at Godthaab, on the west coast, he guessed that Britain would hold out and America would come into the war in the end; and that when she did, the Americans would want air bases along his west coast, as stepping stones on the shortest route from America to Europe. [In April, 1941, the Danish minister signed an agreement with the United States which said that America would protect Greenland against aggressors; also, it gave the United States the right to establish military bases on Greenland.—ED.]

The very fact that Eske Brun had defied the Germans made it seem all the more likely that they would come there sooner or later. The populated west coast was quite safe from raids; the sea and the air on that side of Greenland were firmly under American control. But along the wild 1600 miles of the east coast there was nothing whatever to stop the Germans from landing.

Eske Brun, without a single soldier or any weapon more dangerous than a hunting rifle, consulted the Americans about this problem. They were not yet at war, but they were interested in the possibility of a German foothold in Greenland. However, short of committing a vast organization of ships and planes, they could not do much at that time.

Their first reaction was to ask Eske Brun to order everybody then on the northern half of the coast to come south to the settlement at Scoresby Sound. They pointed out that the coast would be easier to patrol if it was known to be totally uninhabited, so that anyone who was found there could be treated as an enemy on sight. After some hesitation, Eske Brun agreed.

At that moment, scattered along the 700 miles of coast beyond Scoresby Sound, there was a total of twenty-six men and one woman. There were twelve hunters, some Danish and some Norwegian. Each of them lived alone, except the one man who had his wife with him. These men very seldom saw one another. Besides the hunters, there were three Danish weather stations, which had radio transmitters, and one Norwegian one, and each of them had a staff of three or four men. By radio through the weather stations, the order was sent out. Gradually, in the course of the summer, all the hunters drifted in to the weather stations or to Scoresby Sound.

Eske Brun had invited the Americans to patrol his coast, and they had hesitated, so he offered to do it himself. Possibly, he thought, a few men who knew the arctic well could do more than an army and a navy and an air force. Armed only with hunting rifles, they could not prevent a landing, but they might be able to detect it, so that he could tell the Americans where it was. By radio to Scoresby Sound, he asked for volunteers, and chose fifteen. He called them the North East Greenland Sledge Patrol, and as their headquarters, because it was near the middle of their beat, he selected the red wooden house at Eskimoness.

The house at Eskimoness was on the south side of Clavering Island; its window looked out across a wide open bay to the mountains of the great headland with the curious name of Hold With Hope. From season to season, everything in this prospect alters except the outline of the mountains. In July and August, the waters of the bay are blue, the mountains brown and gray except for the snow on their summits and the glaciers among them. All through the summer, from the great glaciers at the head of the bay, a stately procession of icebergs drifts slowly toward the open sea.

The sea freezes quite suddenly in the autumn. Whatever icebergs are passing at that moment are frozen in and become part of the landscape. There is no movement then except the movement of the sky, and no sound except the sound of the wind. The birds have gone, the animals are seldom to be seen.

The seven men who had wintered at Eskimoness were members of the sledge patrol. The eight other members were stationed at Ella Island and at Scoresby Sound. Each man had a sledge and a team of dogs, and their assignment from Eske Brun was to patrol the coast from just south of Scoresby Sound up to the farthest limit which is ever navigable—that is to say, from seventy to seventy-seven degrees north. As the crow flies, their beat was 500 miles long. If anyone had the patience to measure the length of the coastline they had to patrol, along each of the fjords and round each of the islands, it might be 10,000 miles. But it did not seem to them an unreasonable task. Some of them thought it was unnecessary, but none of them thought it was difficult.

The leader of these men was a Dane named Ib Poulsen. He was a slightly built, quiet, self-contained young man, the son of a bookseller in a provincial Danish town. After he had finished his apprenticeship in bookshops, some latent spirit of adventure had made him take a temporary job in Greenland. He never went back to bookselling.

When the Germans invaded Denmark, Poulsen had been at home on leave. By then he had spent four years in Northeast Greenland, mostly as a radio operator in the service of Count Eigil Knuth, one of the great men of Danish arctic exploration. Count Knuth had an arctic station of his own, one of the four stations in Northeast Greenland which broadcast daily weather observations. Even in the summer of 1940, after the invasion of

Denmark and after Dunkirk, all these stations were still transmitting in plain international code, simply because nobody had told them to stop. Accurate weather reports from Greenland were equally important to both sides in the battle between German submarines and British convoys. Anybody could pick up the Northeast Greenland broadcasts, and the British and the Germans were both using them. Yet the British seemed not to have thought of supplying the stations with secret codes, and nobody in Denmark could send them a signal without the Germans' consent.

The men at Count Knuth's station were due for relief. Poulsen and he discussed the situation and agreed that the open transmissions had to stop. Then the Count applied to the Germans for permission to send Poulsen back to Greenland, with two other men from Denmark: Kurt Olsen, a seventeen-year-old radio operator, and Marius Jensen, a man of about thirty who had been a hunter in Northeast Greenland before the war. Of course, the Germans wanted this free gift of weather information to go on as long as possible, and so they agreed to allow a small ship to sail from Norway to Greenland. The ship was supposed to bring back the men who were being relieved, but nobody on board had the least intention of coming back at all.

The ship could not reach Count Knuth's station, which was in seventy-seven degrees north, because the ice did not open that summer, but once Poulsen was clear of German control, he was able to send a radio signal which stopped the unciphered broadcasts. The ship eventually reached Greenland and in the following winter Poulsen reached the station by sledge. He was still there when Eske Brun gave the order for everybody to come south. So this former bookseller became the leader of the sledge patrol and, at the age of thirty-two, found himself in charge of 100,000 square miles of Denmark's colony. Nobody ever had a more isolated command than Poulsen or more tenuous authority. He had never met Eske Brun; he had no uniform or military status; nothing but a radio telegram in code to say that a sledge patrol was established and that he was the head of it.

Poulsen took his command very seriously. Certainly his position gave him plenty to worry about. When he had cut off the international weather reports, he had known that the German navy or air force might try to do something to fill the gap. In September, 1941, in fact, the United States Coast Guard cutter *Northland* had captured a three-man German weather station that had just begun operating on the northeast coast. But in spite of this episode, Poulsen found it difficult to explain the danger to his hunters; nothing could quite persuade them that it was not a lot of nonsense.

By the time the sledge patrol had assembled at Eskimoness, Kurt Olsen, a tough, handsome young man, had impressed the old hunters as never being afraid of anything, and Eske Brun had appointed him second in command. Jensen, like Poulsen, was slightly built and extremely reserved. The other members of the patrol were two young Eskimos named William and Mikael; Peter Nielsen, a young Danish hunter; and Henry Rudi, one of the arctic's great experts on bear hunting. Rudi, a Norwegian, was a cheerful man in his middle fifties and he had lived in the arctic for most of his life. He was said to have shot more polar bears than any other man alive—somewhere in the neighborhood of 1000. These men may have had little in common, but at Eskimoness they felt the unspoken brotherhood which unites men in the arctic.

This brotherhood is not a sentimental fiction, it is real. Unless one understands it one cannot entirely understand why the men who got caught up in the extraordinary events at Eskimoness behaved as they did.

There is nothing to struggle for in the arctic, except to keep alive in difficult surroundings, and in this all men are in co-operation, never in competition; and so mutual distrust has almost died away. There is no crime worth mentioning in the true unexploited arctic. Nobody ever locks a door. A traveler may walk into anybody's house and stay there, whether the owner is at home or away. Political and social quarrels seem absurd, and nobody takes much account of nationality.

Besides this, nobody who has ever lived in the arctic for long has remained unmoved by its harmony and beauty. Even the least sensitive of men, alone in the arctic, feels nearer to whatever God he worships. So the arctic paradox arises: that, although a man must be physically tough, his relations with other men are gentle, trustful and peculiarly innocent.

With these traditions, the winter passed pleasantly at Eskimoness. The hunters were away most of the time and they were reasonably conscientious in carrying out the job which they had scoffed at. At Eskimoness the sun is seen for the last time about the end of October. After that, around the middle of each day, there is a sunrise glow in the sky above the mountains of Hold With Hope, but each day the glow becomes less, and in December, even on clear days, it is hardly discernible. The sun rises again at the beginning of February. But to say it is dark for three months does not mean one can never see. When the weather is clear there is starlight or moonlight or the light of the aurora, and the gleaming white country reflects all the light there is. There is no color at all in the nightlit landscape. The moon shadows on the ice are gray.

Poulsen and Kurt Olsen had to make weather observations and encode them and transmit them every six hours and, because they were the only radio operators, they could seldom leave the station for more than a few hours. They envied the others when they watched them go. There is something irresistibly exciting in driving a dog sledge out across the sea ice in the starlight and hearing the sledge runners hissing on the snow or rumbling with a deep bass echo on the hard ice.

At Eskimoness, there were sixty or seventy dogs, not counting the puppies, when all the men were at home, because each of them had a team of eight or ten. A dog team is driven by four Eskimo words of command and a twenty-five-foot sealskin whip. The signal to go or to hurry is an urgent "Ah, ah," like the bark of a dog. To stop is a more soothing, long-drawn "Ai." Right is a high-pitched, quickly repeated, "Illi, illi, illi." Left is "Yu, yu." Right and left are backed by a crack of the whip on the opposite side to the way the team is supposed to turn.

It is surprising that this archaic kind of transport, which Eskimos have used since before the beginning of history, should still have been the best kind in 1943, but so it was. A Greenland dog never suffers from the cold. It does not need anything which is not provided by nature on the Greenland coast, and it never breaks down. A ten-dog team can pull a weight of about

800 pounds. With a light sledge on hard ice, they are said to be able to gallop at twenty-five miles an hour for a short distance. With a normal load on a long journey, fifteen to twenty miles a day is an average, and forty miles is a good day's run.

There were two reasons why the members of the sledge patrol had tackled the job with so little misgiving; and one of them was that they knew the dogs would do most of it for them. Downwind, they can scent a man or a bear or a hut that is lived in, two or three miles away. They will always make towards the scent, unless the driver can stop them, to see what is going on. All the men had to do was to drive along offshore, and rely on the dogs to smell out an enemy.

The second reason why the job was not impossible was that nobody can move around in the arctic without leaving tracks. On the sea ice, the snow is seldom thick; the wind blows it away as soon as it has fallen. But a sledge or skis or even a pair of boots compress the snow so that it cannot blow away. Fresh tracks appear as hollows in the snow, but after a wind the loose snow collects in drifts and the tracks in wind-blown places are left as hard, raised ridges which often stand where they are until the spring. So the patrols did not look for human figures or for huts. They looked for tracks.

The men kept up their patrol all through the winter. Generally, in the dark time, there is between forty and ninety degrees of frost—about ten degrees below zero to sixty below—and appalling blizzards tear down the icecap to the sea. It is usually thought to be too dangerous to travel. But it can be done if the traveler is prepared to live as simply as Eskimos have lived for centuries, and if he is never careless. He carries a tent and two primus stoves—one for cooking, another for heat. He carries matches and primus prickers—fine needles used to clear the stove jets—in a very safe place of their own, such as a bag on a string around his neck, because a man once nearly lost his life by losing his primus pricker. His gear includes a sleeping bag and ground sheet of reindeer skin, and a rifle—besides, of course, his sledge and skis. With this primitive equipment, the patrol men sometimes journeyed for two months away from Eskimoness.

Usually, they slept in huts. Before Eske Brun's order had put an end to ordinary hunting, each hunter had had his own district, about sixty miles square, with a fairly elaborate hut called a hunting station in the middle of it. Also, he had a lot of smaller huts, about six feet square, spaced about ten miles apart, a day's march for a man who was working traps. In 1943, all the stations in the neighborhood of seventy-six degrees north were deserted, but the stations and some of the huts were still stocked with coal and driftwood, and in some the patrol had laid depots of dog food and paraffin.

The seven men on their tremendous winter journeys were physically isolated by hundreds of miles of utterly barren mountains, but perhaps their mental isolation was even more complete. That was the winter of Stalingrad, North Africa, Russian convoys, air raids on England, talk of the second front. Poulsen at Eskimoness used to hear of these things on his radio. Sometimes when the men came back to their base he remembered to tell them some odds and ends of news about the war, but for them there was no reality in world events. They never quite forgot that they were to search for other human beings, but as the winter passed they could not believe they would ever meet anyone in that beautiful wilderness, or that if they did, the strangers would not be as friendly as all men had always been in Northeast Greenland. But in that they were wrong.

The German trawler *Sachsen* had sailed from Kiel in the summer of 1942, under orders of naval headquarters in Berlin. The ship had nineteen men on board. Her captain was Hermann Ritter, a reserve lieutenant in the German navy, and besides her crew, she carried a doctor, two radio operators and a team of meteorologists. When Poulsen and Count Knuth between them had put an end to the international weather reports, it had made a gap, as they expected, in the Germans' forecasts; the *Sachsen*'s mission was to fill the gap. By 1942 Russia was in the war, and the British had started their convoys to the Russian arctic ports. Submarine warfare and long-range air reconnaissance had spread north to the arctic, and the convoys were being helped and the Germans hindered by the lack of German weather observations.

For Lieutenant Ritter, this voyage in the middle of the war was something like a homecoming. Ritter was a man of fifty, graying a little, very tall and thin and aquiline. He was a

German only by a chance of politics. He came of mixed French and Italian and Scandinavian stock; his birthplace was in the part of the Austrian Empire which became Czechoslovakia after World War I. Then, in 1939, when the Germans invaded Czechoslovakia, his nationality was changed again. This time, he was simply told he was a German.

By then, Ritter had had several jobs, mostly as an officer in merchant ships of various nationalities. But about 1930 he had been one of the crew of the Prince of Monaco's yacht on a cruise to Spitsbergen, and Ritter was yet another man who had fallen in love at first sight with the arctic. He went back to Spitsbergen and lived there humbly for five years as a hunter. Those had been the only perfectly happy and carefree years he could remember since his childhood.

He had been delighted to be given command of the *Sachsen,* an appointment which would take him back to the arctic. As it happened, the appointment had also saved him from a difficult situation. He had been captain of a naval auxiliary vessel running between the North Sea and the Baltic ports behind the Russian front, but he had suddenly been removed from his command by the Gestapo. He did not know why he was under suspicion. A good many people knew he was not a Nazi, but he had always done his duty as an officer. Nobody had ever told him what went on behind the scenes, but it seemed to him afterwards that the navy had defied the Gestapo by quickly finding him a new command. When plans were made for the *Sachsen*'s voyage, Ritter, who had been an arctic hunter, was an obvious choice as her commander.

The Gestapo affair had scared Ritter, not for himself so much as for his wife and his only daughter. But he had hopes of making a great success of the *Sachsen.* His orders were to establish the meteorological party ashore in Northeast Greenland. It was left to him to choose a place. If he could get his ship out of the ice again after the landing, he was to come home; if not, he was to winter there himself.

Ritter was the only man on board who knew the arctic, and the others were eager to listen to everything he could tell them, and he poured out his recollections of his years at Spitsbergen. He confided most in the senior meteorologist, Doctor Weiss, and the expedition's doctor, whose name was Sensse, and in a man called Schmidt, who seemed to be educated. Back in Germany, he had been worried about Schmidt, because he was a keen Nazi Party member. Now, in his own excitement at returning to the arctic, his doubts seemed unfounded.

None of these Germans had ever been to Greenland, and nobody in Germany knew very much about it. They had been given some excellent Danish maps, taken from Copenhagen, and in July, Doctor Weiss had flown over the northeast coast in a Focke-Wulf reconnaissance aircraft from Norway. On that flight, they had specially looked at the meteorological stations which were marked on the maps. At Eskimoness the Danish flag was flying, so they knew somebody was living there, but none of them knew whether the coast was patrolled or guarded.

The *Sachsen* passed well north of Iceland without being detected by enemy ships and then turned farther north to penetrate the ice before she closed the coast of Greenland. On August twenty-sixth Ritter sighted land. It was the southern point of Shannon Island, at seventy-five degrees north latitude.

He had hoped to go farther north than that, but between Shannon Island and the mainland he saw an unbroken mass of solid polar ice. So he turned south, determined to land wherever he could find a sheltered anchorage. The first point he approached was Sabine Island, and there he saw open water close inshore. On the northeast corner of this island, there is a tiny fjord called Hansa Bay. It was free of ice. He turned the *Sachsen*'s bow towards it and steamed slowly in. In the middle of the bay she ran aground.

Sabine Island was not a place which Ritter would have chosen if the ice had not forced him there. It was only seventy miles from Eskimoness, the only place on the coast which he knew was inhabited—a next-door neighbor, as distances are reckoned in the arctic. But, in fact, it was a very lucky choice. It was notorious as a bad hunting ground, so the men of the sledge patrol never went there unless they had to.

The *Sachsen* was floated again without much trouble, and anchored farther in, near the head of the bay. But on their way north, in a storm, one of their lifeboats had been smashed, and with only one boat left, it was clearly going to take a long time to get all the meteorologists' gear ashore. Anyhow, the freeze-up was imminent. To make a thorough job, Ritter could only wait till the ship was frozen in, and then land in comfort across the ice. Besides that, the radio transmitter which the meteorologists had brought turned out to be inadequate, so the ship's transmitter had to be used to send the weather reports. Ritter was glad to have such a good excuse to winter there.

In the meantime, they covered the ship with white camouflage sheets to make it look like an iceberg, and began to explore Sabine Island. The island is nine miles square; it has several flat-topped hills about 2000 feet high, and Hansa Bay is surrounded by them. There are two huts on the island: a very small hunting hut on Hansa Bay itself, and an old Danish hunting station on the south end of the island, near a small bay appropriately called Germania Harbor.

Hansa Bay was a good place for defense. The steep hills protected it from the air, and anyone coming across the open ice from the north or south would be at the mercy of a sentry with a machine gun in a prepared position. But in any case, Ritter's first line of defense was simply to avoid being seen, and that was easy. His ship froze in and snow drifted over her till she was buried. The huts which were built on shore were buried too. By October there was nothing to be seen in Hansa Bay except a slender radio mast, some mounds of snow and a network of human tracks. By then the base was sending reports three times a day to the German navy.

It is hard to say exactly when trouble began up there on Sabine Island. There were too many men ashore and they did not have enough to do. It was dangerous to let them roam around, not only because they might have got into difficulties but because of the tracks which they would leave for any traveler to see, if there were any travelers. But after a time Ritter had to take that risk and let them go on short hunting trips toward the open sea, partly to provide fresh meat, but more in order to occupy their minds and give them exercise.

But that was not a very serious trouble; far deeper was the difference between the characters of Ritter and of Schmidt. At first he went on naïvely confiding in Schmidt. But Schmidt remained aloof; sometimes he even seemed hostile. It seemed that he must have thought from the very beginning that the expedition should be commanded by the senior Nazi Party member, not by the senior naval officer.

Ritter felt some sympathy for Schmidt and, to make things easier for him, he made a point of deferring to his wishes. The Nazis, for example, wanted to give a weekly political lecture to the men. Privately, Ritter thought it a ludicrous idea, but he agreed. Then, of course, he had to attend the lectures and to give the impression of endorsing what they propounded. They were embarrassing occasions. Ritter had heard it all before, but suddenly, as he heard it again in the arctic night, the doctrine of Nazism doubly nauseated him.

During the winter he fell into the habit of spending a lot of his time alone, trying to recapture his old feeling for the arctic. Ritter was a deeply religious man, a Catholic by birth and upbringing; and he was introspective. The belief soon began to crystallize in his mind that his duty as an officer and his duty to God could never be reconciled. Slowly, all through that arctic night, a suspicion grew clearer and clearer in his mind—the simple suspicion that the German cause was wrong.

It was later in the winter that Ritter began to be afraid. He was sitting in his cabin reading a book about the arctic when some of his men knocked on his door and came in. Looking at them, he realized that they were a Nazi deputation. When he put his book down, one of them looked at the author's name and said, "You know this man is a Jew." Ritter shrugged his shoulders. They took the book away.

As Ritter pondered over this incident, he was gradually overcome by a sickening sense of dread. He thought he had left the Gestapo behind in Germany, but he began, with horror, to suspect that he had not. He thought bitterly back over the last few months, of all the confiding things he had said to Schmidt, all he had told him about the friendship of the arctic, the liberal concepts he had tried to put into words, all the ideas which meant so much to him. And, now that he came to think of it, these ideas were the opposite of Nazism.

Now that it was too late, he saw how unwise he had been to let his enthusiasm carry him away. Schmidt had made no comment, but had he been carefully noting it down against him? Ritter was not afraid for himself, but the old fear rose up again for his wife and daughter. He made up his mind to be careful not to offend his Nazis any more. But a week or two later, the doctor, Sensse, came into his cabin.

"Ritter," he said, "I think you ought to know that some of the men are trying to send a telegram to Berlin to say you are not to be trusted."

The doctor said that, so far as he knew, the telegram had not actually been sent. One of the Nazis, he said, had given it to the radio operator with instructions to send it without telling the captain. The radio operator, caught between two authorities, had asked the doctor for advice, and the doctor had decided that Ritter was in command and ought to be told. Ritter thanked him. He had always liked Doctor Sensse, and had never been able to believe he approved of the Nazi Party. Yet Ritter did not dare question him more closely.

Later, thinking about the telegram, Ritter took it for granted that Schmidt was at the back of it; but he wondered if Schmidt had really wanted the telegram to go. It was hardly likely that Berlin would have acted on it without any further inquiries. But on the other hand, if Schmidt had not meant to send it, but had planned that the doctor should tell him about it, then the thing had a point: it was a final warning to Ritter, a way of suggesting to him that he had better do as he was told.

Whenever Ritter tried to plan what he ought to say to Schmidt, he came up against a block: Schmidt suspected him of disloyalty to Nazism, and he was right. The difference was that, for Schmidt, that meant disloyalty to Germany, and for Ritter it did not.

By February, when the dark time ended, the German camp was confused by rival loyalties and distorted politics. Its commander was a lonely, bewildered and frightened man. He dared not confide in anyone. Nevertheless, for six months, the German transmitter in Sabine Island had been sending out daily reports, unknown to the British or Americans; they were guiding German submarines and aircraft in their attacks on the arctic convoys.

It was about the beginning of March when Poulsen said to Marius Jensen, "You'd better have a look at Sabine Island."

This was the busiest time of the year for the sledge patrol. The worst of the winter storms were over, and the daylight was rushing toward the equinox, increasing by twenty minutes every day from the darkness of early February to the midnight sun of early May. Spring is the most brilliant of the seasons in Northeast Greenland. It is still very cold, and the thaw is still far away, but the land is deluged with light of superb intensity, and visibility is tremendous. On a clear day one can see at least 120 miles; mountains which are thirty miles away seem no more than four or five.

It is in this cold flood of light that conditions are best for sledging. It is not too cold for the men or too hot for the dogs. So in March and April, Poulsen had planned to cover the whole of the coast and patrol all the places which had been inaccessible in the winter.

In those early days of March, six of the seven men were at Eskimoness. Peter Nielsen had spent most of the winter alone in the district of Hochstetter Forland, 100 miles north of Eskimoness, and at the end of April he had gone even farther north. Marius Jensen was to take three sledge loads of stores up to Peter, and it was on this journey that Poulsen suggested he should make a detour to Sabine Island, which had not been patrolled for nearly a year.

Marius did not want to go to the island. "You know it's a hopeless place for hunting," he said to Poulsen. "And the weather's bad out there. There's nothing but fog at this time of year."

But it was only a token protest. On March eighth Marius started on his journey with the two Eskimos, William and Mikael. Like all Eskimos, they were perfectly peaceable, easygoing and friendly. The idea of great nations at war was very difficult for them to grasp. To meet a hostile man was just as unlikely, in their experience, as to meet a friendly bear. Because of this natural limitation, Eske Brun had allowed the Eskimos to be enrolled in the sledge patrol only as assistants, to drive sledges and hunt, and lay depots of food. Eske Brun, from the very beginning, had decided never to let Eskimos be involved in anything so unnatural to them as fighting.

On their first day out of Eskimoness, Marius, William and

Mikael made their way to an old hunting station called Sand-odden, which stands on the shore of Wollaston Forland. The patrol had used it fairly often because it was thirty miles from Eskimoness, a good first day's journey.

Each of the men was using a team of eight or nine dogs, and their sledges were more heavily loaded than usual. At Sand-odden, where they spent the first night, it was a temptation to go straight on over the Kuppel Pass, the usual route to the north, instead of going the long way round the outside of Wollaston Forland and Sabine Island.

Apart from the weather and the hunting, there was another bad thing about Sabine Island—just south of the island is one of the worst stretches of ice on the coast. The current from the north makes an eddy round the side of the island which breaks up the ice from time to time all through the winter. There may be leads of open water at any time of the year, and there are always pressure ridges where the ice has broken and buckled; so it is always a dangerous, difficult place to pass. But Marius had promised Poulsen he would try it, so that was that.

As the three men went on, all their thoughts were on a single subject: bears. The defect of Sabine Island as a hunting ground was that herds of muskox were not usually to be found there; but there were bears. The muskox is the main source of food for travelers and their dogs. It looks like a small buffalo, stands about four feet high, and is very good to eat. There is nothing exciting about shooting a muskox, but a bear is a very different thing. Hunting a polar bear from a sledge is exciting and fairly dangerous, and a bearskin is worth quite a lot of money; and a traveler may meet a bear at any minute on the outer coast, even around Sabine Island. This possibility shortens the longest journey.

But Marius and the two Eskimos, on their way toward Sabine Island, saw no sign of bears. For the third night of that journey, Marius had decided to stay in the hunting station at Germania Harbor, on the south side of Sabine Island. They approached it across the sound which separates the island from the mainland, after a hard day's driving between ridges and pinnacles of broken ice. The weather was still crystal clear, and from right across the sound, five miles away, they could see the black speck of the hut at the foot of the Sabine hills.

About halfway across, Marius saw his dogs prick up their ears. Their pace began to quicken. Marius thought, *A bear.* He could not see anything, so he called his dogs to a halt and got out his field glasses. He swept the horizon, searching for the slightly yellow speck which he hoped to see. But all he noticed was that Mikael, away to the right, had halted and was examining the ice.

Marius focused his glasses on the hut, and then he saw the quite incredible thing: in the still clear air, a small wisp of smoke was rising from the chimney. Marius stood there, amazed. It was years since he had seen a track in the snow or a sign of life in a hut without knowing at once who had made it. Then Mikael came dashing up, and he was shouting: footsteps— human footsteps—boots—boots with heels. Nobody Marius knew wore boots with heels, except ski boots, and nobody walked about in ski boots. Marius looked again toward the hut, and he saw two specks appear beyond it. Through the glasses they were two men, running. They climbed the hills at the back of the hut and disappeared over a col toward the middle of the island.

After they had got over their first surprise, Marius and the Eskimos drove up to the hut at Germania Harbor. There was nobody there. It was nice and warm inside. The stove was still alight, and there were two half-empty mugs of coffee on the table. Lying on one of the bunks were two daggers, and there was a jacket of an unfamiliar greenish color hanging on the door. Marius looked at it and on the breast of it he saw the swastika.

The three men poked about inside the hut and looked at the tracks outside it. There was an uncured bearskin and half a bear's carcass. There were two eiderdown sleeping bags in the hut. There was very little food or fuel and no traveling gear at all. Everything suggested a short hunting expedition from a base not far away; and when Marius came to think of the map, and the direction the two men had taken when they had run away in the hills, there was only one place that the base was likely to be, and that was in Hansa Bay, five miles away.

Once he had come to this conclusion, Marius realized they could not hang about at Germania Harbor. They stirred up their tired dogs and started to drive slowly back across the sound. It did not occur to any of them to take the swastika jacket or the German daggers. In the ethics of war, one talks of capturing booty, but in the arctic, war or no war, stealing was stealing.

Even at that stage, the things that really mattered to Marius were the things that always matter in the arctic: the state of the ice and the weather, and the welfare of the dogs. It was getting dark by then, and ahead of them was all the difficult ice they had crossed in the morning. Eskimoness, the headquarters of the sledge patrol, was sixty miles to the southwest. The dogs had to be rested somewhere, and the sooner, the better. The first hunting hut on the way home was straight across the sound, on the point of the mainland which faces Germania Harbor. It is called Cape Wynn; and there, Marius, William and Mikael decided to spend the night. None of them really had any idea that the information they possessed was about as dangerous to live with as a time bomb.

The routine of a night stop in the arctic is always the same. The sledges are unloaded and everything is taken into the hut. The dogs are unharnessed and picketed on long chains, and then they are fed. Somebody lights the stove and somebody gets snow to melt for coffee. As the hut warms up, the traveling clothes are taken off and hung in the ceiling of the hut to thaw and dry. Everything begins to steam comfortably.

After they eat, the sleeping bag is overwhelmingly attractive, but the sledge patrol always had one other chore which Eske Brun, the colonial governor of Greenland, had ordered, and that was to write a log of the day's journey. It bored them. But that night at Cape Wynn, Marius at last had something of interest to put in his logbook, and after supper he settled down laboriously with a pencil.

It was midnight when the dogs began to howl.

When the two German hunters came breathlessly in from the outpost at Germania Harbor, Lt. Hermann Ritter, commander of the German weather-reporting expedition of Greenland, was in bed with a temperature, but the news which they blurted out soon brought him to his feet.

The story they told him was so stupid from a military point of view that it was almost funny. If they had only waited in the hut, they could perfectly easily have shot or captured the three sledge drivers as they approached across the open ice. But something of the arctic spirit had got into those two men. They had run away and come back to base, they explained, because they had not been able to bring themselves to shoot: and that curious explanation was one which Ritter, a veteran of the arctic, could easily understand. Even the Nazi, Schmidt, when he was told, knew what they meant.

Anyhow, Ritter wasted no time on remonstration. The main question was whether they had been seen. They said they were afraid they probably had, as they climbed the mountain. Ritter guessed the three sledges had come from Eskimoness, and he took it for granted that Eskimoness had a radio transmitter. Therefore, if the three drivers, or even one of them, got back to Eskimoness alive, the Greenland Government and the Americans and British would all know where his base was hidden.

Five minutes after the two hunters came in, eight Germans set off, in two separate parties, armed with submachine guns, rifles and revolvers, with orders to get the three sledge drivers and bring them in, preferably alive, but if necessary dead. One of the parties was led by Ritter, who was still feeling ill, and the other one by Doctor Weiss, the senior meteorologist. Schmidt was in Doctor Weiss' party.

When Ritter got to Germania Harbor, it was getting dark, and Doctor Weiss had already arrived with his party and discovered there was nobody in the hut. Nothing had been touched. On the face of it, it was ridiculous to try to catch sledges by following them on foot. Besides, Ritter's men were wearing leather boots instead of fur ones, which is one of the surest ways of getting frostbite.

But Doctor Weiss, who knew much less than Ritter about the dangers and had never seen a dog sledge, was eager to try to follow up the tracks, and he was supported by Schmidt and several of the others. Ritter knew that if anyone went, he ought to go himself, but even the five miles from Hansa Bay had taken a lot out of him, and he could not face the idea of going any farther. But he knew better than to argue, especially with Schmidt, who had made it plain that he suspected Ritter of disloyalty to Germany; so he reluctantly let them go while he stayed at the hut.

The Germans were halfway across the sound when they saw a light in the hut at Cape Wynn. Marius and the Eskimos, in their innocence, had not thought of blacking out the window.

The men spread out in a quarter circle and crept very quietly in toward the light. The moon was shining above the steep hills behind the hut but in the shadow of the hills it was dark. They stumbled through the shore ice. They heard dogs growling.

Suddenly the light went out. They all ran forward; the sound of the dogs turned to furious howls and they found themselves among what seemed a milling mass of dogs. In the darkness it was some seconds before they saw that the dogs were chained and that they could reach the hut by going round them. Weiss dashed for the hut. It was empty.

Weiss was annoyed and baffled. For the moment, the men had slipped out of his grasp, but he had firmly captured the sledges and the dogs. When he looked around more closely inside the hut he found three sets of fur clothes and boots and gloves. He reasoned that the three men would have to come back to get their equipment before they froze to death. He posted a sentry and he and the others went into the hut to get warm. They were hungry, and there was white bread and a pot of marmalade laid out for them, and coffee on the stove. They were delighted to discover American cigarettes. They amused themselves by trying to read Marius' logbook, which was lying open on the table. Confidently, they settled down to wait. That was the Germans' only mistake, because Marius, William and Mikael never thought of going back to get their gear.

Eskimoness was in one of its quiet periods; nearly everyone was away. Kurt Olsen, the young radio operator, was patrolling Hold With Hope with an Eskimo whose name was Aparte, and Henry Rudi had gone round Clavering Island. Ib Poulsen, the leader of the sledge patrol, was sending the weather broadcasts at six-hour intervals and was also teaching the job to Eli Knudsen, who had been in charge of the station at Ella Island all winter. The patrol had a radio set down there, but there had been nobody there who could work it. And so Knudsen had come north for a few weeks' lessons in Morse and maintenance, and he had brought his two Eskimos with him. The only other person near Eskimoness was the fourth of the Eskimos, Evald, and he was away hunting.

It was eleven o'clock in the morning of March thirteenth when Poulsen looked out by habit across the ice and saw a dark speck. He knew what it was even before he had reached for his field glasses—one man, about three miles away to the eastward, and he was walking. He shouted to Knudsen to harness a few dogs and go out to bring the man in, and he began to get first-aid things ready in the hut, because a man without dogs could mean only disaster. He went outside as Knudsen came across the shore ice, riding the sledge with an almost lifeless man lying on it—Marius, gray with exhaustion, tattered, dirty.

Poulsen and Knudsen helped Marius indoors and noticed he had lost his boots and had been walking in his socks. They worked over him and found he had nothing wrong except first-degree frostbite, which would cure itself; and they warmed him up and gave him a drink and some food and put him to bed, and questioned him harshly before he fell asleep because they had to know what had happened.

From the incoherent story Marius gave them, there seemed to be every chance that in less than six hours the Germans would be there at Eskimoness. The minute Poulsen had pieced the whole story together, he sat down and wrote a report of the events at Germania Harbor and Cape Wynn and began to work against time to put it into cipher. At noon, Scoresby Sound was on the air, and he started to send the first half of his message for onward transmission to Eske Brun. The second half of the signal had to wait till 1800, because he had not had time to encipher it.

Between the transmission of the first and second halves of this signal, quite a lot had happened, and the second half had been rewritten several times. The final version included the information that Poulsen expected Olsen back on Wednesday, and that, unless ordered otherwise, he would leave then for further re-connaissance. William and Mikael arrived in the afternoon, bedraggled and weary, but otherwise not much the worse. With so much to think about, it was some time before anybody asked Marius how he had got back to Eskimoness.

The bare facts make his journey unique of its kind in arctic travel. At the end of a very long day, in which he had already traveled something like forty miles, at one o'clock in the morning of March twelfth, Marius left Cape Wynn. In thirty-four hours, without any food whatever, he had walked fifty-six miles across the ice to Eskimoness. Somewhere on the way he had passed William and Mikael, who had stopped in a hut and gone to sleep. Somewhere his skin boots had fallen to pieces. But it always happens, when a man drives himself to the very limit of endurance, that his memory of his experience is dim, and nobody will ever know much more than that of the journey which Marius made.

Once Poulsen had got his signal away, he supposed the American Air Force would be getting under way and would take charge of the whole situation within a day or two. In the meantime, his first idea was to collect as many men as he could at Eskimoness. That same afternoon he went out on the ice to have a look toward the east. With glasses, a sledge can be seen at twenty miles; so far, there were no Germans coming. So he took the risk of sending the only other able-bodied man, Eli Knudsen, round toward Henry Rudi's hut to try to find the old man and bring him back, and during that same evening they returned; Rudi was anxious and rather more subdued than usual. There was nobody who could go to look for Kurt Olsen, and Peter Nielsen was so far away up north that he would have to be left where he was for the moment.

The first thing was a plan to retreat. They were not feeling defeatist, but they had no idea how many Germans there were or what their intentions were. Three of the four remaining dog teams were picketed some distance away from the house behind a hill. Poulsen's team was kept by the house as watchdogs for the night. A depot of tents and provisions and traveling gear was laid in the hills, so that if the worst came to the worst, they would be able to get away to safety. All the patrol's written orders, accounts and messages were hidden in a hole in the rocks and all the ciphers and codes except one were buried.

For the more active defense, they blacked out the windows and began to build breastworks of sandbags inside them, and bit by bit they put up barricaded firing points at strategic places around the house. That night one man was set on watch outside the house. It was the first time an enemy attack had ever seemed imminent at Eskimoness or anywhere else in Greenland.

Poulsen did not even try to sleep that night. The trouble was that he was only a civilian, and so were all his men. All he had been told to do was to try to find a German landing if there was one, and the general idea had always been that once it was found, the Americans would deal with it. To look for Germans was a different thing from shooting them. Personally, Poulsen was not yet in a frame of mind for shooting anyone.

The next morning an enormously long signal came from the west coast, and as Poulsen plowed through it with his cipher book his spirits rose.

To Poulsen Eskimoness   March 14th
From Eske Brun

Your main task till further notice obtain fullest most reliable information and if possible without prejudice to main task also to eliminate enemy forces by capture or shooting. You are authorized use any means to this end and your weapons should be used rather than run least risk of being captured yourselves, or at the least sign among prisoners of resistance or attempts to escape. Immediately you have in your own judgment assembled enough men at the station, you may make journey proposed with necessary companions. Keep radio watch for possible detection enemy radio in neighborhood. Be prepared for air attack. How many men will be at station when Olsen returns? Inform me, for sake of identification from air, how many men leave with how many sledges immediately on departure. Signal condition of fjord ice with regard to possible plane landing. Signal winter-ice and pack-ice conditions. Energy and judgment of great importance our future position in East Greenland. Remember enemy probably resolute, so take no chances, but shoot first.   BRUN.

Some of the other men were out when he finished deciphering the signal, and to make sure that they all saw it, Poulsen stuck it up on the wall inside the door—an action with consequences which nobody could have foreseen.

The only Americans whom Poulsen had met in Greenland were the men on the United States Coast Guard ship which had supplied him in the summer, and one of the officers on board had told him he could count on American Air Force help whenever he needed it. Now, Eske Brun's signal seemed to confirm it, and the men at Eskimoness began not only to watch the ice, expecting Germans, but also to watch the sky. Everything Poulsen did in the next few weeks was done in the belief, which dwindled slowly, that the American Air Force must be on the way.

The truth was that Eskimoness was 750 miles from the nearest Air Force base, which was in Iceland. There were American air bases on the west coast of Greenland, but in actual distance they were much farther than the planes on Iceland. There were not very many aircraft then which could do a round trip of 1500 miles carrying bombs or even parachutists. There were no parachutists nearer than America or Europe, and nobody would have taken the chance of landing a heavy bomber on the ice. The only direct help they could have given might have been to drop a few machine guns. So Poulsen was really hundreds of miles beyond the range of help. But he did not know it, and he signaled the governor the local ice conditions and added that he was sure a plane could land safely.

In the meantime, Eske Brun had begun to worry about the order he had sent. What he had done, in legal terms, was to incite civilians to murder. When he thought it over, he hit on an answer which pleased him enormously. He decided to found an army—the Greenland army. He wrote out a set of commissions and appointments, and then sent a signal to Poulsen to tell him what he had done. Poulsen was made a captain, and the senior Dane at Scoresby Sound, Carlos Ziebell, a lieutenant. Kurt Olsen, as second in command at Eskimoness, became a sergeant. All the rest of the Europeans were made corporals: Marius Jensen, Eli Knudsen, Peter Nielsen, and even old Henry Rudi. In lieu of uniforms, Brun told them to make armbands for themselves in blue and white, with a number of stars according to their rank. The six Eskimo sledge drivers were considered as noncombatants.

The whole arrangement had a charming element of farce in it, but it also had a perfectly serious intention. The Germans on Sabine Island could hardly know that the Greenland army was on the small side and a comparatively recent institution. Also, if the worst came to the worst, its members could claim to be treated as prisoners of war.

Anyhow, the founding of the new army gave Poulsen an official rank at last, and it gave all the men at Eskimoness something to laugh about. When they had sewn their armbands and got tired of saluting Poulsen, they went back to work on their fortifications with extra confidence. The Greenland army. It did not want to fight, but if it had to, every man in it had a rifle and could hit a musk ox at a thousand yards.

Ritter had also sent a signal back to his headquarters in Germany, reporting that his base had been discovered. He also asked for orders, but the answer he got was not nearly so satisfactory as Poulsen's. It simply told him to use his own discretion, and in all the circumstances that was just what Ritter did not want to do.

Poulsen and Marius had been surprised that the Germans did not attack Eskimoness the very day that Marius returned. The reason was so simple that they had not thought of it. The Germans had captured three excellent dog teams, but they did not know how to drive them. The ten-mile journey back to Hansa Bay had been a series of comic accidents. Ritter would have liked to go to Eskimoness at once, but until his men had learned to manage dogs, it was impossible for him to get there.

The Germans set to work at sledging with enthusiasm. Ritter taught them the little he had learned about dogs in Spitsbergen, and also put in some practice on his own; and between his sledge practice, he began to read through Marius Jensen's logbook. In his travels he had learned a good many languages; one of them was English, and another was Norwegian, which he had picked up in Spitsbergen. Anyone who can speak Norwegian can also read Danish which is very much like it. When he had read it all, he knew the strength of the sledge patrol and guessed it was armed only with rifles, and he knew more or less where all its members had been when Marius had started on his journey.

From a psychological point of view, however, the captured logbook did him more harm than good. It told him far too much about his opponents. They were exactly the kind of people he had known in Spitsbergen and come to like so much.

He found himself almost wishing he was with them, driving freely about the coast instead of sitting imprisoned with his Nazis.

Nevertheless, he had to look at the situation from a military point of view. Now that the base had been detected, he took it for granted that sooner or later it would be bombed. He had done all he could to make it difficult by camouflaging his installations and tucking them away among the hills. There were only two other things that he could do. One was to move the base and hide it somewhere else. The other was to smash up the radio transmitter at Eskimoness to make sure that the Americans, when they came, would not have any weather reports to guide them, and his conscience had nothing to say against it. Of course, he could not expect the Danes to agree, but he hoped to persuade them it was not worth shedding blood about it. But both jobs depended on mastering the dog teams.

By the end of the week, the Danes at Eskimoness were beginning to feel secure. Nothing had happened, the defense works were complete and the first feeling of alarm was wearing off. The Eskimos, on the other hand, got more and more alarmed. The whole conception of war was terrifying to the Eskimos. Nothing in their upbringing had prepared them for fighting. They had only the vaguest idea of European geography, and none at all of politics or ideologies. On the other hand, they knew their Bible well, and the Christianity which was the whole basis of life at Scoresby Sound was simple. It merely said to its people: "Thou shalt not kill."

Poulsen knew he could not expect them to take any part in defending the station, and anyhow he had been told not to get them mixed up in fighting. He sent Aparte and Mikael away with their sledges to Ella Island, to tell any of the men who happened to be there to come north as reinforcements.

Kurt Olsen had come back from his trip to Hold With Hope, but Peter Nielsen was still somewhere in the far north, round Hochstetter Forland. The only way to warn him about the Germans was to go up north to try to find him. Poulsen would have liked to send the other two Eskimos, but he knew, without bothering to ask them, that he would never be able to persuade them to go.

He decided to let Marius and Eli Knudsen go for Peter while he and the Eskimo, Evald, using Evald's sledge, would go on a reconnaissance farther east. As they were short of dogs, the teams had to be divided to give Marius enough to travel with.

Poulsen gave strict orders to the others. They were to go north by the usual route by Sandodden and the Kuppel Pass, and they were never to approach a hut without driving right round it first to make sure that no tracks led into it. They were to come back by a different route, longer and more difficult, but farther from Sabine Island. They agreed, but he knew from experience that the hunters, once they were out on their own, would interpret his orders pretty freely.

The two parties went together as far as Sandodden and spent the night there. The next morning Marius and Knudsen set off for the Kuppel Pass. Poulsen and Evald turned back and started to follow the shore to the eastward—exactly the route that the Germans would probably take if they ever came in to attack.

From the very beginning, there was an eerie feel about the coast beyond Sandodden. Evald was very nervous. The sea ice was so rough that sledges or Germans might easily have been hidden among its ridges, and the black cliffs which brooded silently above it on the left seemed menacing. To try to calm him, Poulsen walked along the snow-covered scree at the cliff foot, a hundred feet or so above the ice, while Evald followed him with the sledge, down on the ice and a little way behind. But it was slow work and by nightfall they had covered only a dozen miles.

They pitched a tent that night in a gully at the foot of the cliffs. The darkness only added to Evald's fears; he burst into tears and Poulsen tried to comfort him, but Evald was much too upset to lie down and sleep, and the whole of the night passed in prayers and religious discussion in the Eskimo language. Poulsen saw it was hopeless to try to take Evald farther. By day, their progress would be slow, and by night he would not sleep. There was nothing for it but to go back.

Poulsen returned to the station on the twenty-first of March. It was no good being annoyed with the Eskimos for what looked like cowardice. Poulsen knew he had never succeeded in explaining to them, in the cumbrous Eskimo language, any convincing reason why they should shoot at Germans. So he gave them the simplest possible orders. They were to keep one of the two remaining dog teams well out of sight of the house. If anything happened, they were to harness the team at once and drive to safety, as far as Ella Island if they thought it necessary. They said they understood.

The three Europeans also had their action stations. Poulsen's was in front of the house, Rudi's in a sandbagged post to the west of it, and Kurt Olsen's about fifty yards away to the east on top of a little rise. With all this settled, they relaxed as well as they could to wait for Marius, Eli Knudsen and Peter Nielsen.

On the evening of March twenty-third, before it was dark, Poulsen went the rounds of his station alone, far enough out on the ice to see along the coast, and around to the back of the small peninsula on which the house was built. He stopped to talk to the dogs.

His thoughts were not particularly military. Among other things, he was thinking about a barrel of beer. Danish government outposts were always well stocked with wines and spirits, on the theory that a man who could be trusted to winter there at all could also be trusted not to drink himself to death, but beer was never sent up there becuase it took up too much space in the supply ships. Instead, the stations were supplied with the ingredients for making it, and Poulsen was in the middle of the process. He had an oil drum full of it in the house, and he meant to go through the final stage of brewing before he went to bed.

He finished it at eleven o'clock that night, just about the time when Kurt Olsen was starting the weather broadcast in the radio room next door. He was standing there in his shirt sleeves, looking at his barrel with a feeling of satisfaction, when Henry Rudi put his head in at the door.

"Poulsen!" he shouted, "Poulsen! I think there's somebody on the ice!"

Poulsen snatched up his rifle. "Kurt!" he called. "Outside!"

"I'm just starting the report!" Kurt Olsen answered.

"Get to your post!" Poulsen shouted over his shoulder. He ran to the door.

Outside, it was pitch dark, for the sky was overcast. Everything was as silent as ever. Rudi had gone. Poulsen stood alone and listened. The dogs were stirring. And then, out on the ice beyond the shore, he heard a stealthy movement.

"Who's there?" he shouted.

A voice in broken Danish shouted, "Who are you?"

That answer told Poulsen everything. "What do you want here?" he asked in German, and there was another silence.

"I want to speak to Herr Poulsen!" the bodiless voice replied.

Poulsen was astonished and shaken to hear his own name. A defensive instinct told him not to give himself away. "You can't talk to him tonight!" he shouted. "You can come back in the daylight!" He stood there tense, with his finger on the trigger, trying to catch a glimpse of his opponent.

"Can I speak to Herr Olsen or Herr Rudi?" the voice asked.

Poulsen's thoughts were racing ahead of his words. The Germans knew exactly who was at the station; then they must have broken the ciphers; they must know how few men there were and how weakly they were armed.

He heard movements again and shouted, "Get back from the beach!"

"I must speak to Herr Poulsen, or else Herr Rudi, or Herr Olsen!" the voice insisted.

"What about?" Poulsen asked. "How many of you?"

The voice replied with something that sounded like a name.

"One man can come across the beach!" Poulsen said. "Unarmed!"

The voice said, "Do you intend to offer armed resistance?"

"Yes!" Poulsen shouted; and at that word machine-gun fire burst out and tracer bullets flew at him from the ice. He dropped to one knee and raised his rifle and fired toward the muzzle flashes a hundred yards away, but it was so dark he could not see the sights of his rifle, and the flashes from his own gun seemed to draw the fire down on him.

He had never in his life seen tracer bullets, but he knew what they were, and he knew from the very first moment that they were a weapon he could not fight against: for a machine gun with tracers can be aimed like a hose, but a rifle in the dark when one cannot see the sights is perfectly useless and cannot be aimed at all.

He ran round the house to try to find the others and met Henry Rudi standing there as if he were paralyzed. Another burst of fire came overhead, and he pushed Rudi down and went to look for Olsen.

A concentration of bullets was pouring over Olsen's post. Poulsen shouted to him, but there was no answer. He turned back toward the house and got a clear sight of the flash of a machine gun again, and he shot at it. Again it seemed that when he fired the machine gun was turned on him.

Rudi had disappeared. The hammering of the machine guns and the crisscross of bullets soaring over the flat ground beside the house confused Poulsen and he thought he was surrounded. He went back for Olsen, but his post was still under fire, and Olsen did not answer when he shouted. He could not find anyone or do anything more, and if he stayed where he was for another few seconds he was going to be killed or captured; so he ran across the level behind the house, still under fire, and went a little way up the hill beyond it.

There he stopped to look back. Most of the firing died away, and only one gun went on in occasional bursts from the eastward.

He began to be conscious of something else—the cold. And slowly, as his nerves calmed a little, he began to realize more fully what had happened. In less than ten minutes the house had been lost, and everything that was in it. His men were dead or scattered. He was still wearing only a shirt and trousers and a pair of sealskin boots which he had used as bedroom slippers. There were approximately forty-five degrees of frost—about thirteen degrees below zero—and the nearest help was at Ella Island, 200 miles away.

Lt. Hermann Ritter, leader of the German expedition, was sick at heart. When he had attacked the sledge patrol, he had hoped to avoid bloodshed by frightening them into surrender.

But that had gone wrong. When the men he had brought with him had taken up the shooting, he had seen they were shooting to kill. He could not tell them to stop; they were too widely scattered and there was too much noise. It was exactly what he had been afraid would happen: he was faced with a military duty which his conscience said was wrong. In the seven minutes that the shooting lasted, Ritter had accused himself of murder, and found nothing to be said in his defense.

Before the firing stopped, Ritter began to advance toward the house. He had not bothered to reload his machine gun. He did not care in the least by then what happened to him. Let the Danes shoot if they were still alive. As he walked up the sixty yards of shore he was thinking, with a despairing cynicism unusual in him, that a death which could be called a hero's death would be convenient, because it would silence the Nazis in his command who suspected him of disloyalty to Germany, and would make sure of the safety of his wife and daughter, back at home in Germany.

There was no corpse by the door; nobody shot at him; nobody answered his shout. He walked straight to the door and threw it open. He flashed his torch round the room, found the electric-light switch and turned it on. Almost the first thing he saw was the signal from Greenland's colonial governor, Eske Brun, still hanging where Ib Poulsen, the leader of the sledge patrol, had pinned it to the wall for all his men to see. Ritter read it through: "Eliminate enemy forces by shooting or capture; take no chances, but shoot first." There was no compromise there, no possible hint of a peaceful solution. The message reminded Ritter that whatever he might want himself, he had put himself outside the pale of the arctic community, which he had learned to love before the war, simply because he had become a German naval officer.

Having captured Eskimoness, Ritter had to decide what to do with it. Eske Brun's signal suggested that Eskimoness might be used not only as an advanced radio station to help the United States Air Force, but also perhaps as a base for an attack against Ritter's own weather-reporting station at Hansa Bay, seventy miles to the northeast. He could only play for safety and put the whole place out of action once and for all. He did not want to do it. It offended his sense of arctic propriety.

In the end, Ritter decided to wait, to give the Danes a fair chance to come back if they were still in hiding in the hills. Also, he decided to leave one small out-building standing. To some extent, that salved his arctic conscience. If any traveler happened to come along after he had gone, depending on Eskimoness for rest or shelter in a storm, the smallest of the huts would be enough to save his life.

Ritter and his men stayed there for two days. Ritter inspected every item of equipment in the house. There were dumdum bullets—standard ammunition for hunters after big game.

There was a mass of old letters, family photographs, a certain amount of money and all the sentimental odds and ends which men accumulate. There was also another logbook—Kurt Olsen's —which told Ritter of Poulsen's plan to spy on the German base from the Sabine hills, and here and there, a very large collection of valuable furs. Ritter took the logbook, but he collected all the personal possessions of the Danes, including the furs, and put them in the little hut, which had been used for curing skins. As a symbol, he also hauled down the Danish flag and put it with the furs; and then he wrote a message and nailed it up inside the little hut:

The U.S.A. protects its defense interests here in Greenland. We do the same. We are not at war with Denmark. But your governor had given orders to capture or shoot us, and you are giving weather reports to the enemy. You are therefore making Greenland a theater of war. We have stayed quietly at our post without attacking you. But if you want war, you shall have war. Remember that if you use illegal weapons (dumdum bullets) such as we have found here, you must take the consequences, because you will put yourselves outside the rules of war. Note that we have put all personal property of your hunters and all furs in this hut, while we have destroyed the radio apparatus operating for the U.S.A.

Signed: H. RITTER
Commander of the Wehrmacht Unit,
Eskimoness.

But it was nearly six months before this note was found, and it never came into the hands of the sledge patrol.

After they had finished these preparations, Ritter and his party smashed the radio, shot some of the dogs because they could not take all of them away, and set the wooden house on fire. Soon there was nothing left at Eskimoness except the hut and the ashes of the hunting station.

If Ritter had known exactly what had happened to Poulsen, he would have had a good reason for feeling remorseful, because nobody, on that night of March 23, 1943, could have said that Poulsen had any reasonable chance at all of saving his own life.

The temperature was about thirteen degrees below zero. Poulsen, standing on the hillside above Eskimoness that night, in his shirt and trousers and his skin shoes with no socks inside them, had no protection at all against frostbite, and he knew it. But he did not go back to the house. By then, he was so angry with the Germans and with himself, for what he regarded as his own failure, that he would have gone through any ordeal which might have helped to retrieve the situation. So, in his absurdly inadequate clothes, Poulsen turned away from his captured home and began to walk, although he knew that nobody in the history of the arctic had done such a foolish thing before.

First, he went to a place where he knew Henry Rudi had hidden a rucksack, and he was thankful to find it gone. So the old man had at least got away from the house. He took it for granted that the two Eskimos, William and Evald, had escaped with their dog sledge. Next he ran to the cache he had laid in the hills. He was encouraged to find that somebody had been there before him and taken some of the food. It might have been only Rudi, but he hoped it was Kurt Olsen too.

The cache contained tents and sleeping bags and food, but no clothing. Poulsen was very cold already. A tent was of no use to him, because he had no sledge and the tents were too heavy to carry; so he cut one up into pieces with his knife. He wrapped a large piece round him like a cloak, with a flap of it over his head, and he tied it in place with some bits of the guy ropes. He took two smaller pieces and wrapped his hands in them, tying them round his wrists with difficulty because his hands were already getting numb. He put some food in a sleeping bag and rolled it up and hoisted it on his back. Before daylight Poulsen began to stumble away toward the west.

His first objective was Henry Rudi's hut at Revet. A portable radio transmitter had been left there in the autumn, and if it was still in working order, he might be able to send a signal to the settlement of Scoresby Sound, 350 air miles to the south. Secondly, the three members of his patrol who had been up north—Peter Nielsen, Eli Knudsen and Marius Jensen—had been told to come back that way. If he was very lucky, he might meet them, but in any case he had to leave them a warning not to go on to Eskimoness. Thirdly, he hoped he would find some cast-off clothes there.

It was thirty-five miles to Revet. Of course, Poulsen could

have walked that far without stopping, but along the shore of Clavering Island he would have been visible for a long way in the daylight, and he expected the Germans to make a sortie with their sledges to round up prisoners. So in the early dawn he stopped at a hunting hut and had some food, and then, in case they found the hut, he climbed a little way up the mountains and got wearily into his sleeping bag.

The second night's walk can have been only agony. Sharp edges of ice and rocks along the shore cut the soles of Poulsen's feet through the soft thin skin of his shoes. The first stages of frostbite showed in his hands and face and ears and feet. He had a feeling of unnatural lassitude and could hardly keep himself awake. Luckily, it was only twenty-three miles more to Revet from the place where he had slept. That night, when at last he reached the hut, Poulsen was so exhausted and his hands were so bad that he could not move his fingers to turn the door knob. He went down on his knees in the end, and got hold of the knob between his wrists and at long last he turned it and crawled inside.

The stove was warm. Somebody had been there, and only gone that night. In the dark, Poulsen held his frozen hands against the stove and felt the searing pain come into them as they thawed. As soon as he could move them, he fumbled round for matches, and lit the fire which was laid, and the paraffin lamp; and then he saw a scribbled note which was lying on the table:

Don't go to Eskimoness. Germans have captured it. Think Poulsen was killed. We others all right.

OLSEN. RUDI.

That took a weight off his mind. It even made him smile, and before he left the hut, he crossed out the words, "Think Poulsen was killed," and wrote at the bottom: "Am O.K."

Actually, he was in poor shape. He had patches of first-degree frostbite all over him, but in the first degree, before the tissues are damaged, frostbite heals itself after the extremely painful process of thawing is over. He was also very tired and his feet were very sore. But the worst of it was that Poulsen knew quite well that his difficulties had only just begun.

The words "We others" in Olsen and Rudi's note made him

think that Olsen and Rudi and the two Eskimos were together, and if they were, they presumably had the Eskimos' sledge. But he was simply unable to go out again to try to track them in the darkness. So Poulsen ate, and thawed himself, and tried the portable radio; its batteries were flat. He found a few dirty, worn-out clothes, including an *anorak*—a hooded jacket—and a pair of boots; and then, because Revet was one of the most likely places for the Germans to look for him, he took the sleeping bag up into the hills and slept in the snow again.

That evening Poulsen felt a lot better, and he was able to look squarely at the fact that he had no option: he would have to try to walk the 200 miles to Ella Island just as he was, alone and without any equipment at all. The most urgent thing was to send a radio report to Eske Brun, and then to collect his scattered forces into a unit again.

Shortly, before it was dark on March twenty-fifth, Poulsen went down again to Henry Rudi's hut. The boots he had found were much too big for him, and he still had no socks. He cut up some old sacks and made them into stockings as well as he could, tying the loose ends round his legs. He found an old pair of skis and took some matches and an empty meat tin so that he would be sure to have something to melt snow in in the huts on the way. He wrapped the tin and the food in the sleeping bag and lashed it on the skis so that he could tow the whole lot behind him like a sledge; he had nothing to carry except his rifle. Then he went out and shut the door. On the door he drew three circles, which was a private sign to the northern party which meant: "I have gone south." He fastened a string to the front of the pair of skis and tied it round his waist, and then went down onto the ice and turned southward.

Poulsen knew the way to Ella Island well, because he had traveled it several times by sledge. To begin with, it led across the bay called Godthaabs Gulf, which is twenty-five miles long and about the same in breadth; and the second stage was up the narrow fjord which is called Loch Fyne—another twenty-five miles to the head of it.

When it was daylight and he got to the mouth of Loch Fyne, he began to see old tracks here and there. He tried to identify a recent track among them which might be the Eskimos' sledge, but all he found was the footmarks of two men walking south.

These puzzled him, because they suggested that all four of his men were not traveling together, but it was easy enough to think of explanations. Two of them might have gone on with the sledge, perhaps to gain time in taking a message through. Here and there, during the rest of his journey, Poulsen saw the tracks, but he never did catch up with the men who made them.

There were hunting huts in the fjord, one at the mouth and one halfway and one at the head. It was twelve miles from hut to hut. He walked on right to the head of the fjord, with only short rests in the huts on the way. At the end of a night and a day and half of another night, the first fifty miles of the journey were behind Poulsen.

In the third of the huts there was another portable transmitter. He decided to stop there and make a determined attempt to signal Scoresby Sound. It was a forlorn hope, because the set was only a small affair which was meant to reach Eskimoness or Ella Island, and Scoresby Sound was a long way beyond its normal range.

Besides lack of food, the thing that was troubling Poulsen most by that final stage up Loch Fyne was the state of his feet. The sacks they were wrapped in were hard and coarse, and the oversize boots rubbed up and down at every step. When at last he came to the hut, he unwrapped his feet and found a disgusting mess, the toes and heels raw and bleeding, and dirt and fibers from the sacks ground into the open sores. He melted some snow in the tin and washed his feet in it. After that, he assembled the radio and waited for the time when Scoresby Sound was scheduled.

That transmitter was a most exasperating piece of machinery. It had really been designed to be operated by two people—one to crank the generator and the other to work the Morse key. Singlehanded, the receiver would work all right, but the transmitter was almost impossible. At midnight, Poulsen cranked it up and heard Scoresby Sound vainly calling him at Eskimoness. When Scoresby Sound sent "Over," Poulsen tried to crank with one hand and send Morse with the other. But it was no good. The operator went on calling Eskimoness over and over again, and took no notice of Poulsen's frantic attempts to cut in on the wave length. When this was added to his loneliness and weariness and pain, he could have burst out crying.

Poulsen would have been even more discouraged if he had known how completely the Germans were in control of the tactical situation just then. Before Lieutenant Ritter burned the sledge patrol's headquarters at Eskimoness, he had had a chance to study Kurt Olsen's logbook. He did not fear any immediate counterattack from the men he had routed from Eskimoness. Also, he now knew that Jensen and Olsen had gone north after Peter Nielsen and had not returned. So he gave orders for strict precautions against surprise. If the three Danes showed up, the Germans would be ready for them.

Poulsen persevered with the transmitter for two nights and a day, but all this time was wasted. During the second night, he gave up hope and carried the radio up into the hills and buried it, so that the Germans would not destroy it if they ever came that way. At dawn, he got ready to start on his journey again, with more than 150 miles still to go.

From the head of Loch Fyne, Poulsen went west to the head of Musk Ox Fjord, and then through the inner fjords and sounds. As soon as he left Loch Fyne, he got into difficult going. There is a stretch of ten miles between the heads of the two fjords, and it is a notorious place for deep, loose snow. The whole of Musk Ox Fjord is sometimes just as bad.

Poulsen put on his skis and carried his sleeping bag. But the ski bindings did not fit his boots and were always on the verge of coming off. The skis sank ankle-deep in the powdery surface. The reindeer-skin sleeping bag made such a bulky, awkward bundle that he gave up carrying it, and tried hauling it behind him on the snow. The ten miles over land seemed endless. Small obstacles loomed large, and he was surprised to find how difficult it was to overcome them. It was sometime later before he realized why: It was five days since he had had anything that could be called a decent meal. That afternoon he reached the first hut in Musk Ox Fjord. He had gone only fifteen miles, but could not go any farther.

Sometimes a man has a stroke of luck which he remembers all his life, and Poulsen never forgot that hut. It was as small and bare and sparsely furnished as any kind of human lair could be, but on a shelf in it, forgotten, he found a packet of beans. It might be too much to say that those beans saved Poulsen's life, but at least they made him feel well-fed that evening, and there were enough to take him the forty long, tedious miles down Musk Ox Fjord in the next two days.

At the mouth of the fjord he got back into better country, with hard ice underfoot, among the headwaters of Kaiser Franz Joseph Fjord. There he had to pass the foot of a glacier which is seven miles wide. On the far side of the fjord, and ten miles or so below the glacier there is a hut, and it had been well stocked with food when Poulsen had last been down that way. It was still the same, and when Poulsen got there, he had no more fear of going hungry. He sat down to an orgy of tinned meat and oatmeal and coffee.

Beyond that hut his walk took a better turn. He was still getting weaker day by day, and the sores on his feet were deeper every evening when he washed them. But beyond a certain degree, the pain of raw feet cannot get very much worse. The whole of the rest of the way was along the tremendous fjords of Andree's Land. Each day Poulsen traveled two stages, about twenty miles.

On April fourth, in the evening, he came within sight of the Bastion of Ella Island, a vast rock which rises behind the station there. He had walked 230 miles in eleven days, including the trip to Revet and the day and a half which he had wasted in Loch Fyne.

When he was still some miles away, still dragging his bleeding, suppurating feet across the ice, he saw a sledge approaching. But the driver was not one of the four men whose tracks he thought he had been following; it was the Eskimo, Mikael, whom he had sent south with Aparte before the trouble at Eskimoness had started; and from Mikael's astonishment at seeing him, Poulsen slowly and unwillingly understood that nobody had come through from Eskimoness, and the people at Ella had not heard what had happened.

Mikael and Aparte fed Poulsen, and doctored him in their own rough and friendly way, and the scraps of the story which he told them grew in their imaginations to a tale of irretrievable disaster. If Poulsen had been able to think at all, he would have reassured them, but the only idea which he still had in his head was the idea which had urged him on so long: to get a signal off. He had no cipher, but he had decided to send the signal in Eskimo, which would be just as good as a cipher, because no German would understand it. He could speak Eskimo, but he could not write it; so during that evening he told the two Eskimos what he wanted to say and got them to write it down, and at midnight he raised Scoresby Sound and sent a brief situation report.

As soon as Scoresby Sound had acknowledged it, they replied that they knew about the attack on Eskimoness. Kurt Olsen had got through a short signal ten days before, on the emergency transmitter in Rudi's hut at Revet. Since then, there had been silence. On hearing this, Poulsen told Scoresby Sound to cancel the signal he had just sent—the signal which he had walked so many miles to send—and he closed the transmitter down.

After midnight he slept, but not for very long. By six o'clock in the morning he had recovered enough to try to think ahead. He had reasoned that there was really no harm in sending an unciphered message about something the Germans had already done; and he called Scoresby Sound again in his own language and got off a more complete signal:

0625. April 5th

From Ella Island
To Brun Godthaab via Scoresbysound

After difficult fluid situation got number two emergency transmitter going and informed of Olsen's report of 26th March. Green code number 27 with March code word and weather code number 920 captured. Suspect that green code was already known to opposition. Believe everyone present March 23rd uninjured, but have lost touch with the others. Regard situation as very critical for our divided team and for the stations and supplies in the whole district. Can information be given in clear either Danish or Eskimo whether help may be expected and whether I may send further information in clear? Forced to move from present position, but can probably keep regular radio contact.

POULSEN.

He had added this last sentence because as soon as he had heard that his men had not arrived, he had made up his mind to turn round at once and go north to look for them. He could not walk any more, but he thought he could take a lightly loaded sledge and ride on it. While he was waiting for an answer from Eske Brun, the Eskimos sighted another solitary figure on the ice.

It was Evald, the Eskimo who had been at Eskimoness when the shooting started. When he and William had seen the tracer bullets soaring over their heads at Eskimoness, they had run away without their sledge. Their only impulse had been to go home to Scoresby Sound, 400 miles away. They had had two days' start over Poulsen, because of his walk to Revet, and they had had the advantages of being properly dressed, of having their own skis and of getting the first pick of the food in the huts on the way, and yet he had nearly caught them up. On the previous day, they had by-passed Ella Island, because they were afraid the Germans might have got there, but during the night, Evald had felt ashamed of himself and decided to take the risk of going back there, so that if the Germans had not arrived he could warn the people there that they might be coming. William had gone straight on, to carry the warning, as he thought, to Scoresby Sound.

This story at least cleared up the puzzle of the footprints, but it made Poulsen even more concerned for Kurt Olsen and Henry Rudi. Now it was clear that he had passed them somewhere right at the beginning of the walk, near Revet. The two Eskimos, as he knew to his cost, had not left much food in the huts when they had passed them, and he had finished what little there had been. He reached new depths of self-accusation, imagining his old companion of two winters exhausted and starving amid the deep snow of Musk Ox Fjord or the empty huts of Loch Fyne.

In the fight at Eskimoness, Henry Rudi had fired a few aimless shots; Kurt Olsen had fired none because he had not seen anyone to fire at. They were soon convinced that it was useless to resist. They had set off independently to Revet, but had met in a narrow gorge among the hills, and they had gone on there together to try to make the transmitter work, and to leave a warning for the three men who were still up north.

On the day when Poulsen got to Revet and slept in the hills

behind the hut, Rudi and Olsen were also sleeping, not more than a mile away. That evening, as darkness fell, they began to walk south along the hillside above the fjord. It was then that they saw a man walking far below them on the ice, and also going south; there was no one it could have been but Poulsen. They thought he was making for a hut in a small fjord which opens off the head of Godthaabs Gulf, and they went there themselves in the hope of meeting him. But in the darkness he had gone straight on across the gulf, and they never managed to catch him up again. It was by this small margin that he failed to hear that Olsen had sent his signal to Scoresby Sound.

Rudi and Olsen had escaped with all their clothes. In that respect, they were better off than Poulsen; and they were also not obsessed, like him, by any desperate need to hurry. If fact, they could not have hurried. Henry Rudi was willing and as tough as a man of fifty-five can be, but at that age, with the best will in the world, one cannot march as far or as fast on an empty stomach as a man of thirty can.

All the way round Godthaabs Gulf and along Loch Fyne, Henry Rudi had fretted that he was holding his young companion back. He did his best to persuade Kurt Olsen to go on ahead and leave him, but, naturally, Kurt would never have thought of leaving him to his fate, whatever happened.

Because there was nothing left to eat in the huts, they had to waste days in hunting. Kurt went out with his rifle, while Henry rested and kept the fire going. They kept themselves going on hares and musk-ox steak, and so, in the course of ten days, they covered some ninety miles, and got to the second hut in Musk Ox Fjord.

Rudi and Olsen had a shock that night: they heard dogs outside. They listened while Olsen covered the doorway with his gun.

The door opened and a tired voice said, "Kurt? Don't you start shooting," and the man came into the room—Peter Nielsen, the man that Marius Jensen and Eli Knudsen had gone to look for.

"Peter!" Kurt Olsen said. "Are Marius and Eli with you?"

"No, they're not here," he said. "I'll tell you what happened. Eli Knudsen's dead."

When Marius Jensen and Eli Knudsen had parted from

Poulsen at the hunting station at Sandodden, and gone northward over the Kuppel Pass to look for Peter Nielsen, they had started to have trouble with their dogs. Eli Knudsen was driving his own team, but Marius had only eight assorted dogs which he had borrowed at Eskimoness. The animals fought more than usual among themselves, and drove Marius to exasperation and Eli Knudsen was always miles ahead.

It took them three days to reach Hochstetter Forland, and then they had to push on for another twenty miles before they came on Peter's tracks and ran him to earth in another hunting hut. They stayed there one night. Poulsen had told them to come back by the route past Revet, but that way was probably two days longer than the way they had come. The right thing to do, they all agreed, was to take a chance on Sandodden and the Kuppel Pass; and so, in spite of Poulsen's orders, they started back in that direction.

This journey also became something of a procession, with Eli Knudsen ahead and Marius and Peter lagging far behind. On the third night, they had agreed to camp on the northern side of the Kuppel Pass, so that the next day they could pass Sandodden without going too near it, and reach Eskimoness the next evening.

However, when Marius and Peter arrived at the pass, Eli Knudsen was not waiting there. Sandodden had been his own hunting station before the war, and they guessed he had gone there. They were tired and hungry, and so were their dogs. They were very annoyed with Eli for not sticking to the plan they had agreed on, and because all their food had been packed on his sledge. All the same, they decided to camp. They found a secluded place between two steep moraines and pitched their tent there, and spent a hungry night.

This, as it happened, was the evening of the twenty-fifth of March—the day on which Eskimoness had been reduced to ruins.

When the fire had burnt itself out, Ritter and his six men had started a fairly leisurely journey back toward Hansa Bay. For the first night stop of the journey to Hansa Bay he chose the most convenient place: Sandodden.

The evening when they arrived there, he and his men

picketed their dogs, of which they now had over fifty, out of sight among the high drifts of snow which surrounded the station. They had hardly settled down in the hut when the sentry shouted that a sledge was coming. The Germans seized their automatic arms and hurried out, and took up positions hidden behind the house and below the snowdrifts.

When the sledge was a hundred yards away, Ritter stepped out into view and shouted, "Halt!" He saw the driver give him a startled glance and heard him shout to his dogs and crack his whip. The dogs swerved to the right and came on faster, heading for a bank of stones and snow which would have hidden the sledge if it could reach it.

"Shoot the dogs!" Ritter shouted, and as the sledge swept past the station the machine gun opened fire. Some of the dogs in full gallop rolled over and over. The machine gun fired again, and the driver fell off the sledge face downward in the snow and did not move. The sledge careered on, dragging dead and wounded dogs in their tangled traces.

They carried Knudsen into the hut. Doctor Sensse was in the party, and he stripped off Knudsen's *anorak* and plugged the bullet wound high up in his chest, but he was unconscious, and in half an hour he died—the first man in all the recorded history of the northeast Greenland coast who had died there at the hand of a fellow man.

This sudden, violent, unnecessary tragedy was a shock which haunted Ritter's memory for months. The other Germans also felt more or less ashamed that seven well-armed men should have had to slaughter an enemy who was almost defenseless, and the machine gunner kept repeating his excuses that his gun had jammed when he fired his first burst at the dogs. When he had cleared the jam, it had fired again before he had aimed it; one of the magazines of the gun was defective.

The defective magazine had been reported to Ritter some time before, and he had given orders that it should be thrown away, but he had never bothered to see that the order was carried out; and so, he told himself, his own carelessness had been an additional cause of this useless waste of life, for which, in any case, he, as commander of the party, was to blame.

But there was immediate action to be taken before Ritter

could be alone to listen to his conscience. It was an easy guess that where one man had come down from the north, two others were likely to follow very soon. He sent some men out to drag in Knudsen's sledge and dispatch the wounded dogs and clear up the mess, and he doubled the guard and set up an ambush. One cannot dig a grave in frozen soil, so they put Knudsen's body in a tiny sod shack which was close by. They were unaware of the rather ironical fact that Knudsen had built the shack himself, as a store for frozen meat, when he had lived there as a hunter.

Ritter was not the only one of the German party whose human feelings were offended by Knudsen's death. One of them, that night or the following morning, made a wooden cross and put it on the shack, and inscribed it with Knudsen's name, which he had found from the papers in his pocket, and the words: "He died for his country." Ritter never saw this emblem. If he had, the inscription might have struck him as sententious, but he could hardly have failed to see that at least one of his party, Nazi or not, had some instinct in sympathy with his own.

The next morning, Marius Jensen came driving down from Kuppel Pass. Knudsen's sledge tracks led him on, and it never crossed his mind that if Knudsen had gone there the night before it might not be safe to follow him. He was within a few yards of the house when German soldiers rose up from the drifts of snow all round him and a warning burst of fire went over his head. There was nothing he could do but stop his dogs and put his hands up. The Germans searched him and took him inside the hut, and in exactly the same manner, an hour later, Peter Nielsen drove into the simple trap.

The fifteen members of the sledge patrol knew little of world events, but they had heard fearsome stories of the ruthlessness of Germans. In talking things over, they had all agreed that they could expect only to be shot if any of them were ever captured by the Germans who had established a meteorological base in Greenland. Even so, Marius and Peter were shocked to learn that the Germans had killed their comrade, Eli Knudsen.

However, because neither Peter nor Marius had had anything to eat for twenty-four hours, not even the prospect of being executed could quite make them forget that they were extremely hungry. When Peter was dragged in and confronted by Lt. Hermann Ritter, the commander of the Germans, he immediately asked for some breakfast. At that, the Germans began to laugh, and he and Marius were fed.

Afterward, Ritter began to question them. Both of them pretended to be much more stupid than they were. They said that Ib Poulsen, the leader of the sledge patrol, just gave them their orders, and they never asked about things that did not concern them; they did not know how many men there were at Ella Island or how many there were in the sledge patrol. Ritter said he had heard that there were Americans at Scoresby Sound, a settlement far to the south. They said there might be, for all they knew; Poulsen would never have told them a thing like that.

Ritter was able to make them tell him a little more than they intended, but he could also see that they knew much less than he had expected. There is nothing much that a questioner can do against studied stupidity unless he uses threats or some kind of third degree, and Ritter was too badly upset by Eli Knudsen's death to be able to contemplate more violence. During the interview, he told Jensen and Nielsen he had burnt down their headquarters at Eskimoness, but that did not startle them into any more admissions. Ritter could not help adding, to relieve their anxiety and perhaps to excuse himself, that so far as he knew, their friends—Poulsen and Henry Rudi and Kurt Olsen—had all got away. After an hour or so of interrogation, Ritter left Marius and Peter under guard in the hut and went outside alone.

Some of Ritter's men had noticed that he seemed distraught. In fact, the past twelve hours had been a turning point in his life. By all the standards Ritter had been brought up to respect, the killing of Eli Knudsen was a crime and a sin. Of course, the machine gunner had not meant to shoot Knudsen, but the crime lay in the circumstances which had made Ritter bring weapons of war to the peaceful arctic—a peace he had learned to love as an arctic hunter before the war. The sin was that he had ever accepted a job which in any way served Nazism—a system he abhorred. Back in Germany it had seemed wise to take that fortunate chance to go to the arctic again, for the sake of his own security and his family's. Now he could see what a dreadful mistake he had made.

As Ritter stood outside the hut at Sandodden that morning he made one definite resolution: he would not repeat this crime. If it came to the test again, he would pray to be guided by Christian, not Nazi principles, whatever the consequences might be.

Sandodden had become a hateful place for him, and he gave orders to journey on to Hansa Bay. The Germans harnessed their dogs and drove away, taking their prisoners with them, and peace and quietness settled again on this scene of violence. The remains of Eli Knudsen were left lying in the shack beside the hut, and they still lie there today.

The Germans had captured every single dog which had been at Eskimoness, except the ones they had shot, and part of Knudsen's team too. They now had the makings of eight teams, and so they could take them all back to their base at Sabine Island only if they let Peter and Marius drive one each. Ritter divided this cavalcade into two groups and sent Peter with the first while he and Marius traveled with the second. One party went south along the shore of Wollaston Forland, and the other north over the Kuppel Pass, to approach Sabine Island from the other side.

Before they left Sandodden, the prisoners were told that if one of them gave trouble on the journey or tried to escape, the other one would be punished. But Ritter took all the sting out of the threat for Marius by giving him back his old team, the one he had lost at Cape Wynn.

After Peter and the first three men had gone, Ritter told two Germans of the second party to start. They both set off with a practiced air, but after a few seconds one of these teams caught sight of the other, and at once the two orderly teams disintegrated into a tangled mass of snapping, yelping dogs, the sledges collided and overturned and one of the most comprehensive dogfights Marius had ever seen was under way. Ritter told Marius to go and sort them out. Marius ran to the sledges and waded in and laid about him with an expert hand, and very quickly the dogs separated, panting and pleased with themselves. To discover that the Germans were far from efficient at the all-important art of driving dogs immediately restored Marius' self-confidence.

The two parties met again at the hut on Germania Harbor—the very place where Jensen had discovered the presence of the

Germans in Greenland. There Peter and Marius were left under guard, while Ritter and most of the others went on to the base, which Marius now knew for certain was hidden in Hansa Bay.

For Marius and Peter, a most curious kind of imprisonment began. Ritter knew there was no need for him to lock his prisoners up. He had no inclination to give them the ruthless treatment he guessed they had expected, and he picked the older men of his trawler crew, rather than the young Nazis, to look after them. The hut was small and the guard had no option but to live on terms of equality with the prisoners. The German sailors, at the end of their first winter in the arctic, were glad of the chance to pick up tips about arctic crafts from the experienced Danish hunters. But although their captivity was quite comfortable and even had its enjoyable moments, Peter and Marius plotted from the very beginning to get away.

Ritter, in those few days, was at Hansa Bay. To some extent, as soon as he had clearly stated to himself his fundamental disagreement with Nazi aims, he had found it easier to deal with Schmidt and the other Nazis. Whatever he had done and whatever he did in the future, it would be wrong in Nazi eyes; therefore, he could give up any efforts to appease them. He was convinced that when his trial came, as he supposed it must, he was certain to be condemned. His self-examination had given him moral courage. All that was left for him was to try to do God's will.

Even a week before, he might have been tempted to treat the prisoners as he imagined Schmidt would think they should be treated. But now he was able to use his common sense. On the journey he had admired Marius' expert handling of his dogs. With eight teams and enough competent men to drive them, he could have moved his entire camp so they might have been able to dodge the American bombing which he still expected day by day. With this idea half formed, he went back to Germania Harbor and asked Marius if he was willing, during his captivity, to train the Germans and act as a kind of pilot.

Marius refused, but he used the opportunity of this talk with Ritter to try the simple plan which he and Peter had thought out. He appealed to Ritter to let Peter take a dog team and go back to Sandodden to make a proper job of burying Knudsen. Also, he said that Peter was such a second-rate driver that he would not be able to escape; although this was not true, Marius half believed it. Ritter refused.

When Ritter got back to Hansa Bay, however, he thought over what Marius had suggested. If he let Peter go as far as Sandodden, he would probably try to escape, and he suspected that Peter could not be quite so incompetent with dogs as Marius had pretended. The question was whether it really mattered if he escaped or not. Even if Peter got away and succeeded in getting to Ella Island and was fitted up with a new rifle, one rifleman hundreds of miles away would only make a negligible difference to the strength of an opposition which included the United States Air Force. On the other hand, as long as Peter stayed where he was, he had to be guarded and fed.

Thinking further, Ritter reasoned that if Peter was allowed to go to Ella, he would be certain to tell the rest of the sledge patrol that the Germans were well organized, and that this warning might deter them from trying an attack on Hansa Bay or searching for his base again if he managed to move it.

A day or two later Ritter and Marius had another meeting. By then, each of them had decided in his own mind to make a bargain; and in the upshot, Marius agreed to pilot Ritter on a reconnaissance northward toward Hochstetter Forland, and Ritter agreed in return to let Peter go to Sandodden; he told him to wait there until a German party came to fetch him back.

To let one of the prisoners go alone on a long journey seemed to Schmidt and the other Nazis the worst depth of incompetence to which Ritter had yet sunk. Ritter merely pretended that he expected Peter to obey his order to stay at Sandodden. But by then, Schmidt and Ritter never spoke to each other if they could help it, and the question was not discussed between them.

At about this time, Doctor Weiss, the meteorologist, put forward a plan of his own. He wanted to go to Ella Island with Doctor Sensse, Schmidt and a few of the best of the German sledge drivers and put the place out of action as a weather station. Actually, Ella Island was too far away to give local reports of the Sabine Island weather to the United States Air Force.

Ritter suspected that what Weiss and Sensse really wanted, now that they had more or less learned the art of driving dogs, was the pleasure of a really long arctic journey. Ritter could not help sympathizing with that, and he agreed with the plan. The journey would take several weeks; for the base, it promised several weeks of peace from internal strife.

So preparations were started for three journeys from Sabine Island. Peter was given a small team of six dogs and enough provisions to take him to Sandodden and keep him there for a few days. Ritter was getting ready to travel with Marius on his reconnaissance to the northward; and, unknown to the prisoners, Weiss, Schmidt and Sensse were fitting out two sledges for an attack on Ella Island. Peter was the first of them to start.

This was how it had come about that Peter caught up with Henry Rudi and Kurt Olsen on their weary walk to Ella Island after they had escaped the Germans at Eskimoness. Peter had been to Sandodden and hastily grubbed up stones and heaped them over the small shack where Knudsen's body lay. He had exchanged the sledge which the Germans had given him for a lighter one which had been left there, and he had set off again without wasting a minute. For Henry and Kurt, his arrival in Musk Ox Fjord saved the situation. They all went on together, taking turns on Peter's sledge.

But meanwhile, at Ella Island, there was still no news of what had become of them, and Poulsen, as leader of the scattered sledge patrol, was becoming more anxious day by day. As things turned out, he had had to put off his plan to go north to look for the missing men. When Eske Brun, the colonial governor of Greenland, had heard the first brief news of the capture of Eskimoness, he had ordered the senior man in the sledge patrol at Scoresby Sound to go north at full speed to Ella to give what help he could. Poulsen now heard by radio that this man, whose name was Carlos Ziebell, was already well on the way, with eight sledges driven by Eskimo volunteers.

It was just as well that his delay was forced on Poulsen, because, although he would not have admitted it, he was too ill to travel safely. Apart from his raw feet, he was covered with half-healed frostbite sores, and he was so tired after his 200-mile hike that several days of rest was what he needed.

While he waited with his three Eskimos, Poulsen himself was in a vulnerable position. The house at Ella Island, he knew, would be the Germans' first important objective, if they were bent on ravaging the coast. So, on the day after he got there, he sent two of the Eskimos, with the sledge, to set up a depot on the south side of the island, the opposite side to the house. They put up tents and stored some food in them, together with the station's portable emergency transmitter; and the next day Poulsen and the others drove round there, and they left the station empty.

Just after Poulsen had unpacked his sledge at the depot, five of Ziebell's Eskimos arrived; Ziebell and the others were back at the station. In a hurried exchange of news, it turned out that one of the five Eskimos was the brother of William, who was walking to Scoresby Sound; he left at once to try to catch up with William and help him home. The four others and Poulsen's three Eskimos settled down at the depot, while Poulsen drove back to the station, anxious to meet Ziebell.

Ziebell had brought new orders from Eske Brun which were not very welcome. As soon as everyone possible had been gathered in to Ella Island, they were to retreat to Scoresby Sound. That settlement, with its homesteads and radio station and peaceful people, was the only place on the coast really worth defending.

Ella Island in the next few days fell into a state of complete confusion. During the night at the depot, Ziebell's Eskimos and Poulsen's had talked things over. Evald's story of the tracer bullets and the downfall of Eskimoness, in passing from mouth to mouth, had had horror upon horror added to it; and in the morning all the Eskimos with one accord announced that they were going back to Scoresby Sound at once. It must not be thought that the Eskimos were cowards, for they were not. But Scoresby Sound and the peaceful, empty coast were the whole of their world, and beings whom so far they had never seen, armed with mysterious weapons, had appeared in it from a land they had never heard of. After a first panic, they wanted to go home to die with their families.

Poulsen and Ziebell spent most of the next two days in arguing and explaining and persuading, all in the Eskimo language, while the Eskimos argued among themselves. Somebody pointed out that it was not only the men from Eskimoness who were missing; for two Norwegian brothers named Akre had been based at Ella Island, and had been away on a patrol round Geographical Society Island, and should have been back by then. Because they were late, it was only too easy to jump to the conclusion that they had been captured, and that therefore the Germans were only just around the corner.

At any rate, eight of the ten Eskimos finally started back to Scoresby Sound; some were frightened, some had to return for family reasons, and Mikael and Evald, who had lost their dogs to the Germans at Eskimoness, were sent, too, because they were of no use without their sledges.

While the last echoes of this tremendous discussion were still dying away, three of the men who had been the crux of it came driving in to Ella in good heart: Peter Nielsen, Henry Rudi and Kurt Olsen. Peter had reached Musk Ox Fjord in four days from Sabine Island, and taking the two other men with him he had got to Ella Island in four days more, a total distance of about 270 miles. With only six dogs, this was a remarkable achievement by any standards.

He brought Poulsen the first news that Eskimoness had been burnt down, the news of Eli Knudsen's death and his own and Marius' capture, and, above all, the first definite confirmation that the German base was in Hansa Bay. He had, too, a fairly accurate idea of the number of men in it and the kind of armament they had.

All this was information which had to be sent to Eske Brun, but the only code which Poulsen had at Ella was the one called the green code, a copy of which had been captured at Eskimoness, so it was certainly unsafe to use it now. Poulsen therefore made up his mind to send more sledges south, to take Peter's news in writing to Scoresby Sound.

Luckily, he was able to intercept two of the departing Eskimos at the reserve depot on the south side of the island. On the next day, April tenth, he sent them off with light sledges to travel fast and carry his dispatch, and behind them, with two more sledges, went all the others. Poulsen and Ziebell stayed behind at Ella, with two teams, to cover the retreat.

On that same day Marius was right up on Hochstetter Forland, 300 miles away from the nearest of his friends, alone with the German commander, and he could not understand why Ritter had taken him there or what he was looking for so far to the northward.

When he started, Ritter had had a definite objective: to investigate the hunting stations within reach of Sabine Island, and to see if any of them could house his men and his equipment in case they had to move from Hansa Bay. Suddenly, as if he had waked from a nightmare, everything was exactly as it had been in his happy Spitsbergen years before the war. Once again, he was free, in the incomparable arctic freedom; again he was lapped in the beauty of the arctic scene. All the commonplace details of an arctic journey filled him with new delight.

He and Marius traveled together out over Hochstetter Bay and they entered tremendous tracts of fjord and ice and mountain which even now only a handful of men had ever seen and which never have been disturbed by the faintest echo of war. Neither of them spoke very much on their journey, not even at night in huts or in the tent, when the dogs had been fed and the two men cooked and ate together and shared the chores and slept within an arm's length of each other. When they spoke, Marius spoke Danish and Ritter Norwegian. Ritter was thinking again in Norwegian, instead of in German; and that served to complete his illusion that the horrible events of the past few months had been a dream, and to make him feel that now, in those blessedly impersonal surroundings, he could be himself again.

In this curiously twisted frame of mind, Ritter had a single mad desire: to go on north, away from Sabine Island and away from humanity, to travel on and on and never to come back.

If a psychoanalyst had been watching Ritter in the first days of that pilgrimage, he might have diagnosed a nervous breakdown. But Marius was no psychoanalyst; he saw only that the German commander was unpredictable in his decisions and very often inclined to change his mind. When Ritter asked him if it was possible to travel right up to the north of Greenland, and round the north coast and down toward Baffin Island and Hudson Bay, Marius hardly took the question seriously. But what surprised him most was that Ritter was so unlike what he had expected a German commander to be. He seemed to be a vague, gentle and friendly person.

For about ten days this ill-matched but strangely congenial pair drove aimlessly here and there about the deserted huts in the distant north. Marius began to get a little impatient at the delay of his plans to escape. He had promised to drive Ritter on this journey, in return for permission for Peter to go to Sandodden, and he could not break his promise, provided the journey did not go on forever. Besides, he could have escaped only by killing Ritter or leaving him alone up there to die. They had only one sledge between them. Ritter had one rifle and one revolver, and Marius had none. Perhaps, by warlike standards, it was Marius' duty as a prisoner to get away and congratulate himself on having rid his country of an enemy, but Marius did not know much about the duties of a prisoner of war, and it never seriously occurred to him to do it.

Although the sudden shock of freedom had been the final cause which almost pushed Ritter over the edge of reason, freedom was also his cure. Slowly, as the peaceful days passed by, he began to think in a balanced way again. Suddenly and inconsequently, about the twelfth of April, he realized how much time he had already wasted in his search for another base for his men. At once he told Marius to turn and drive him south again.

They went down by way of the Kuppel Pass without going to Hansa Bay; and then, avoiding Sandodden with its sinister memories, they turned inland and went to Revet. Then Ritter directed Marius farther south, into the mouth of Loch Fyne. In the loch, as they drove hurriedly along it, there were two new sledge tracks going south. Each of them speculated in silence about these tracks.

As they went down Loch Fyne the weather began to break; as Ritter and Marius approached the mountains of Loch Fyne and Hold With Hope a strong wind was blowing and heavy snow was falling. At the head of the loch all the old sledge tracks turned west toward Musk Ox Fjord, but the two new ones led on to the southward, toward the Badlands valley and toward Mosquito Bay. At the hut where the routes divided, Ritter ordered Marius to press on to Mosquito Bay. He had seen the hunting stations at Hochstetter Forland, Sandodden and Revet; Mosquito Bay was the last within range of Sabine Island as a possible retreat.

So Marius led on, across the watershed and down the valley through the heavy, deep snow. Whoever had made the tracks, Marius knew he would have to follow them to the station. The Badlands valley was a kind of cul-de-sac. In a northerly gale it was impossible to think of driving beyond the end of it, out across the forty miles of sea ice at its foot, and impossible also to turn and drive up it again with the wind ahead. The hut at Mosquito Bay was the only shelter he could hope to reach.

They were quite close to the hut before he saw it through the driven snow. He saw dogs outside and recognized them, and he cursed himself for having left his escape too late, for they were dogs which the Germans had captured. As he and Ritter drove up to the house, it was Schmidt, with a submachine gun in his hand, who made them welcome.

The whole of Doctor Weiss' party was in the house; they had been stormbound in Mosquito Bay for nearly a week. That night, suspicion smoldered and enmity was on the verge of breaking into violence. Marius, the prisoner, was probably the only one who was more or less unmoved by what was happening, because he could not understand the Germans' conversation. Ritter, imprisoned by the storm in the little house with Schmidt, the man he believed was the author of all his problems, the man he mortally feared, tried to defend himself by offering only the vaguest explanation of what he had been doing and why he had decided to come south.

Ritter told them that now he had seen Mosquito Bay he was satisfied, and meant to return to Sabine Island, and, as a matter of fact, that was true. He never thought of desertion. Whether Schmidt believed the statement or not, it suited him to accept it for the present.

Yet another subject of disagreement came to a head that night. On their way to Mosquito Bay, Doctor Weiss, Schmidt and the others had spent a night at Sandodden themselves, and had seen the sledge which Peter had exchanged and left there. On their way up Loch Fyne before the storm, they had identified his tracks, and so Ritter had to swallow Schmidt's hints that a humble hunter had made a fool of him.

It was on that night of bitter, suppressed dissension that Marius first learned for certain that Weiss and the others intended an attack on Ella Island. They asked him, through Ritter as interpreter, which was the better route for them to take—the short way across the open ice or the way back through the Badlands and then through Musk Ox Fjord. Marius advised them at once to go back through Musk Ox Fjord, and told them the open sea ice at that time of the year would be dangerous. Ritter passed on the advice and persuaded them to accept it. When the weather cleared, Doctor Weiss and Schmidt and the others harnessed up and set off.

Certainly Marius knew about the loose deep snow in Musk Ox Fjord, and he knew in the split second when the Germans asked his advice that he had it in his power to thwart them. It worked: the inexperienced drivers, who had come down through the Badlands without much trouble, found it a very different matter to go up, after a week of fresh snowfall and wind. Their heavily laden sledges bogged down and the dogs floundered. When at last they had crossed the stretch of land, they found that Musk Ox Fjord was worse.

Indeed, it was worse than Marius could have expected. A warm wind called the *foehn,* which sometimes mysteriously flows down from the ice cap, was sweeping through the funnel of the fjord. This wind can raise the temperature within an hour from fifteen degrees below freezing point to fifteen degrees above it, and it plays havoc with the ice. The Germans found slush and salt water on the ice in Musk Ox Fjord. Two days later they were still only halfway down the fjord. They must have been very angry and blamed Ritter for all their delays.

In Mosquito Bay, an hour after the others were out of sight, Ritter was baking bread in preparation for the journey back to Sabine Island. He told Marius he could go out to feed the dogs; Marius went and saw what he had hoped for. When they had arrived and the house had been full of Germans, Ritter had left his rifle on the sledge. Marius took it and went to the door with his finger on the trigger. Ritter was kneading dough; he looked over his shoulder and made a movement toward his revolver on top of the cupboard.

"Stand still," Marius said to Ritter, and he got the revolver too.

Ritter stood scraping the dough from his fingers. All he said was "What are you going to do?" and he probably knew the answer.

"I'm going to Ella Island," Marius said.

When Ritter had watched Marius, with his eight splendid dogs and an almost empty sledge, driving down to the ice and out across the bay which he had said so convincingly was dangerous, he had not the slightest doubt that Marius would get to Ella first and warn its garrison. What would happen? The Germans were much better armed than the Danes, and would probably fight their way out of the ambush; and Schmidt, at least, would never believe that Ritter had not planned to get him killed.

It was so obvious. Ritter had spoken to Marius in a language the others could not understand. Between them, they had given the advice to take the longer route. It would appear to the Germans as high treason and attempted murder, and Ritter would never be able to argue against the circumstantial evidence. Even the motive was there, and was sufficient. The prosecutors would point out that Schmidt was the man who had assembled all the evidence of Ritter's earlier crimes, and that Ritter knew it. By plotting the death of Schmidt, they would suggest, he was hoping to destroy the previous evidence and return undisputed to his command.

Yet Ritter felt peaceful. He had thought himself guilty of the death of Eli Knudsen. Now, he was prepared to be condemned for trying to murder Schmidt and his companions as expiation for the death of Knudsen.

He felt peaceful also because there was nothing left for him to do. Events had moved out of his hands. Hansa Bay was 130 miles away. Unarmed, he would have had to carry all his food and equipment for the journey on his back. There was an excellent chance of meeting polar bears. For Ritter in his present condition such a journey would have been impossible. Even the effort of imagining the details of the journey was beyond him.

There was plenty of food of limited kinds in the house at Mosquito Bay—sacks of flour and coffee and sugar which had been left there two years before when the weather station closed down. Perhaps, after months, he would die there, of scurvy if nothing else had killed him first. Perhaps one day someone would come and find him. But he could not concentrate his attention on such things; he could not care.

Some time after Marius had gone, Ritter stood up and noticed that the dough he had mixed was still on the table. It had risen. He stoked up the fire and put it in the oven, and he began to tidy up the house, entirely absorbed in trivialities.

Marius drove like the devil; there were ninety miles ahead of him. He was confident that, barring accidents, he would get to Ella Island first, but he had to get there in time for his warning to be of some use. So he drove on, urging his dogs without mercy, through the afternoon and through the night. It was only ten days or so before the midnight sun began, and there was not much more than a hint of dusk at night; there was no darkness left at all.

Marius went straight down the open coast to Cape Franklin and across the mouth of Kaiser Franz Josef Fjord to Cape Humboldt, and into the narrow entrance of Sofia Sound. On the evening after he left Mosquito Bay, he saw the Bastion of Ella Island a dozen miles away and cursed his dogs on toward it. They were dead beat, and so was he. An hour later Marius could see the house. But no sledge came out to meet him; no movement, no smoke from the chimney. With a sinking heart, he drew up to the house.

He went into the empty living room. It was quite cold. When he had opened the shutters he saw a note and a map on the table. The note was addressed to him and signed by Poulsen and dated the nineteenth of April, two days earlier. It said they had given up searching for him and were going south to Scoresby Sound. The map showed Marius the route to Scoresby Sound, which he had never traveled before, and Poulsen had marked the places where he would leave the food depots.

Marius put the map in his pocket. So they had all gone, and his rush of ninety miles had been wasted. He was alone with exhausted dogs, and Schmidt and his fellow Germans, with luck, were a couple of days behind him.

The Eskimo settlement of Scoresby Sound was in a state of desperate apprehension when Ib Poulsen and Carlos Ziebell finally reached it on April 30, 1943. Nothing like the German threat from the northeast coast had ever happened before and it seemed at the time, to the people of Scoresby Sound, that Armageddon was coming.

There were nineteen Germans on the northeast coast of Greenland, and upwards of eighty able-bodied Eskimos at Scoresby Sound. Poulsen knew that whatever happened, the Eskimos would not fight; they would passively turn the other cheek, as their Christian religion had taught them. He did not pretend to know what whims of strategy guided the Germans, but he knew that if they attacked Scoresby Sound, they would burn the village down. They had done this to his former headquarters at Eskimoness; and Scoresby Sound, like Eskimoness, was sending weather reports on its civil radio to the Americans and British.

Scoresby Sound could hardly have been more difficult to defend. It had only a system of air-raid warnings, which Ziebell had instituted, and a few shelters. Its thirty or forty houses extended over several miles of shore, and it had two opposite approaches—down Hurry Inlet and down the outer coast. Its nearest neighboring village is Angmagssalik, 450 miles farther south. Scoresby Sound's people depended for their food and livelihood on hunting journeys, and hunters in the distance on their sledges could not be distinguished from attackers. Poulsen's fighting force consisted of five men with rifles: himself, Ziebell, Kurt Olsen, Peter Nielsen and Henry Rudi; and even of these, Henry Rudi's position was rather equivocal. He had signed on as a civilian in the sledge patrol, but when the patrol had been converted into the Greenland army nobody had asked Rudi if he wanted to join it. Rudi was Norwegian. Poulsen knew he had some doubt, which was more than justifiable, whether he ought to be serving in time of war in a foreign army. Henry was also the man whose arctic trust of all his fellow men was most deeply a part of his character, perhaps because he had been in the arctic much longer than the others. Certainly, after the burning of Eskimoness and the news of Eli Knudsen's death at the hands of the Germans, his trust had been shaken, but he would probably still have found it hard to aim his gun at a fellow man and fire it. Poulsen had to rank Henry halfway between the rest of his companions and the Eskimos.

By the end of May, the thaw would have started, and for most of June, when the fjord ice was turning to slush and the land was under flood, nobody would be able to threaten the village except by air; and what happened in July, when the seas were open, was too distant to worry about. Another hard fact was that although the sledge patrol had been sent back to Scoresby Sound to defend it, any active defense would have to take place outside it. A gun battle in among the houses would be certain to kill more Eskimos than Germans, and would give the Danes no chance to make use of their only kinds of superiority, a knowledge of the country and a knowledge of sledges and dogs.

The ideal defense position, they reckoned, was right up in King Oscar's Fjord, beyond the place where the possible routes to Scoresby Sound divided. They also decided to make one last appeal to the Americans to send over an aircraft and drop them a machine gun.

Poulsen decided to lead the somewhat forlorn expedition himself, and to take Ziebell, Kurt Olsen and two Eskimos with him, leaving Henry Rudi and Peter Nielsen to encourage the Scoresby Sound people and help them to build themselves new shelters. But before they could start the weather broke and made travel impossible. On the whole, this storm was welcome. It did nothing to soothe the fears of the Eskimos, but each day of impassable storm was one day nearer the finally impassable thaw.

The weather began to clear on the ninth of May, and on the tenth Poulsen was on the way up Hurry Inlet, with his four sledges close behind him. At the head of the inlet there is a hut. They stopped a couple of miles away and looked at it through glasses; there were sledges and dogs outside it. These could only be sledges from the north, and so they surrounded the hut at a distance and approached it cautiously. Poulsen, half expecting some trap, crept right up to the house, trigger-conscious, before the dogs woke up and howled at him in furious alarm. Then the door opened and two sleepy but apprehensive men peered out—the missing Akre brothers.

They had one important piece of news. After they had found Poulsen's notes in the huts round Sofia Sound, they had come south without stopping at Ella Island, but they had crossed a lot of fresh sledge tracks which led toward it. Working it out, there was only one answer: the tracks were German. This news and the acquisition of two more rifles made Poulsen change his plans. He sent Ziebell and Olsen on, with the portable transmitter they had brought from Ella Island, to establish the outpost somewhere in Carlsberg Fjord. Poulsen went back to Scoresby Sound with the two newcomers to report to Eske Brun, the colonial governor of Greenland, and to try to organize a second line of defense.

Two days later, things came to a crisis. Kurt Olsen and Ziebell had got to Carlsberg Fjord and had been in communication with Scoresby Sound radio. They had pitched the tent at a place where they had a good view to the northward, but Kurt reported that the weather was getting foggy. Then, suddenly, his transmitter went off the air.

Poulsen waited for news with some anxiety while they tried to make radio contact again. It was likely enough that Kurt's sudden silence meant nothing worse than a fault in the portable transmitter, but it might have meant, also, a German attack.

While he waited, Poulsen got a confusing report from a young Eskimo hunter and the assistant priest of the settlement. They had just come back from Hurry Inlet. They had seen two men in the hut there, one of them in uniform. The priest had spoken to one of them, who said his name was Marius Jensen, but the Eskimo had not been able to understand him very well. There were at least nineteen dogs, the Eskimos said, and four pairs of skis and one sledge.

The significance of nineteen dogs and one sledge was the crux of this story. Twelve dogs was the maximum which would be used with one sledge, and eight or ten was more usual. Therefore from seven to eleven spare dogs had been seen. Other sledges must have been away somewhere, each with only a part of its team. The report suggested to Poulsen a force at the very least of five or six men. There was only one conclusion: that the

Germans who had been at Ella Island and captured it without a fight were now aiming at Scoresby Sound.

The sledge patrol went out to meet them: Poulsen, Peter, Henry and the Akre brothers. As they drove westward out of Scoresby Sound, Poulsen looked back beyond the little houses, and there, rolling in swiftly from the open sea, he saw the fog—the fog which had blinded his outpost at Carlsberg Fjord and let the Germans past. Poulsen saw looming in it his ultimate defeat, for his last hope had been to ambush the German forces at the mouth of Hurry Inlet, but now, if the fog came in and filled the inlet, he would hardly have the slightest chance of seeing them. There was a moment then when everything seemed lost.

Unexpectedly, sledges came hurrying out to intercept Poulsen, from the last houses in the settlement. Their Eskimo drivers called him to come in. Two strangers had arrived with only eight dogs. The hunter's and the priest's imaginations had added eleven more. The man called Jensen, the Eskimos said, was little, but he must be very strong. He must have been beating the tall man, because he was crying. Poulsen followed them in, quite unable to imagine what he would find.

There was Marius with his sledge, and another man, a stranger.

"Marius!" Poulsen said. "Who's that?"

"My prisoner," Marius said. They were men of few words.

The tall man, Lt. Hermann Ritter, commander of the German expedition to Northeast Greenland, had been tearing the medals and distinctions off his uniform, and now he was sitting with his face buried in his hands.

It took Poulsen a very long time to gather the story of Marius' escape, but even the few facts which Marius could bring himself to put into words were enough to suggest he had made a rather remarkable journey; for he had left Sabine Island on April fifth and got to Scoresby Sound on May thirteenth, and he had traveled on every day of those five and a half weeks, and covered a distance of about 800 miles, mostly with Ritter, but partly alone.

After Marius' escape from Ritter and at the end of his ninety-mile dash to Ella Island, when he had found that the sledge patrol had gone south, the obvious thing for him to do was to follow them and waste no time about it. The Nazi, Schmidt, and his squad were only a day or two behind him. But Marius went back to Mosquito Bay, instead, to see what had happened to Ritter.

When Poulsen asked Marius why, he replied with an amiable grin, "Because I knew you'd ask such a hell of a lot of questions. I thought I'd better get Ritter to answer them." And for years afterward, there the matter rested.

Marius was not simply being obstinate; the fact was that he hardly knew why he had done it himself. Poulsen's probing had forced him to delve in his own mind, and Marius had glimpsed the truth and covered it up again: for, although he did not care to reveal his emotions, he had gone back out of simple kindness. Also, in wartime, it is hard to say in so many words that one likes the enemies' commander.

Marius had already traveled a long way with Ritter, man to man. Ritter had treated him fairly and decently. By all arctic standards, Marius felt he had played Ritter a dirty trick by leaving him; Marius was afraid Ritter might not know how to look after himself, now that he was alone, and that he might die at Mosquito Bay. Marius did not stop to think much about the risk to himself, which was tremendous; he just set off to help a man who might be in difficulties.

Five days after he had left Mosquito Bay, Marius was back there again. Ritter, seeing the sledge approaching, had not really been surprised; he was almost beyond surprise. In the solitude of the house, his mind had faded into a kind of half-deliberate daydream which excluded all thoughts of war. He had been thinking only of his family and of peaceful arctic things.

But Marius roused him. As he came in at the door, he just said, "Get your clothes on. We're going south." Within a few minutes they were away again, but before they went, Marius asked Ritter to promise not to give him any trouble, and Ritter, still bewildered, said he would. So began the most curious journey recorded in the arctic; for Marius had to escort the enemy commander alone for 290 miles, through territory which the enemy, if anyone, controlled. It took him fifteen days.

Could Ritter have escaped? The literal answer must be that he could. Marius took all the precautions he could think of to prevent it, but of course there were moments, especially in the first few days and nights, when Ritter could have taken Marius unawares and got the rifle back. Those chances could not be avoided. But Marius had tied his prisoner with a subtler bond. Ritter understood that Marius had risked his own life and his own freedom to come back and look after him; so that Marius had shown him at last that the old arctic principles of conduct were still alive. It was Marius' achievement not that he cowed his prisoner into going quietly, but that he showed him just by being himself, an example which made his prisoner unable to raise a hand against him.

So they traveled in a kind of unspoken truce. The danger for Marius all through the first few days was not from Ritter at all; it was from Schmidt. By the time Marius got back to Mosquito Bay, Schmidt and the four other men might just about be expected to have got to Ella Island. There was absolutely no way of guessing how long they would stay there when they found the place deserted. Above all, Marius could not tell whether the Germans would go back by the way they had come to try the short cut through Sofia Sound themselves. So, day after day, he had to expect to meet them face to face.

They passed Ella Island without being challenged by the Germans, and after that every mile they traveled made them safer, and every mile made the idea that Ritter might escape seem more remote. One night, in one of the huts down in King Oscar's Fjord, Ritter said, "Well, the war's finished now for me." After that, they were not a prisoner and an escort any more; they were just two travelers. All that either of them wanted was to get to Scoresby Sound and get the journey over.

A bare report of what Marius had done was transmitted to Eske Brun, and eventually traveled to the British and American high commands. Somewhere, somebody added to it a strictly military motive for Marius' gallant action. He was promoted to sergeant in the Greenland army and awarded the British Empire Medal and the United States Legion of Merit. No medals are awarded for simple human kindness.

Ritter and Poulsen, as was only to be expected, treated each other at first with reserve and suspicion. The Danish prisoners had been looked after well enough in Sabine Island, and Poulsen made things as comfortable as he could for Ritter in return. But Ritter refused to give Poulsen any military information. Poulsen imagined that a German officer's idea of duty might make him try to do some damage in Scoresby Sound, and especially perhaps to sabotage the radio station; so he kept him strictly under guard. It was a nuisance. The capture of Ritter, so far as Poulsen could tell, had not ended the chances of attack. On the contrary, the Germans now had an extra reason for coming to Scoresby Sound: to rescue their commander. For the first time, the whole of the sledge patrol was gathered together, except its one dead man, but that meant only eight rifles, and guarding the prisoner day and night took two of them.

Still, Marius' successful coup had put new spirit into all the sledge patrol. Their blood was up. They had never liked the retreat from Ella Island, and now it seemed a feeble policy to sit in Scoresby Sound and wait for the thaw. They began to talk of going back to Ella Island. The idea was put up to the government, and Eske Brun, never a man for retreat, agreed at once.

By then, there was not much time to waste. It was past the middle of May, and they could not depend on much more than a fortnight of sledging. The journey to Ella would have to be a journey without a retreat; for if they got to the station and found the Germans in possession and failed to turn them out, it would probably be too late to get back to Scoresby Sound—the ice would have melted behind them.

Ziebell, Kurt Olsen and Marius were chosen for the Ella expedition. Exactly a week after Marius had come in at the end of his marathon journey, he started again for the north with these two new companions. The sledge patrol had taken the initiative at last.

It was only a few days after they had gone that Poulsen received the very first sign that anyone in the outside world, except Eske Brun, was interested in his private war. A signal came to warn him to expect a friendly aircraft, and soon afterward an American bomber zoomed over Scoresby Sound and threw out a container attached to a parachute. Poulsen unpacked it and found four machine guns. At once he sent a signal to the Ella expedition to tell them to wait where they were, and he sent two Eskimo volunteers after them with a gun and ammunition.

Four days later, the Eskimo sledges were back, still carrying the machine gun. North of the head of Hurry Inlet, the rivers were running. The thaw had begun and the sledge route was impassable. Scoresby Sound was cut off from the rest of the coast. The guns had arrived when it was just too late to matter.

Poulsen, sitting impotently now in Scoresby Sound, was relieved to hear, on the second of June, that Ziebell's force had got to Ella Island and reoccupied the house without any opposition. For a long time he heard no more than that. Kurt Olsen had taken the emergency transmitter with him, but the sledge had been loaded up with camping gear for a whole summer, and they had had to cut down on radio batteries and agree only to exchange essential signals.

Ziebell and Marius and Kurt Olsen, ten days out from Scoresby Sound, had made a wary approach toward Ella Island. The house looked exactly the same as ever. The shutters were closed and there was no sign of life. After they had watched it for long enough, Ziebell told Kurt and Marius to stay there and cover him while he advanced.

As soon as the dogs saw the house ahead of them, they took charge and began to gallop gaily in toward it. Halfway there, Ziebell saw that outside the house there were over a dozen rifles standing in a row, stacked in threes in orderly parade-ground fashion. And then he saw something else: in the shadow of the doorway a man in uniform was staring out to sea.

Frantically, he tried to turn his dogs and get away again, but they took no notice of his shouts or his whip and bounded straight on toward the house. Still nothing happened. The house was silent, the man stood like a statue. The dogs swept right up to the door, and then Ziebell saw that he had been looking at a dummy stuffed with straw. The rifles were an old Danish pattern which had been obsolete for years and had been left in the loft at Ella because nobody had any ammunition for them.

Ziebell signaled to the others to come up, and then went in. The eight-day clock was ticking. On the stove was a pot of stew which was beginning to go moldy. The pictures of American pinup girls that had graced the walls for years had disappeared, and in their places were two photographs, one of Hitler and one of Mussolini. Below the one of Hitler, someone had written: WE ARE THE BEST SOLDIERS IN THE WORLD.

It hardly seemed worth while to use up batteries to send these tidings to Poulsen, peculiar though they were. A rational explanation was invented for the dummy and the rifles: they might have been put there, with no intention of being ridiculous, in case a reconnaissance aircraft was sent to photograph the station.

More important, though less amusing, were the other things the Germans had done at Ella. The radio transmitter and its batteries and generator and the lighting installation had all been damaged, and so had the motorboat engine, and a large hole had been blown in the boat by a hand grenade. The wooden aerial masts, ten inches thick, had been felled, cut through by machine-gun fire. The supplies of food in the station were rather depleted, as if they had fed several men for quite a time, but what was left was in good condition.

Altogether, the damage was much less than anyone had expected. It had all the appearance of a delaying action. Even the motors which were damaged had not been thoroughly destroyed; nobody had taken a hammer to their castings. A few days' work was enough to get the lighting motor going again, and the motorboat engine was also repaired on the spot. The hole in the boat was more difficult, but only because there were no materials at the station for shipwright's work.

There were two interpretations to be put on the Germans' halfhearted sabotage. One was that they were only interested in stopping broadcasts from Ella till the summer was well advanced. The other possibility was that they intended to come back. The latter idea was supported by the mystery of the ticking clock, for the Danes took this as conclusive evidence that the Germans had been at Ella less than a week before. As a matter of fact, it was nearly a month since Weiss and his men had done the damage and gone away, and one can only suppose that the banging of doors, or footsteps, had started the clock again.

So Ziebell and Kurt and Marius settled in. The rivers had started to roar again, avalanches were falling in the mountains and the ice on the fjord was getting wet and dark. Very soon, wherever the Germans had gone, they would have to stay there, and Ella Island, surrounded by miles of slush, would be safe from invasion by either ice or sea.

Scoresby Sound was also safe, unless it was raided by air. Henry Rudi and the Akre brothers became air-raid wardens. The sledge-patrol Eskimos started their summer jobs of mending sledges and harnesses and skis, and hunting to feed the dogs. Peter Nielsen guarded Ritter, relieved by Poulsen when he could get away from the office work which had piled up for months.

It would have been fitting if Ritter and Poulsen, in the weeks they spent together in Scoresby Sound, had discovered in conversation that they had never wanted to fight each other. They both suspected it, but neither of them put it into words.

It was not till later years that either of these men could come to understand the other and appreciate his qualities. However, Henry Rudi, a shrewd judge of human beings as well as of bears, remarked quite early in Ritter's imprisonment that the man was a gentleman, and he said in his forthright way that even if Ritter did try to escape, it would be wrong to try to shoot him. Peter also, to his own surprise, had begun to feel a profound admiration for Ritter. Marius, Henry, Peter—perhaps none of them quite knew why they unwillingly liked their enemy, but perhaps it is fair to guess that what they had seen in Ritter, and what they admired, was the probity which made his German uniform seem insignificant.

As for Ritter himself, after all the spiritual distress that he had suffered, his conscience was calm and his fears were ended now. Perhaps he was glad he had been captured. Looking back on his record as an officer, he would have admitted he had treated Marius as his prisoner too leniently. Certainly he had been careless and foolish to leave his rifle on the sledge at Mosquito Bay. But if that could be forgiven, he felt he had done his duty to the German navy as best he could. Above all, he felt supremely thankful that the war was over for him, because for him that simply meant that never again could the power of military law or of party politics be used to coerce him to do acts which seemed to him to defy the will of God.

His imprisonment at Scoresby Sound gave point to these

reflections. He had never been in an Eskimo settlement before, and he would have loved to join in its daily life, but, of course, that was denied him. To watch the Eskimos could only make him more aware that he was the only man in the whole community who did not have the trust of every other, the only outlaw.

Yet he could not make a show of his feelings. It was not a matter of pride or of being afraid of being rebuffed; it was a matter of humility. He had given the Eskimos plenty of reason to mistrust him, and for what he had done he had to be willing to pay the price of ostracism. It was also in his own interest, as it happened, to behave consistently and correctly as a prisoner of war. So, at Scoresby Sound, he retired into his own thoughts and made no friendly overtures. After a few weeks, when the sound had thawed, a seaplane came in and took him away to a prison camp in America.

But just before it came there was a rifle accident—an Eskimo child had got a bullet in her leg. Somebody had heard that Ritter was clever as a doctor, and the Eskimos asked the Danes to let him come and help them. He went with his guard. It was almost his last act in Greenland, and perhaps it is appropriate as a final impression of this strangely attractive man. Perhaps in the Eskimo house a true glimpse of Ritter may be seen, trying to soothe the pain of a child he had never seen before and would never see again, wholly absorbed in the gentle, delicate operation on the wound.

The end was coming quickly, not only because the thaw was imprisoning everyone, each in his little corner of the coast, but also because in Europe and America vast forces were stirring at last to intervene.

The bombing of the German camp on Sabine Island was a difficult undertaking. It required Liberators and Flying Fortresses fitted with long-range tanks and it also required air crews trained in arctic flying. The Americans' leading expert for a raid of that kind was the veteran former Norwegian pilot, Bernt Balchen, who was a colonel then in the United States Air Force. He knew more about polar flying than anyone else in the world at that time, and indeed he still does.

On May twenty-fifth, unknown to Poulsen and the other members of the sledge patrol, the heavy force of bombers reached Hansa Bay. For three hours, the arctic quiet was shattered by engines and bombs and gunfire as plane after plane roared over the Sabine hills. The Germans fought back with .50-caliber machine guns. When it was all over, none of the American planes had been damaged and Bernt Balchen reported that he had done great damage to the huts and the ship. However, according to German reports the *Sachsen* was not hit, and certainly not one of the Germans was hurt.

Doctor Weiss was in charge by the time the bombers came. When he and Doctor Sensse and Schmidt and the two other men had got back from Ella Island, they had been very surprised to find that Ritter had not come back, and Weiss had appealed to the German air force to come to the rescue. When the American bombers came over, a German flying boat was already waiting in the north of Norway. Sometime in July, as soon as the sea ice broke up and sufficient open leads of water could be seen, it came to Hansa Bay and picked up all the men except Doctor Sensse, who could not be found, and took them back to Germany. Before they left, the German records say, they set Ritter's ship on fire and burned some more of the huts.

Later still, two United States Coast Guard ships, the *Northland* and the *North Star,* forced their way up the coast. At the same time, Ziebell and Kurt Olsen and Marius, who had patched up the motorboat at Ella Island, were making their own way north. They came up Musk Ox Fjord, which was free of ice, and hauled a dinghy over the ten miles of land to the head of Loch Fyne, and rowed all the way down the loch and across to the desolate ruins of their former headquarters. It was some satisfaction for the sledge patrol to get back by themselves to the very place where their retreat had started, but the *North Star* got to Eskimoness first, and it was the American crew who found the small outbuilding full of furs, with the Danish flag among them and Ritter's defiant note pinned on the wall. Afterward, the crew of the *North Star* built a temporary base for the sledge patrol seven miles from Eskimoness.

At Hansa Bay, during this period, the crew of the *Northland* had been told to look out for German survivors, but there was nobody there. The huts were in ruins and the *Sachsen* was a blackened hulk.

But that was not quite the end of the whole affair. On the day after the *Northland* got to Hansa Bay, three of the American crew went to Germania Harbor, and there, to their surprise, they took a prisoner—an emaciated bearded man who was dressed in rags. The tattered hooded jacket he was wearing had a bullet hole in the shoulder. He said his name was Sensse, but the name on his clothes, when they searched him, was Eli Knudsen.

When Doctor Sensse and Weiss had got back to their base, it was nearly a month since they had left Ritter with Marius at Mosquito Bay. Everyone wondered what had happened to Ritter; probably some of them thought they were better off without him, but Doctor Sensse was not content to wonder. The thaw had started and open leads were showing along the coast, but Sensse harnessed five dogs—not more, because the Germans were short of dog food—and started alone for Mosquito Bay.

It is not recorded whether Sensse ever got there. Somewhere along the way, the melting ice broke under his sledge, and he and the dogs and the sledge went through. He managed to drag himself out, but the sledge sank and took the dogs down with it. Sensse was not very far from Sandodden when this happened, and he succeeded in walking there. In the hut he found Eli Knudsen's clothes, and he put them on.

He lived there alone on the scraps of food which were left in the station, in the macabre company of Eli Knudsen's body, which he and the other Germans had left in the meat-storage hut. There was an old boat at the station, and when at last the fjords were free of ice, he launched it and rowed the fifty miles back to Germania Harbor, to find his compatriots gone and American sailors in possession of Sabine Island.

One is left with the question of why the German doctor made this dangerous journey. It seems unlikely that he would have gone alone if he had been going as a Nazi, to corner Ritter and bring him back to answer for his crimes. The alternative remains that he went as a doctor and a friend, and risked his life because he imagined that Ritter was lying, sick or injured or starving, down at Mosquito Bay.

In the fight in Northeast Greenland, diverse opinions of the morality of war had been revealed: Schmidt, whose dream of Nazi greatness had been proof against the arctic charm; Ritter, whom arctic beauty had led back to the paths of God; Poulsen,

Marius, Peter, Kurt and the others, who had loved the arctic peace and made war to preserve it as well as they were able; the Eskimos, whose whole world was pitched in the arctic splendor and whose whole morality was in the Sermon on the Mount. Where among these did Doctor Sensse stand? The facts suggest that Sensse had wanted to be offered Ritter's confidence and was ready in the end, though Ritter had held aloof, to acknowledge the noble tradition of the arctic and endure the final test of human friendship.

So the story ended where it had begun, with a surprising encounter at the hut in Germania Harbor. On the day after, the American ship steamed out of Hansa Bay. The Germans were not done with Greenland, as it later turned out; they continued to send weather-reconnaissance planes up along the coast and they had battles with the Coast Guard ships from time to time. A year later they even established another base farther north, at Shannon Island, but that, too, was detected and destroyed. At any rate, when the Americans sailed away from the German camp late in July, 1943, Sabine Island was left deserted, as peaceful as it had always been since long before mankind began to fight. It is still deserted and perfectly peaceful now.

U-Boat into Scapa Flow

BY BURKE WILKINSON

No setting gives men a better chance to display the quality of daring than the arena of war. Much as we may dislike their ideals and their goals, intrepid men deserve our admiration. Gunther Prien, one of Hitler's ablest U-boat commanders during World War II, slipped through the supposedly impregnable defenses of Scapa Flow to wreak havoc on the mighty British fleet—and escaped to receive the acclaim of the Third Reich.

A feat of arms such as his will, in all likelihood, never be repeated, for since those days techniques of harbor defense have advanced tremendously. So Prien rates a niche in history, for his qualities of cold skill and hot courage, perfectly juxtaposed on the night of October 13, 1939, enabled him to carry out one of the most dangerous missions in the long, scarred annals of war.

ON THE NIGHT of October 13, 1939, Gunther Prien, one of the youngest and most daring of the German U-boat commanders, slithered his submarine into Scapa Flow and torpedoed the British battleship *Royal Oak*. More remarkable still, he slipped out of the heavily defended fleet anchorage again, and within a few hours was riding in triumph down Unter den Linden.

Gunther Prien, square-jawed, jaunty Saxon, became the first hero of the Third Reich. Nor was any enemy more popular in England than the cocky-looking little kraut who tied so tight a knot in the tail of the British lion. For the British have always his exploit "must be regarded as a feat of arms," and there were admired courage, even enemy courage. Churchill admitted that pictures of Prien that fall in the better British magazines. Since that night, the mantle of many myths has settled over Prien—the folklore of heroism has shrouded the glittering deed itself.

Without special knowledge, it would have been impossible to maneuver a full-sized U-boat through the elaborate defenses of the Flow. How did Gunther Prien know there was a flaw in these defenses? Stranger still, how did he make good his escape after pumping six torpedoes in leisurely fashion in the direction of the *Royal Oak?* From here on, the fog thickens even more. What happened to Gunther Prien himself? Did he fall out with his Nazi masters? Is he alive today?

Now the story can be told in detail, using captured documents—including the log of U-47 on that fateful night—and interviews with German naval personnel as the main sources.

Gunther Prien was a child of the depression. His widowed mother, ruined by the inflation, struggled hard to maintain the shreds of middle-class respectability in the midst of the most dire poverty. The Prien family lived in Leipzig. The mother turned out cheap paintings and also peddled laces sent her from the mountains. The three children learned the lessons of survival early.

When he was fifteen, in 1923, young Gunther Prien struck out for himself. He took what money he had saved—some ninety crowns earned by guiding Swedish visitors through the Leipzig Fair—and enrolled in a three-month course at the German sailors' school in Finkenwaerder. Then he shipped out as a cabin boy on the old sailing ship *Hamburg.* His first cruise was exciting enough—fire on board off Pensacola, shipwreck near Dublin. On his return, he filed for officer candidate.

By January, 1932, Officer Candidate Prien was well up the ladder of merchant-marine success. He passed his examination for a master's certificate and looked around for a command. But the depression had deepened; his failure was complete. His savings gone, he crept back to Leipzig—to odd, humiliating jobs, and finally the dole. To him, as to so many other unemployed, the Nazi Party offered solace to his pride and a promise of better things. He joined it in the summer of 1932.

Prien's next move shows that he was made of sterner stuff

than many of his ersatz fellow party members. He enrolled at a Volunteer Work Camp at Vogtsberg. Prien, then twenty-four, attracted the attention of the camp commandant, one Lamprecht, by his willingness to volunteer with a much younger age group. Lamprecht promoted Prien to squad leader, troop leader, and finally his own deputy.

Within the year, the German Navy sent out a call for former officers of the merchant marine. Prien enlisted, and once again found himself on the lowest rung of the sea ladder, as officer candidate. But his quickness and confidence stood him in good stead. The course completed, he went to sea as first watch officer of a U-boat. In the autumn of 1938 he married the daughter of an officer and took command of his own submarine—a durable young man of thirty, with natural powers of leadership and a kind of security at long last.

Prien never lapsed from party membership—a fact which Goebbels later put to good use. In the 1930's the navy—especially in the officer class—resisted Nazi infiltration even more than the army. Only much later, when Doenitz took over in 1943, did it come to be regarded as "reliable." So it is somewhat surprising to find that Lieutenant Prien remained a good party member during these years of naval advancement. Surprising, until his original reason for joining is recalled—to Prien the appeal of Nazism was social, not military. At a time of near despair, it restored his confidence in himself.

When war came, Prien and his pig-boat were on an extended training cruise in the Atlantic. In his sketchy life story, published after his most celebrated exploit, he tells us that he heard the news of war through the general announcement over the German radio. But he admits that he knew the exact area in which he wanted to operate.

Prien's first kill was largely the victim of his enthusiasm. She was a lumbering old Greek freighter, unmistakably neutral, and, moreover, headed for a German port. But on the third day of the war he torpedoed a sulphur-laden British freighter, Glasgow-bound.

It was in the second month of the war that the star of Prien's destiny rose like a rocket. Admiral Doenitz, the ferretlike commander of Germany's underseas flotillas, personally selected him to carry out the most dangerous and desperate mission in his power to give—the penetration of the British fleet anchorage at Scapa Flow in the Orkney Islands.

Doenitz summoned Prien on a Sunday morning in early October. The U-boat skipper found his chief before a wall map of the Orkneys. Doenitz pointed out to him the seven entrances to Scapa, the estimated location of the British defenses and the place where the German submariner Emsmann was killed in attempting to carry out a World War I raid there.

Doenitz expressed the conviction that a determined submarine commander would be able to make the penetration despite the swift and treacherous currents.

"What do you think of it, Prien?" he fired at his subordinate. "I do not want any reply now. Consider the matter at leisure. Take all the data with you and calculate everything carefully. I will await your answer Tuesday noon." The ice-cold eyes studied Prien for a moment, appraisingly. "I hope that you understand me correctly, Prien," Doenitz continued. "You are completely free in your decision. If you decide that the enterprise cannot be carried through, tell me so. Absolutely no shadow will fall on you. For us, you will always remain the same."

Doenitz shook hands with Prien and the latter took up the charts and papers, saluted and left the room. Why did Doenitz pick Gunther Prien? In his queer, sparse little autobiography, Prien gives but slight indication that the submarine admiral inspired in him the almost fanatical loyalty which he aroused in many of the U-boat commanders. Yet Doenitz, no mean judge of men, did sense in Prien the qualities most needed for the raid on Scapa—conscientiousness almost amounting to caution, coupled with sudden bursts of extreme daring under pressure.

And the Prien life story affords definite clues to this duality in his nature. Twice in his youth he answered the call of the sea. Yet each time he did so, it was not in a spirit of adventure, but as a sober, considered choice in his search for steady employment. In writing of life at sea he keeps the exotic and adventurous side to a minimum, and stresses the discipline and rigorous daily labor of a sailor's life.

It is significant, too, that the episode which obviously impressed him most—and which he tells in exhaustive detail—was a collision with another steamer in the approaches to the Weser—not so much because of the accident itself as because of his fear of losing his hard-won fourth officer's certificate as a result of the investigation. His descriptions of naval training and even actual combat are stamped with the same sober conscientiousness.

But Doenitz saw more, and more there was. Spurts of sudden rebellion, outbursts of temperament are in the fabric of Prien's youth. At sea as a cabin boy, he took issue with the captain over the bad food. In the labor camp he quelled, by swift action, a dangerous revolt over the dismissal of a thief. In the navy his nickname became "Little Hothead"—and nicknames are usually honestly come by.

Witness, too, an illuminating episode in the life story, and one that could hardly have been filled in by the clammy hand of a ghost writer:

On the way to the labor camp, Prien's train stopped awhile at Plauen, a pleasant town of cobbled streets and whitewashed houses. Sauntering about the streets, Prien spotted an extremely pretty girl in the front garden of a villa. On a sudden impulse, he put down his suitcase, crossed the street to a florist and bought a bunch of roses. Entering the garden of the villa, he pressed the bouquet into the surprised girl's hands, kissed her . . . and away to his train and his camp.

Years later, Prien thought he recognized the girl in a group picture shown him by a fellow naval officer. He wrote the girl, again on impulse. The fact that she had never even been to Plauen became irrelevant, and they soon were married.

So, not without inspiration, Doenitz picked Prien. For two days Prien studied the charts and made his calculations. But from the very first his will was clear. He wanted this mission for his own; he wanted the British battleship. His life at long last was in full focus. He reported back to Doenitz that he was willing and ready. His orders were to prepare his boat and wait at Kiel for final sailing instructions.

On October 8, 1939, at 1000 of a fine clear autumn morning, the U-47, Lieutenant Prien commanding, pointed her long, thin nose to seaward, course NNW.

Why was Doenitz so dead sure that Scapa Flow was vulnerable to U-boat attack? "I hold that a penetration on the surface at the turn of the tide would be possible," his statement, as quoted in Prien's log, reads. One plausible answer is now known. Doenitz had information of the most specific kind that there was a loophole in the massive network of defenses to the fleet anchorage. Scapa had an Achilles' heel.

Which brings us to a subplot, often hinted at, widely distorted. Title: The Little Watchmaker of Kirkwall. To trace the subplot to its source we must go back to 1923. Study for a moment the dilemma of a certain Alfred Wehring, a German naval officer with a fine World War I record. One of the youngest captains on the list, he had served with distinction in the Battle of Jutland. Although his name was still on the pay list, he had been idle for four years.

It so happened that in 1923 Admiral Canaris, the sinister and shadowy figure often called the father of modern German Intelligence, was almost single-handedly reconstructing, spy by spy, the German espionage system. Canaris had formed a high opinion of Alfred Wehring during the war, and now persuaded him to take up a new line of work. First off, Wehring became a salesman for a German watch firm. In the course of the next three years he visited many European countries as the distinguished representative of this well-known firm. If his diversion on these trips became, increasingly, an interest in new naval construction, it was discreetly done and caused no comment.

Wehring next turned up in Switzerland, apprenticed to a Swiss watch company. He learned his trade thoroughly and soon became an expert craftsman. In 1927 he emigrated to England, equipped with a shiny new passport thoughtfully provided by Admiral Canaris. Alfred Wehring now answered to the typically Swiss name of Albert Oertel. But some of his old love of the sea apparently persisted. For Oertel settled down at Kirkwall, in the Orkneys, not far from the British fleet base in Scapa Flow. He worked for several small jewelers, repaired watches in his spare time. He lived frugally, for he had a dream to fulfill—to open his own small store in Kirkwall, dealing in watches and gifts. The good people of the district liked Oertel and wished him well in his dream.

In due time, Oertel opened his own store and prospered modestly. Landlubber that he was, from a landlocked country, he loved the sea, and his neighbors laughed tolerantly at his obsession. He was even loath to leave his coastal town to see his relatives in Switzerland. Instead, many of them, all speaking with a marked Swiss accent, came to visit him. Some shared his enthusiasm for the Orkneys and settled there too.

In 1932 Albert Oertel became a British subject. If the post-office officials in Kirkwall had not known that Albert Oertel was a fervent family man, they might conceivably have felt some surprise at the amount of mail he received. Any possible suspicion was further disarmed by the fact that the mail invariably included some Swiss chocolate for the children of the town.

Once a month, Oertel, the family man, wrote his aged father in Switzerland. Rather technical letters, perhaps, if anyone had cared to scrutinize them, for they dealt with such matters as gun emplacements and antisubmarine installations. But then, the father was none other than Admiral Canaris, whose family had by now increased out of all proportion.

When war came, Albert Oertel was among the first to hang the Union Jack over his door. He bought war bonds with quiet pride. Less obviously, he kept a sharp eye on the naval activity in the great Flow. His fellow Swiss who had settled in the islands were particularly helpful in keeping him posted on what they, too, saw and heard. Albert Oertel learned that Kirk Sound, one of the eastern approaches to the fleet anchorage, was not yet roped off with underwater cables of high-tension steel. The three blockships positioned there were believed adequate for protection, while the work of maintaining antisubmarine nets in the other entrances went on at high priority. The British had every reason to believe that a submarine would not be able to negotiate the narrow, shallow channel with its sluicing tides and strategically placed blockships.

On the October afternoon on which Albert Oertel had marshaled all his facts, he closed his shop early and went home. From a cupboard he took a pair of earphones which belonged to an old-fashioned radio—complete with large dials and knobs—set into the cupboard itself. Albert Oertel made ready to listen to the afternoon news.

But an observer would have noticed that he was having trouble getting the right station, for his hands seemed very active indeed. In actual fact, Albert Oertel's great moment had come. His fifteen years of apprenticeship were nearly over. His short-wave sender, instrument of destiny, flashed the message: *There is a flaw in the defenses of Scapa Flow. There are capital ships lying in the anchorage.* Oertel tapped out the details with a steady hand.

For the purposes of this account, we will leave Oertel hunched over his short wave. Some say Prien picked him up off the Orkneys and took him back to Germany, but there is no official record of this in the secret log of the U-47 or elsewhere, so he bows offstage at the high point of his dubious career.

From Prien's log and his life story, it is possible to reconstruct the cruise of the U-47 in considerable detail:

The skipper alone knows their tremendous target. He is under orders not to reveal it until just before the run-in. Yet excitement runs high, nonetheless—the excitement of a war patrol. They sight a trawler soon after leaving port, and dive. Smoke just over the horizon tells them there are targets aplenty ahead. The men sense something unusual, look at their commander questioningly. But Prien maintains course and his own counsel. He is hunting far bigger game.

The weather, fine and clear when they left Kiel, worsens rapidly after nightfall. Falling barometer and rising winds carry the promise of really dirty weather ahead. Running surfaced through the dark night, the submarine plows into the whistling wind and across the white-streaked billows. For a short distance to port and starboard the lookouts in the conning tower can see white crests glowing. The pounding of the Diesels sounds very loud.

In course of time they raise the islands, at first glimpse only a darker, steadier shadow above the dark sea. Having made his landfall, Prien turns seaward again, goes to the bottom and orders his crew assembled in the bow room. It is time to tell them of the mission ahead.

"We enter Scapa Flow tomorrow." Prien wastes no words. In the light of the shadeless lamps, the faces are chalk-white, with deep shadows under the eyes. For a moment the silence is complete, except for water dripping somewhere, suddenly loud.

Prien proceeds with instructions. All except the watch to turn in for some sleep. The watch to wake the cook at 1400. Dinner for all hands at 1600—last warm food for the duration of the operation. After that there will be sandwiches and chocolate bars only. Absolutely no smoking. In the everyday details, the enormous central fact comes into focus: They are going into Scapa Flow.

All unnecessary lights will be turned off, says Prien in his calm, quiet way, for current is precious. They will lie on the bottom until after dark. No one to make any unnecessary motion, for air, too, is precious. During the operation there will be absolute quiet. No order will be given twice. Understood? The chorus of ayes is reassuring to the skipper, somewhat less confident than he appears.

The long day wears itself away. Prien, unable to sleep, prowls the boat. In the officers' mess he finds Spahr, his tall navigator, studying his charts of Scapa and its seven entrances. Spahr is apologetic. "Sir, I had to see the charts once more before sleeping." Heavy silence. "Sir, do you really believe we will get in there?"

"Well, Spahr," Prien answers, "am I a prophet?"

"And if it turns out otherwise, sir?"

"Then we just had bad luck, Spahr."

By seven in the evening all is ready, the last warm meal eaten and the final phase ahead. Three men go through the boat, setting explosive charges to blast her to high heaven in case of capture. Curt orders crackle out, "Diving stations! Leave ground!" The submarine drifts upward from her daytime lair. Cautiously, with infinite care, the periscope is raised. Prien sweeps the whole horizon. Something bothers him. Although night has fallen, it is still curiously light, with a lightness not from searchlights or the moon. The overcast to the northward seems fluorescent.

The answer hits Prien like a blow. Aurora borealis! No one, it would seem, had thought of that contingency when the night of a thin new moon was selected for the operation. The twilight grows stronger as the northern lights flame like huge pale fires behind the drifting clouds. Should he go to cover again and wait for another, darker night? Do the northern lights recur two nights running? Prien is shaken. So are his two navigation officers and boatswain's mate, with him in the conning tower. But not for very long.

"Well, gentlemen, what do you think?" asks Prien.

"Good shooting light, sir."

"It'll be a fine show tonight, captain."

Prien has his answer. The spirits of the men are at their peak. Another day at the bottom will make them logy and dispirited. He steers for Holm Sound, eastern approach to Scapa Flow. Their course is now due west. The hills come closer against the light sky. Thanks to the diligence of Albert Oertel, sometime naval officer, Prien knows where the three blockships are tethered and how the cables between them are strung. The blockships are in Kirk Sound, a narrow bottleneck at the top of Holm Sound. Kirk Sound, in turn, on its western side, widens into the broad expanses of the Flow itself.

Now is the time for all Prien's skill. The tide is swirling and eddying through the narrow gut, the steel cables are waiting to enmesh him like a fly in aspic, the blockships loom. The lamp of a bicycle, pedaling down a lane along the cliffs, momentarily catches him in its swinging arc, reminding him of his helplessness in case of discovery.

Sickeningly, shudderingly, U-47 goes aground between two of the blockships. Then her stern chafes against a mooring cable of the northern blockship. (Stop port engine. Starboard slow ahead. Rudder hard to port.) The bad moment has passed now. She floats free and the cable releases its clutch. The wide reaches of Scapa Flow stretch before him.

"We are through." He passes the word down the hatch. Prien has done what no mariner on a warlike mission has ever done before. Now for the kill.

Although a north wind has scattered the overcast, the northern lights are still throbbing right up to the zenith of the sky. "It is disgustingly light," Prien notes in his log, just after clearing the blockships. "The whole sky is lit up." Yet it is a night for great deeds, with mystery and magic abroad.

First Prien, peering hungrily ahead, spots a few lights close to the water line. They are only tankers sleeping at anchor. Then, quite close to the shore, he makes out the powerful silhouette of a battleship, and behind her a second vast superstructure. They are as familiar to him as a well-loved form and face—a battleship of the *Royal Oak* class, and, secondly, the individual bow turret and bridge of the *Repulse*. He decides on the long shot for the bow of the *Repulse* first. Nearer, nearer his submarine creeps. No alarm clangs out, no sound is heard but the hiss of air pressure, the click of a tube lever, terrifyingly loud in the deep silence of the anchorage.

Los! The boat shudders slightly as the torpedo leaves its tube. Then the waiting again. Five seconds . . . ten . . . fifteen. Prien watches the steel fortress for what seems an eternity. Abruptly the bow of the battleship disappears in a leaping column of water. Almost simultaneously, the detonation of the war head is heard. No time to waste now. Prien jockeys for his sure target, the closer ship.

Next tube ready. Fire!

The third torpedo completes his first salvo. He slips eastward down the Flow again to avoid the expected countermeasures. When none develop, he reloads, maneuvers into firing position again and lets fly at the damaged dreadnought with three more torpedoes. Here is Prien's own description, perhaps somewhat colored by time and excitement, of what he saw as his second salvo crashed into the steel flank of the battleship:

"Again the recoil as the torpedo is launched. Again Spahr's voice begins quietly to count, 'Five . . . ten . . .'

"Suddenly something happens which nobody who saw it will ever forget. Yonder, a curtain of water rushes upward. It is as if the sea had suddenly risen. Detonations sound in rapid succession like the drumfire of battle. They merge into a single deafening crash. Jets of fire spurt up, blue, yellow, red. Huge pieces of the mast, the bridge, the funnels hurtle through the air. We must have scored a direct hit on one of the ammunition lockers."

Prien calls down the hatch that the kill has been made. A moment of silence, then a deep, guttural cry of triumph from the men below, easing the tension of the endless hours.

The bay goes wild. Searchlights cartwheel across the sky, others begin to probe the surface of the water as sub-chasers and torpedo boats swing into action. Prien takes a last look at his night's work. The fires are dying, but the *Royal Oak* is obviously in her death agony. Any minute the waters will close over the listing, twisted hull. It is high time to be off. The current is dead against him now. He is so near to the land that he notices a car parked ashore, headlights blazing. The car suddenly careens away at high speed.

No time for secrecy, even if Prien could maneuver, submerged, through the narrow channel. Speed alone can save him now. Out of the myriad lights in the bay, one seems to be moving directly for them. Prien recognized with alarm the masthead light of a destroyer.

Full speed ahead!

The mountains close in as they near Kirk Sound again. The luck of the daring is with them. The destroyer turns away on a false scent. Her depth charges, when they come, are mercifully distant. Shaking in every joint as she bucks the current, the U-47—engines going full ahead to hold her on her course—slips out through the blockships again. This time Prien chooses to go between the southernmost hulk and a breakwater. He does so, with inches to spare.

At 0058 he had fired his first shot. At 0122 he finished firing. By 0215 he is in open water again.

"To all hands," goes Prien's last command of the night as the depth charges die away and the headlands fade. "One battleship sunk, one battleship torpedoed."

Such was Gunther Prien's night of triumph.

Niña II

BY ROBERT MARX,
AS TOLD TO WILLIAM R. SHELTON

It has been almost five centuries since Christopher Columbus set forth to discover a new world. The trip from the Canary Islands that took Columbus 36 days takes less than a week on a modern luxury liner, less than half a day on a jet. But man still needs to explore the unknown—the mysteries not only of the future, but of the half-forgotten past. And so it was that nine men set out in the summer of 1962 on one of the strangest adventures of modern times. They were determined to conquer the Atlantic exactly as Columbus had 470 years before.

The ship they sailed in was scarcely bigger than a suburban businessman's weekend yacht. The 42-foot replica of the Niña *had no motor, no radio, no modern lifesaving equipment. Its inexperienced crew encountered hardships that might have made Columbus himself turn back. But after a voyage more than twice as long as that of her famous namesake, the* Niña II *sailed into San Salvador.*

Robert Marx, the only American member of the crew, was the vessel's pilot-navigator. The 29-year-old native of Pittsburgh was no stranger to adventure. While a U.S. Marine at Camp Lejeune, North Carolina, he spent his spare time diving in the treacherous waters off Cape Hatteras until he located the long-lost hulk of the Civil War ship Monitor. *Later, as an underwater archaeologist, he spent years on Cozumel Island off Mexico's Yucatan Peninsula, recovering thousands of antiquities from one of the most important Spanish wrecks ever discovered.*

But all this was only a prelude to his epic adventure aboard
Niña II. *In duplicating the voyage of 1492, Marx and his eight*
companions re-created something more important: the courage
and determination that enabled Columbus to reach a new
continent.

WHAT was it like to sail across the Atlantic in one of Columbus'
tiny ships? I don't know. But I do know that a similar expedition today is like this:

It's the sight of a black sky at noon and the sound of the wind
rising and the knowledge that only a thin sheath of leaky
wooden beams keeps you afloat over the surface of death. It's
the sickening feeling as *Niña* suddenly heels over more than 60
degrees, a wall of water gushes over the side, and you fight to
cut down the sails before the gale snaps the mainmast like a
match.

It's the taste of brackish water, in smaller and smaller rations
until there's no water at all, the taste of food that gets so rotten
that you finally eat it in the dark so you don't have to look at it.
It's the taste of freshly caught shark—harpooned, roped and
writhing, and then battered to death on the deck—when you
know that scores of other sharks are on the other side of those
leaky beams, waiting for you.

It's not all a nightmare, of course. It's also the clean joy of a
ship surging forward under sail, and the sound of your crew-
mates singing, and the sense that you're close to a kind of truth
you can't find on land.

In my own case, I'd been ashore in Spain for a number of
months, and I was getting restless for adventure. Not just any
adventure. It was the adventures of the Spanish explorers that
had long fascinated me. I'd read about them and I wanted to
know more about what those voyages were really like.

I had gone to Spain in hopes of building a replica of a
Spanish galleon and sailing it to the New World. Word about
the project must have spread, for I got a telephone call one day
from a young naval lieutenant, Carlos Etayo Elizondo. He had
taken a leave of absence to sail across the Atlantic in his own
replica of *Niña* and asked whether I'd be interested in joining
him. By the time that telephone call ended I had abandoned my
own project.

When I first met Carlos in late June he was dressed in a slightly soiled white Navy uniform and appeared to have a rather casual air, but his dark eyes blazed with a contagious obsession to sail *Niña II* to America. Since 1957, the 41-year-old Carlos told me, he had devoted himself almost exclusively to the reconstruction of *Niña*. After he received a modest inheritance he selected a shipyard in Pasajes, the seaport of San Sebastián, and the work began. The keel of *Niña II* was laid in January of 1962. The 42-foot ship was built of oak and pine from the Pyrenees, just as Columbus' ships were, and held together with wooden pegs and wrought-iron spikes, all driven in by hand. Carlos invested every cent he had to make her authentic—more than $20,000. On June 5 the workmen had ceremoniously launched the bare hull, and now they were building her masts and poop cabin.

"Your galleon is still in your head," Carlos said to me, "but my caravel is in the water. You are welcome to join forces with me." He offered me the job of pilot-navigator, and I accepted without hesitation. I even went a step further.

"Why not go exactly the way Columbus did," I asked Carlos, "eat the same chow, wear the same clothing, use the same arms and navigate by the same methods?"

He said he had considered this but didn't believe it possible. He thought no seaman would sign on with us under such handicaps. We argued about it all night, and he finally agreed to give it a try. My first job was to assemble costumes, cannon, swords and other authentic 15th-century gear for our voyage.

Before setting sail, however, I had another assignment, unlike anything that Columbus' lieutenants faced. Carlos had a suspicion that Americans weren't very brave, and he wanted to be sure of me. He wanted me to participate in the famous festival of the running of the bulls at Pamplona. All I had to do was to get out in front of the bulls in the sealed-off streets and race them to the ring. Without quite knowing what I was in for, I agreed. When the starting gun sounded and hundreds of youths began a stampede toward the ring, Carlos just stood still, and I had to stand with him. Carlos had participated in nearly every run since he was a child, and as the bulls approached he stood there as though he were calmly greeting friends. My heart nearly stopped as the bulls thundered closer. Finally, as the bulls roared down on us, Carlos yelled "Now!" and we took off. I leaped for a window grille. It collapsed in my hands, and I fell back against the hindquarters of one bull. Then there were six more real daddies charging down on me. I ran at Olympic speed for about a mile until I finally scrambled over an eight-foot gate with the six bulls snorting at my heels. Carlos solemnly told me that he thought I had passed the test.

So I was good enough for *Niña*. And when I finally got my first glimpse of her in Pasajes, she looked to me like the eighth wonder of the world. Though far from complete, she had a dignity about her that made her just beautiful.

One of the final tasks of preparation was to find the right crew. What we most needed were authentic seamen, not adventurers. We were swamped with applications, even from females. One of the first authentic types we sighed up was José Valencia Salsamendi, a swarthy, sturdy man of 38 who came from a long line of seafarers. After spending years as a commercial fisherman all over the world he had finally given up the sea in order to spend more time with his wife, but the lure of *Niña II* had been too great. Another authentic type was Nicolás Bedoya Castillo, a white-haired man of 69 with a face like cordovan leather. He suffered from rheumatism, but he had the wisdom of a lifetime at sea in the Spanish navy.

Some of the others were not quite so authentic, but they were equally eager to join. There was Antonio Aguirre Oronoz. He was 42, a harmonica player, a fisherman, a cook, a former professional boxer, strong as an ox. Then there were two carpenters who had helped build *Niña*. Neither of them had ever been to sea before.

Finally, on July 28, under the eyes of a curious crowd, we cast our moorings and set out into the sheltered bay to try our hands at the oars. It was a great beginning. Our oars were so short that they barely reached the water. None of us was used to rowing or keeping a beat. Our oars banged against each other like swords in battle. And the incoming currents kept pushing us against the mudbanks. After a few hours our hands were raw and blistered, and we had barely moved *Niña* 300 yards. As we struggled back to the dock the spectators laughed and jeered at us. "And in this crate which we can't get out of port," José said to me, "we are going to try to cross the Atlantic?"

Crazy as it seemed, that was just what we were going to do. Three days later with favorable winds, we hoisted our lateen sail and prepared to try our beautiful ship against the fierce Atlantic. It was almost a disaster. In defiance of every law of sailing as we knew it, our *Niña* couldn't go 20 feet in a straight line. As we headed her out to sea, she insisted on drifting toward an ominous row of lava rocks. "To the oars!" cried Carlos. And with our oars, which barely skimmed the water, we had to row at double time for more than an hour before we brought her back to safety.

Both of our trusty carpenters were seasick, and one of them got so frantic that he fell into the hold and broke three ribs.

Did Columbus have problems like this? Perhaps. We retreated to port in nearby Guetaria to decide what should be done. The mizzenmast had to be reset and the rudder rebuilt bigger. And we needed two new crewmen to replace our two seasick carpenters, who just faded away once they got ashore. On August 12 we held our second sea trials. The extensive alterations had performed a miracle. *Niña II* held a reasonable course with both the square mainsail and lateen rig. We were the proudest men in Spain that night.

There were a few other last-minute preparations, such as getting more crewmen. At Guetaria we signed aboard a handsome Frenchman, Michel Vialars, a 29-year-old former army officer who was, fortunately for us, a trained veterinarian. Carlos also signed a priest, the Reverend Antonio Sagaseta, 46, of Pamplona. Columbus had no priest aboard, but our *padre* had been an artillery officer and an engineer. The priest, in turn, brought aboard an ancient cat, which I named Chirche. Chirche, perhaps wisely, developed an immediate antipathy to *Niña*. She leaped into the water and swam ashore. Some kids tossed her back to us. For nearly an hour Chirche struggled to reach dry land, even crossing on the lines, but the kids kept tossing her back. Finally she gave up in exhaustion and settled mournfully down on deck.

Our final preparations concerned food. We were determined to leave Guetaria with exactly the same provisions that Columbus had carried: biscuit, flour, lard, water, wine, vinegar, brandy, olive oil, almonds, raisins, cheese, sugar, salt, chick-peas, rice, garlic, onions, beans and sardines. Quite a menu. All the crewman except Carlos and me were heavy smokers, but when we tried to talk the crew into doing without tobacco, on the grounds that tobacco was unknown in Columbus' time, we learned that this was too much to ask. We compromised by asking them to light their smokes with the ancient flints I had obtained in Madrid. I know it sounds crazy, but it was that kind of trip.

On August 23 a strong and favorable northwest wind, predicted to last 10 days, began off Spain's western coast. Since our official voyage began out of Palos, where Columbus had departed from Spain's southern coast, we consented to a two-day tow on the 24th to take us to the favorable winds. We estimated making the 950-mile leg to Palos in six days. That first night in heavy seas was a nightmare. Our caravel wandered behind our towboat like a crazed whale. Often we got so far sideways that we nearly capsized. Leathery old Bedoya exclaimed several times that all was lost. Our tiny lantern on the mast kept going out, and once at three A.M. we came within a few feet of being run down by a freighter. The tiller pulled and tugged at us with such massive force that we were all soon covered with bumps and bruises. One minute at the helm was like five minutes on a bucking bronc. After three days' struggle with *Niña* I had slept less than three hours and Carlos even less. None of us had time for a hot meal.

By then we were supposed to reach the favorable winds. We dropped our tow and were on our own. But the wind unaccountably died on us, and we wallowed in lifeless seas. After six days we felt as if we had lived at sea for months. Our water, stored in uncleaned old wine kegs, was almost completely spoiled; our bread looked as though it had turned to penicillin; we were covered with cat fleas; our cabin was damp and filthy.

On September 11 we finally reached Palos—tossed, buffeted, frightened, undernourished—and we hadn't even started. But we were following in Columbus' course, and Columbus had spent many weeks here as guest of the Franciscan friars at La Rábida Monastery. Could we do less? It seemed only reasonable that we should have dinner at the monastery, lunch with the governor and parties and celebrations without end. We met many descendants of the men who had sailed with Columbus, and they regarded us as national heroes. We got our water from the same well that Columbus had used, heard Mass in the same church and received our food largely from the descendants of Columbus' crew. We also picked up two new seamen. One was Manuel Darnaude Rojas-Marcos, whom we called Manolo, a 33-year-old soccer and spear-fishing buff. The other was José Robles, a comical man of 39 whom we called Pepe ("Joe"), since we already had another José aboard. He joined us with only the clothes on his back and not a cent in his pocket. We lost another passenger—Chirche, who had finally made her way back to dry land.

At sunrise on the 19th of September we started down the Río Tinto, passing La Rábida Monastery where the friars sang Gregorian chants. As we crossed the bar of the river, escorted by scores of yachts and fishing boats, buzzed by Spanish air-force planes, we knew we had finally begun our task of re-creating history. Our next stop—Columbus' next stop—was the Canary Islands, 1,000 miles away.

Our troubles began again almost immediately. For three days we had to fight a wind that threatened to blow us into the Mediterranean. Then the winds died on us, and we sailed with all canvas spread. Around noon of our sixth day out we were all sitting on the quarterdeck eating our main meal of rice and beans and watching a school of porpoises playing around us. Suddenly the hot wind hit us, one of those sudden gusts that sweep off the North African desert. Our authentic wooden spoons and platters spilled all over the deck as *Niña* began heeling over to starboard, and we scrambled to hang onto masts and rigging. We could feel the wind rise by the minute. It was 35 knots, 45, then 60, with gusts of hot air raging even stronger. It all happened so quickly that we had no time to take in sail. The wind tugged and heaved at *Niña* until the ship heeled over almost on its side. Some of us hanging onto the port railing could see her keel knifing up out of the foaming water. Michel grabbed an ax to cut the mainmast, but I held him back. We didn't have to disable the ship; we just had to get the sails down.

The sky darkened ominously, and about every tenth wave washed completely over us. José, our best seaman, whom we sometimes called "the monkey," scrambled out over the churning seas on the yard, adding his weight to our efforts. The rest of us grabbed knives and slashed the sheets that held in the mizzensail. The loose lines now flailed at us like whips. Then the mainsail suddenly ripped, spilling the air and taking some of the pressure off *Niña*. With the mainsail in tatters we quickly lowered it.

But our troubles were far from over. The fierce storm raged on for more than 30 hours. Despite our steadying storm sail and sea anchor *Niña*'s old symptoms began reappearing, and she kept turning broadside to the waves, tossing like a cork. The cabin filled with two feet of water, and everything was a shambles. A four-gallon ceramic jug of olive oil had broken, and the sides and roof of the cabin were as slick as grease.

And now we discovered another major trouble. *Niña*, built with authentic timber from the Pyrenees and held together with hand-carved wooden pegs and handwrought iron spikes, leaked like an old washtub. For hours, we labored at the ship's two crude hand pumps until our bilge water again reached a safe level.

When the seas finally abated we went down to inspect the hold where our provisions were stored. The sight sickened us. Everything seemed destroyed. Jugs containing water, wine, vinegar and brandy were broken. Ceramic containers for rice, flour and beans were shattered. Altogether the storm cost us three-quarters of our water and half our food. As we went about repairing our sails we started the strict rationing that we maintained all the way to the Canaries. Perhaps we had learned a lesson: The sea can be most dangerous when she appears the most benign.

Another casualty of the storm was symbolic—the destruction of the 15th-century hourglasses we used for navigation timing, as Columbus did. I now had to dig down in the damp hold for my automatic pocket watch. We knew we were lost that night as we spotted a light from Africa when we thought we were 200 miles from the coast. My navigation instruments were replicas of the 15th-century quadrants and astrolabes, while Carlos used a sextant. Often my positioning would match that of the sextant or come within one degree (60) miles of the sextant's position. My pocket watch was useful in timing sunrises and sunsets, which helped us estimate longitude.

As we limped along toward what we thought were the

Canaries we gradually became somewhat more comfortable. Our bodies became better conditioned to the sea life, and the weather was warmer. Michel and I occasionally took baths in the sea in an effort to eliminate some of the fragrance of the cramped cabin. On the days we did our washing *Niña* looked like a clothesline on a blue Monday in Brooklyn. Since our bread baked in Palos had gone bad, I learned how to make a strange kind of *tortilla* out of unsifted flour, olive oil and sea water. They looked like mud cakes, but they tasted all right. For breakfast, and again at dinner, we usually had two *tortillas*, a sliver of raw onion and a thin slice of ham or cheese. Lunch was rice and beans or rice and lentils.

On the third of October we finally reached the Canary Islands, and we surprised everyone by entering Las Palmas instead of Gomera, as Columbus had done. I discovered then that my watch was five minutes slow and our anticipated Canary landfall was 70 miles off. As the pilot boat came out for us we put on fresh clothes and combed our long hair and beards. After all our hardships we had still scarcely begun our voyage. But again we underwent the sudden transformation from smelly, laboring seamen into celebrities. Thousands met us at the dock, including bevies of lovely European girls in bikinis. I think it is historically accurate to say Columbus never saw anything like this.

Our first treat was a hot bath ashore, then a 12-course meal in a fine restaurant. Nothing seemed too good for the crew of *Niña*, installed in the palatial Hotel Metropole. For some of our authentic crew this was the first luxury they had ever known, and we moved in like nine ragpickers among all the gorgeous gowns and dinner jackets.

After this round of festivities Father Sagaseta said Mass for us in the same church where Columbus is believed to have heard Mass before his ocean crossing. Then we went to *Niña* to prepare her for sailing. I had located a young nanny goat which we named Pinzona, after a beautiful girl we had all met in Palos. We also took aboard a winsome kitten. Antonio the cook named her Linda, which means "pretty" in spanish. From the beginning Linda's soft eyes and playful ways made her the pride of the crew. We loved her. She had fleas, too, but her beauty more than compensated for her parasites.

After dramatically firing our falconette (a small cannon) we tried to row out of the harbor authentically. But the wind was too much for us, and we embarrassedly accepted a tow. When our tow finally cast off, I think we were all relieved to be at sea again after our revelries ashore. Now we finally began our mission. Now we were really setting out on Columbus' course to the New World. We did not realize it then, but during the weeks ahead we would face more peril even than Columbus on his voyage.

The first problem was food and water. We began with provisions that we estimated were good for roughly 50 days, but our estimates were partly wishful thinking. I suspected that most of the old water kegs we had taken on at Las Palmas were already leaking, and our fresh fruit was sure to rot quickly in the damp hold. To confirm my suspicions, a working party went below at the end of the first week and discovered that two faulty water barrels out of five had already leaked dry. That meant that we were starting with more than 40 percent of our water gone. Carlos ordered immediate rationing and asked that our 200 casks of wine be held in reserve, but our crew, long accustomed to wine, continued to drink it like rain water. On top of all this, we had sailed only 60 miles out of Las Palmas when we found that *Niña* was leaking again. To make it worse, one of our pumps had suction trouble.

Our original plan was to sail due west, never dropping below the 24th Parallel of latitude. But for 14 days the prevailing northeasterly trades never materialized. Instead we had steady westerly winds and calms, combined with southbound currents. I took our position whenever the weather permitted, and I could see we were being pushed steadily southward, even farther from San Salvador than when we began.

But our main worry right from the beginning was our dwindling supply of food and water. Our fruit went quickly. After just five days at sea more than half our supply of melons, bananas, oranges and tomatoes had rotted so badly that we had to throw them over the side. Carlos even started drinking tiny amounts of sea water to test one possible survival measure. Michel, anticipating the worst, began to build plankton nets so that we could scoop up the tiny marine organisms and eat them. Old Bedoya revealed his own anxiety when he reminded me that we shouldn't throw the goatskin away when the time came to kill and eat the goat because we might eventually need to eat the skin.

Such remarks made me wonder about Columbus and us. Which is worse—to know as we did that you have 3,000 miles to go and not enough food to get there, or to think that you have plenty of food and not know where you're going? It's a sort of philosophical question about the means and the end. Would you rather have an end without the means or the means without the end? Don't try to figure out the answer. There isn't any. The sea makes philosophers out of the simplest men, or vice versa.

And then there were other problems that may not have bothered Columbus. It is hard, for example, for a 20th-century man to get rid of the idea that there ought to be some kind of sanitation, or whatever you want to call it. Sanitary facilities aboard our tiny craft consisted mainly of the briny sea. While hanging over the side one day, one of our crewmen looked down into the gaping jaws of a shark just inches below him. This understandably began a shark scare aboard *Niña*. It threatened to curtail the refreshing sea baths that Michel, I and a few others took during calms. This was a minor tragedy, for our tiny cabin smelled far worse than low tide on a hot day. Old Bedoya, for one, had not taken a bath or changed his clothes for months. I could only entice the men into the water after diving beneath the hull myself to prove there were no sharks within range. It was a risk, but I felt it was worth it.

Fishing at first was deplorable. Once we saw some baby whales, and we often saw porpoise, sharks and flying fish, but we couldn't get anything aboard. On the ninth day out Antonio did catch a three-pound yellowtail which had two squid in its stomach, plus three smaller yellowtails. Then on our 12th day out the *padre* suddenly shouted that we had a big one. We had hooked a 10-foot tiger shark, and it was full of fight. It was sheer mass confusion as Bedoya tried to lasso its tail, Antonio tried to harpoon it and Carlos tried to ax it. The goat bleated in terror, and Linda meowed loudly from the rigging. Even after we got the shark aboard, it thrashed about wildly. It was a weird sight to see five or six men with axes, 15th-century spears, harpoons and even sledgehammers, trying to subdue the monster. The shark snapped at the men's legs. Everyone leaped madly about the deck. Then little Linda jumped right into the thick of it, expecting a meal, even balancing herself on the shark's head while it was gnashing away at everything in sight. That night we polished off a bottle of rum, played the harmonica and then couldn't sleep because of all the excitement.

Our bit of luck with fresh meat came none too soon. The next day we discovered that our remaining salt meat was full of worms. We ate our shark meat with sea-water tortillas again, since our flour was already moldy and turning all colors of the rainbow. Several of us were now quenching our growing thirst by alternating small amounts of salt water with Spanish red wine. By the fourteenth day our remaining water was undrinkable. It had turned a horrible shade of brown; it was full of living creatures and smelled worse than gall.

This was all peaceful enough—a little dull and a little disgusting, but peaceful. Yet the primal force of the Atlantic Ocean, Columbus' Atlantic, was never far from us. Sixteen days southward bound from the Canaries, the first really big storm struck just at sunset. It bent the mainmast out of its socket. *Niña* heeled far to port and stayed that way, taking on water with every wave. It was my turn to man the tiller, and this was a tug of war between a man and the powerful waves battering the rudder at the other end of a fragile length of timber. After one hour at the helm I couldn't take it any more, and I collapsed exhausted on the floor. I dreamed that I was tied in the center of a tug-of-war rope with hundreds of people pulling at it from both ends. I dreamed that I had to resist desperately in both directions to keep from being pulled to pieces. Just as I was reviving, *Niña* suddenly heeled violently over to one side and a whole bookshelf full of navigation manuals came crashing down on my head.

By the following morning the storm had abated slightly, but *Niña's* rudder was no longer functioning, and we were wallowing sickeningly in every swell. Pepe went down to inspect the hold and casually reported, "We are leaking below."

That wasn't all. Both our bilge pumps were useless. Constant wear had destroyed the suction. We had to start bailing. We formed a human chain leading up from the hold and passed up buckets and wooden bowls to keep the ship from sinking. And so it went for two days. The constant bailing was sapping our strength and making our thirst and hunger nearly unbearable. It was an endurance contest in which the stakes were our lives.

Finally I decided to go over the side myself and try to patch the hull with crude caulking and wood plugs, as they had to do on the old Spanish galleons. I found the main hole, where a wooden peg had worked loose well below the water line. While Antonio and Bedoya were shaping a new plug for the hole I remembered the story about the Dutch boy and the dike. Like an idiot I put my thumb in the hole, gulping air occasionally as the ship rolled and my head came above water. Suddenly I was pulled deep under water. Then I realized I couldn't get my thumb out. I grabbed my knife. For an instant I thought I might have to cut off my thumb. But *Niña* rolled in time for me to breathe again. Quickly I enlarged the hole with my knife. I finally extricated my swollen thumb and managed to insert a new wooden plug.

But the storm had blown us southward, the wrong direction. And when the winds finally died we realized we were far off course and far behind a reasonably safe schedule, considering our water and food shortages. At first Carlos and I kept the precise record of our progress a secret from the men, as Columbus had done. But finally, as our rations dwindled, we felt we had to tell them. On the seventeenth day out, the point at which Columbus was already over half the distance to San Salvador, we were still wallowing along within insect range of the African coast. That night on deck we held a solemn ritual. First we opened a bottle of brandy, more in sadness than celebration. We all knew the serious implication of the decision we were about to make.

Every one of us faced the possibility of death, and everyone had a right to help decide our course. Should we head for the nearest land for more food and water or should we continue our struggle to make San Salvador? Each man aboard was given a piece of wood of about the same size. If he wanted to vote for San Salvador he was to throw the wood in the sea. If he wanted to vote to proceed to the nearest land he was to place the wood in the goat's empty water dish. It was dark, and each man could vote in secret. I thought I heard a faint splash, then another and another. I was the last to vote, and I found the goat's water dish empty, just as I expected. Unanimously we had voted to continue in Columbus' path. It was San Salvador or nothing, come what might.

Whether this was a vote of confidence or insanity, the northeasterly winds soon picked up and began driving us, for a change, toward San Salvador. In one day we actually went 117 miles, 80 in another, but our average was more like 45. Our decision certainly had done something for our morale. From that point on we set to work in a far more orderly way. Each favorable morning our work day began at 10 as we dried our straw-and-maize mattresses, straightened up the cabin and cleaned up after Linda and Pinzona. We managed to get the starboard pump repaired by sealing its cracks with some pitch, and every morning we performed the ritual of pumping. Life settled into the routine of the sea.

Food was still our principal concern since our rations were now down to the starvation level. To supplement the meager diet we devoted whole days to catching fish. We laboriously converted our 15th-century spears and lances into harpoons, and we struggled hour after hour to spear pilot fish or dolphin. I even tried to harpoon a porpoise, though I had often told the rest of the crew that a porpoise is a true friend of man at sea and shouldn't be killed under any circumstances. I learned then and there that a man with a real empty stomach quickly changes his principles—or forgets them.

Finally we tried eating what we thought was plankton. The result was disastrous. We scooped in our fine mesh dragnets and found only a gelatinous blob in the bottom. Michel, José and I each gingerly took a tiny portion, making faces at the taste but trying to pretend it tasted like caviar. After a few moments José said his tongue was on fire. Michel complained of a sting and rushed to the stern and vomited. Then I too felt it—a sensation like the hottest of Mexican peppers on tongue and gullet. What we had scooped up was not plankton but hundreds of stinging baby jellyfish.

The animals had troubles too. We wondered if Linda had noticed that our dwindling supply of shark meat was tasting stronger each morning. I certainly noticed it. And poor Pinzona was getting more hungry stares every day. She was none too popular these days, for she'd eaten just about everything within reach—including most of the caulking in our skiff. We still loved her dearly, but the day would soon come when our hunger would overcome our love.

Before that day, however, Pinzona had to ride out the worst storm of all. It began on our 23rd day out when we were about 300 miles from Africa. The first storm warnings came at twilight. Lightning snapped on the horizon, and the seas began rising rapidly. So did the easterly wind. Within a few minutes we were plowing along at the unheard-of speed of seven knots, then eight or nine.

This was a storm out of Joseph Conrad. The sound of the wind through our rigging was a whine of fury. The gale whipped the spume of the waves in our faces and bent our mainmast like an archer's bow. *Niña* plunged up out of the water like a rearing horse, then nosed down so low that we couldn't steer. In the darkness we heard Manolo scream that he couldn't hold the tiller. We struggled to get the sails in, but we couldn't handle them. We even tried attacking them with our spears, but the wind finally did our work for us. It tore the bonnet sail to tatters, and in two hours we got the canvas to the deck.

That night seemed endless, but the next morning was worse. By nine o'clock the sky was darker than a gravedigger's foot. The rain pelted us like slivers of ice, and *Niña* plunged through the mountainous seas with the stability of a castaway cork. Poor Pinzona was whinnying in terror.

When I finally got below I found that Bedoya had a bad gash on his right hand and Antonio was feverish. The rest of us looked like zombies, and our ship seemed to be coming apart. The pressure on the mast had ripped open the seams of our top deck, and the rain poured in through the great cracks. But we were able to catch very little of it for drinking. During that second day every loose thing aboard washed over the side, including one of the pump handles. The other pump was useless. At the height of the storm we had to form bucket brigades and bail for our lives. No one said a word; we were desperate, scared men fighting for survival.

On one of my watches during this second day the tiller had suddenly whipped both my wrists painfully against the bulkhead. I knew our great wooden rudder was broken, and without it we were at the mercy of the ocean. For a full day we tossed helplessly as each towering wave danced before our eyes like a waterspout. Seas broke over us from all quarters. The only way to move safely on deck was to crawl.

In spite of the danger of working in the storm, we had to fix that rudder before the seas pounded us to pieces. On the storm's third day we cut two of our rowing benches in half and made a crude sling. Then Carlos lowered me over the side with a supply of nails and line.

That was the most desperate and the most frustrating piece of carpentry I've ever tried. The rudder was split but still hanging together. It had to be firmly nailed. But as I tried to pound in the first nail the ship heaved, and I was under water. Then *Niña* pitched and the nail was out of my reach. As the stern came plunging down, I took a swing at it. Not once in 30 swings could I hit the nail squarely. A few glancing blows bent it. And I knew that just below me in the surging foam were sharks. All I could do was ignore them. It took two hours to pound in the first nail. It took 12 hours to drill three large holes through six inches of wood. When I finished the job on the fifth day I was so weak I had to be brought aboard with block and tackle. By then the storm was all but over, with the wind dying and the waves softening. It required a full 12 hours' rest before any of us could find the strength to put up the sails.

But our troubles were far from over. Just as we were getting peacefully under way again another storm approached. Scarcely a week after the hurricane ended we saw the same dreaded signals in the sky. And when that storm died another one came. This was the hurricane season—a full month after we'd expected to reach San Salvador. We scarcely kept track of when one storm ended and the next began. Our life became one long struggle, fighting with the tiller, fighting with the sails, and always bailing. To make the fight for survival worse, the winds and currents often worked against us, pushing us farther from our goal.

Hot meals were a rarity. Hunger was with us constantly. We all lost so much weight that our trousers threatened to fall off. Now we had to face a small personal tragedy. It was finally coming time for Pinzona to meet her fate.

Each day we eyed her hungrily and vowed to eat her on the morrow, but the next day we could always find a dozen reasons for postponing the slaughter. But Pinzona was growing thin. Her alfalfa and maize were all gone, and she seemed to survive only on salt water, wood and rope. One day Pepe milked her for the last time and gave the milk to Linda. We gave Pinzona a drink of fresh water, like a condemned man's last meal. Then José hit her over the head with a hammer, and Michel slit her throat. Nothing was wasted. The blood was fried with onions and ham fat, and the intestines were boiled for soup. We had to do it, but we hated our deed. So did Linda the cat. She seemed uncommonly sad for the next few days.

The rest of our food was a weird mixture of scraps from our dwindling stores and anything we could catch. We broke out a bottle of warm, foamy champagne when José harpooned a dolphin. Some of us tried to remove all the worms from our remaining raisins, figs and prunes and put the hulks on deck to dry. We discovered that rotten figs cooked with straight rum are divine. But we had to watch our alcohol consumption carefully, because we were all so tense and exhausted that an argument could start in a flash—and often did. Carlos ordered no politics discussed, and we rationed the wine to five *botas,* or goatskins, per day.

Late in November, on our 48th day at sea, yet another storm took us completely by surprise and almost wrecked us. It was a squall that came out of nowhere, and its first mighty breath ripped out one of the bits which braced the mast. This lethal bit, with a vicious spike attached, flailed wildly about at the end of its line, threatening us all. José, our best man in a pinch, knew our mast and sails would be lost in a moment unless we regained the needed support. As we shouted warnings he went after it like a *banderillero* duelling with a fighting bull. Time after time he had to duck for his life as the ugly spike snapped by him. Finally he caught it, nearly breaking his hand, and Carlos and I made the line fast.

And then we caught sight of the end. As the storm subsided we spotted our first floating Sargasso weed. It was just a dollar-sized chunk, but we knew we were at last approaching the great masses of floating weed which extend for several hundred miles near the Caribbean. Within a few hours we spotted patches of the dead-brown seaweed as large as a coffee table, and we mixed up a Sargasso-weed salad with vinegar and olive oil.

The Sargasso Sea also has its sinister side, its deadly calms. The winds which we had come to hate and fear now died away. Our tattered sails hung limp, and we scarcely moved, resting, like the Ancient Mariner's vessel, "a painted ship upon a painted ocean." To take our minds off our hunger and thirst I read from the *padre*'s New Testament while the other crewmen practiced English. Occasionally we caught a triggerfish. We also caught a thin, silvery-blue fish that Michel said was a very rare species. It was about 18 inches long and had the razor teeth of a barracuda. He wanted to save it for a museum. But hungry men have no more interest in scientific specimens than they have love for a pet goat. We ate every scrap of the fish while Michel glared at us as though we were eating a newborn baby.

On the morning of November 30, on our 52nd day out of Las Palmas, there were signs that the calm was ending—but that worse lay ahead. We knew we were in the hurricane "slot," and we could sense trouble. There were fast-running winds aloft, a drop in atmospheric pressure that you could feel in your head, and fish wildly jumping about. In midafternoon, as we were sweating in the hot, humid air, Bedoya suddenly shouted, *"Avión en vista y viene directamente para nosotros,"* or "Plane in sight and headed for us."

I sighted a twin-engine, dark-blue plane which I immediately judged to be a U.S. Navy hurricane hunter. It was roaring in upon us right on the deck. I was overjoyed to see it, but I shouted to Carlos that I was sure it was coming to warn us of a hurricane. As the plane buzzed us repeatedly the crew shouted their joy. We knew now that our families would know we were alive.

On subsequent passes the plane dropped a sonar-buoy radio transmitter, a life raft and a Gibson Girl emergency radio. We retrieved them all by swimming or rowing out in the skiff. We also got a note which asked if we were *Niña II*. "What do they think we are?" José exclaimed. "We look like a floating tree trunk that forgot to sink ten years back." When I finally got the one-way sonar buoy working I asked the plane to buzz us, then climb suddenly if a hurricane were approaching. We were as still as church mice as she buzzed us three times and each time failed to climb. So our fears were groundless, and we waved as the plane went on its way.

That night we sang *Anchors Aweigh* and other Navy songs until exhausted. It seemed incredible to the other crewmen that such a big plane would search for us, and I had to explain patiently that the U.S. Coast Guard and the U.S. Navy would search just as hard for any lost or overdue ship, whether an American was aboard or not. José said solemnly to me, "I'll never, as long as I live, forget the U.S. Navy."

Three days later two other Navy planes buzzed us for three hours. After consulting with Carlos I told the planes on the sonar-buoy radio that we still intended to head not for the nearest land—at Antigua—but for San Salvador. We didn't need any help—except water, for we were down to our last emergency jars.

But we still had to sail our way in and there were some 600 miles—and probably more storms—between us and our destination. There was also a tragedy. One morning we missed Linda. During the night she had failed to cuddle next to me. I took it for granted that she was somewhere else on the ship. The next morning we turned the ship upside down. We unfurled the lateen sail where she sometimes slept. We thoroughly inspected the hold. But Linda was not to be found. She had become more and more brazen about leaping about the rigging and taking chances, and she could only have fallen overboard during the night. Her voice was very weak, too weak for us to hear. Gradually we realized that Linda was gone. We were heartsick. The *padre* solemnly said a prayer for her.

It was strange how much we missed her, this tiny stray kitten who had joined us in Las Palmas and kept us company through all the rages of the Atlantic. Without her mewing and preening and climbing the rigging, our ship seemed curiously lifeless from then on.

Our two weeks' calm finally ended. On our 59th day out the merciful trades that had supported Columbus from Spain finally began in earnest and drove us for six glorious days toward the Bahamas. We sang, jumped playfully around the deck, occasionally opened a bottle of spirits and prayed for water to augment the few gallons the Navy had dropped to us.

From time to time we saw ships or planes, but we were still determined to continue our voyage as "authentically" as possible. We needed water, and we were grateful for tobacco, but when the Navy or Coast Guard dropped radios to us we asked that no ships be sent to aid us. To the world outside our small ship this must seem a foolish dedication to the ideal of authenticity. But to the crew of *Niña II* it was important. We had endured great peril for a historical principle. It would have been a serious matter to forfeit it all in a moment of physical weakness. We knew full well that we still belonged to the 20th century; three times during the last phase of our trip we had seen the awesome spectacle of great rockets rising silently into the skies above distant Cape Canaveral. But we were also members of that ageless fraternity of seamen, each of whom owed a debt of gratitude to all the great explorers of the past.

Two days before our target arrival date of Christmas, we established a lookout on the mainmast, night and day. And just as on Columbus' trip, it wasn't long before somebody thought he saw land, then saw it fade. After a half dozen false alarms nobody paid much attention when José Valencia announced at 3 P.M. on Christmas Eve that he saw something "suspicious" on the horizon. Only this time it didn't fade away. There it stayed, green and solid—land. As we realized what had happened, we gathered and began singing *Salve Regina*. The tears started to our eyes as we looked toward the haven awaiting us.

But it wasn't that easy. Our charts told us little about how to approach San Salvador, and it was sundown, with no sign of anyone awaiting us on the island. We decided to circle the island to reach the town of Cockburn. By midnight, steering toward the lights of the town, we got within half a mile of the pier—but we couldn't get in. No matter what we did, the wind and current pushed us back, the anchor wouldn't hold, and we had no way of signaling the town. All that exasperating night we drifted backward, away from our goal, until by dawn we were 15 miles out to the west of the island. At noon that day I finally used one of the flares the Navy had dropped us to signal a passing airliner. The Navy and Coast Guard sent a small motor vessel out for us, and it finally towed us in. It was not the perfect ending, but by this time we didn't care. As we staggered ashore just before midnight on Christmas, our 77th day, we felt an overwhelming sense of triumph—and relief. José Robles fell to his knees and kissed the earth. The townspeople, by now out in throngs, welcomed us with cheers and calypso songs and started a feast that lasted until 4 A.M.

Now I had at least a small idea of how Columbus must have felt on October 12, 1492. Above all I felt the infinite satisfaction of having accomplished what we set out to do, of following as nearly as we could in the historic wake of the great explorer. In the end that was worth the strain and the terror, the doubts and the endless labor against the sea.